The Urban Calendar

365 Moments That Shaped
Our Urban World

Published by Plusurbia Press
Miami, FL

www.plusurbia.com

For permissions or inquiries, please contact
Plusurbia Press

Design and composition by Plusurbia Design®
Author: Juan Mullerat

Paperback ISBN: 979-8-9990386-0-9
Library of Congress Control Number: 2025913753

2025 Edition

To my wife Megan, the most dedicated and inspiring historic preservationist I have ever known, your passion for safeguarding the past has been a constant source of motivation throughout this journey. Your love for history and tireless commitment to preserving its stories remind me every day of the importance of honoring our heritage.

To my parents Ramón and Margarita, who instilled in me a deep appreciation for those who came before us, you taught me that every step we take is built on the foundation of their achievements. Your wisdom and encouragement have shaped my understanding of the world and my respect for the enduring legacies that guide us forward.

Thank you for your unwavering support and for being the cornerstones of my life and work. This book is as much yours as it is mine.

June 10th, 2025

URBAN THREADS

The Urban Calendar links each daily story to a broader theme that highlights a key force shaping the built environment, offering a lens through which we can explore the many dimensions of city-building— from the laws that govern land to the movements that call for more just, vibrant spaces. Whether it's a groundbreaking zoning ordinance, a visionary idea for a sustainable city, or a cultural milestone that transformed a neighborhood's identity, these themes organize the rich tapestry of urban history. Together, they show that cities are not merely physical places but evolving reflections of our values, struggles, and hopes.

COLONIAL & POST-COLONIAL URBANISM	How colonial expansion, administration, and later decolonization shaped city layouts, infrastructure, and social hierarchies.
CULTURAL & HISTORIC	Milestones tied to art, heritage, historic preservation, and moments that define a city's identity.
GLOBALIZATION & MODERNITY	Events reflecting cities' integration into global economic, technological, and cultural networks.
GREEN, SUSTAINABLE, RESILIENT	Initiatives focused on environmental stewardship, climate adaptation, and urban ecology.
HOUSING & SOCIAL MOVEMENTS	Struggles and innovations to secure equitable housing, address poverty, and empower communities.
LEGISLATION & GOVERNANCE	Laws, policies, treaties, and governance structures that influence urban form and growth.
NEW TOWNS & PLANNED CITIES	The creation of entirely new settlements or master-planned urban extensions, shaping landscapes and future possibilities.
TRANSPORTATION & MOBILITY	Major shifts in how people and goods move within and between cities, from bridges to congestion pricing.
URBAN UTOPIAS	Visionary ideas and experiments imagining ideal cities, from philosophical works to futuristic prototypes.
VISIONARIES & INNOVATORS	Individuals whose ideas or leadership profoundly influenced urban development.

INTRODUCTION

Cities are among humanity's greatest achievements —dynamic expressions of our ambitions, challenges, and ingenuity. They are shaped over time through the vision and effort of planners, urban designers, architects, engineers, developers, builders, activists, policymakers, and everyday citizens, responding to both necessity and imagination. The urban environments we navigate today are the cumulative result of countless decisions, breakthroughs, and bold ideas layered across centuries.

This book began with a personal fascination. I've always been drawn to cities—their energy, contradictions, and especially their layered histories. Walk down any street and you can feel the presence of different eras colliding. A single corner might contain remnants of outdated zoning, a once-futuristic building, a forgotten transit line, or a revived public plaza. These elements often emerge not from a single, unified vision, but from chains of disconnected decisions: a policy enacted without a corresponding plan, a building constructed in response to social pressure, an idea that outlasts its original intent. That crossing—between policy and place, between vision and reality—is what makes cities endlessly fascinating. They are living archives of invention, conflict, compromise, and hope.

This book is a curated journey through time, offering a daily look at key moments that have shaped urban planning and city-building. Each entry presents a milestone—an ambitious new city, a transformative transit innovation, a visionary planning concept, or a pivotal policy decision. These moments are more than historical anecdotes; they are compact lessons in creativity, resilience, and foresight.

At its core, this book is meant to be an introduction to 365 moments. Each entry is a glimpse into a deeper, more complex narrative—just a starting point for further exploration. I encourage you to dig deeper into the events, people, and forces that have shaped our cities. These short reflections are teasers of larger stories that deserve greater attention and critical thinking.

The events included are selected to offer a wide-ranging view—balanced across geography, eras, and themes—to reflect the global and evolving nature of urban development. Whether you are a planner, designer, policymaker, student, or simply someone curious about how cities come to be, I hope these pages offer perspective and inspiration. They serve as a reminder that bold ideas—no matter how imperfect—are what push us forward.

Cities are stories written in buildings, streets, and public spaces. They are never finished, always evolving. May these pages inspire you to contribute to the next chapter—to build boldly, plan thoughtfully, and shape the urban world with vision and care.

As Daniel Burnham, the great city planner, once said: *"Make no little plans; they have no magic to stir men's blood and probably themselves will not be realized. Make big plans; aim high in hope and work."*

FORMATION OF
THE CITY OF GREATER NEW YORK

"A great city is that which has the greatest men and women."
– Walt Whitman, American Poet.

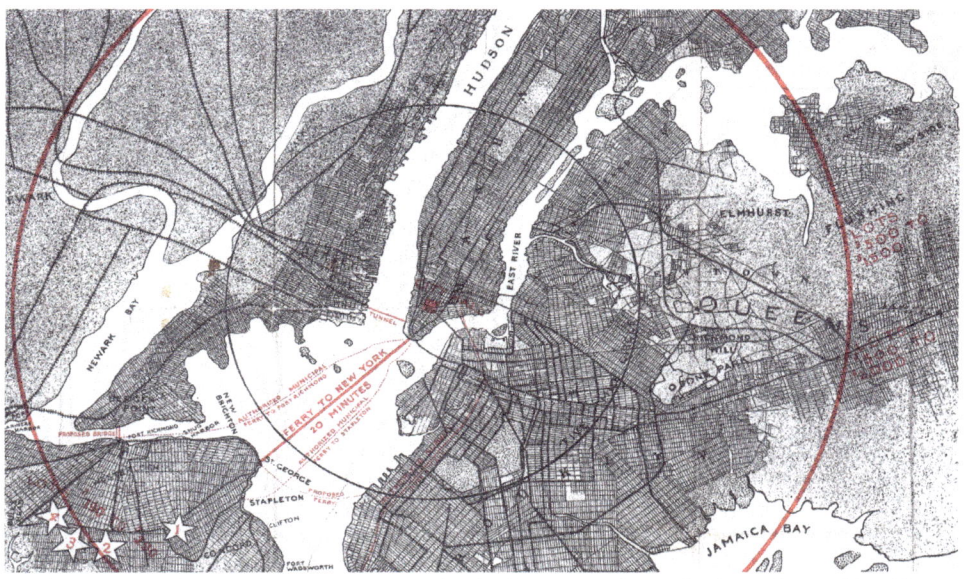

Wood Harmon Map of New York City, 1906 – A promotional real estate map showcasing the newly consolidated five boroughs, emphasizing transit expansion and suburban land speculation during a period of rapid urban growth and infrastructural transformation in early 20th-century New York. By PicturePast. Licensed.

On this day in 1898, New York City annexed land from surrounding counties to form the City of Greater New York, consolidating Manhattan, Brooklyn, Queens, and The Bronx into a unified metropolis. Staten Island joined on January 25, 1898, completing the modern five-borough structure. This transformative event centralized governance and integrated infrastructure, enabling coordinated urban planning, improved transportation networks, and streamlined public services. The annexation positioned New York as a global economic and cultural powerhouse, fostering growth and innovation on an unprecedented scale. It also reflected broader trends in urban consolidation during the Industrial Age, as cities sought to manage expansion and modernize public administration. The creation of Greater New York reshaped the city's identity, laying the foundation for its rise as a global hub while addressing the challenges of managing a sprawling, diverse urban population under a unified system.

How can urban consolidation strategies be adapted to address modern challenges like regional equity and resource sharing?

RAYMOND UNWIN'S: HOUSING, TOWN PLANNING, ETC.: A PRACTICAL GUIDE

"Town planning is not merely an art but a duty, and its aim should be the creation of a better environment for the life of the people." – Raymond Unwin. British urban planner.

The · Garden · City · Principle · applied · to · Suburbs.

Figure 5 from Old Towns and New Needs. The Garden City Principle applied to Suburbs. By Raymond Unwin, 1912. Source: Archive.org. Public Domain.

On this day in 1911, Raymond Unwin, a trailblazer in urban planning, completed the Foreword to his *Housing, Town Planning, Etc. Act 1909: A Practical Guide*. This seminal work provided a detailed interpretation of the 1909 Housing and Town Planning Act, a landmark piece of legislation in British urban development. Unwin's guide offered practical advice on preparing town planning schemes, emphasizing their significance in shaping healthier, more organized, and sustainable urban environments. The book included appendices containing the full text of the Act, procedural regulations, and illustrative examples such as the Hampstead Garden Suburb Act of 1906, a model of garden city principles. By integrating legal analysis with practical insights, Unwin made the complexities of the Act accessible to policymakers and practitioners, facilitating its implementation. His work profoundly influenced early 20th-century urban development, advancing the garden city movement and promoting a vision of equitable and thoughtfully designed communities.

How can modern urban planners balance legal frameworks with creative design to ensure sustainable and equitable city growth?

CONSTRUCTION OF THE BROOKLYN BRIDGE BEGINS

"The great works of bridge building are among the noblest achievements of human ingenuity and courage." – John A. Roebling. Civil engineer, designer of the Brooklyn Bridge.

Brooklyn Bridge New York, ca. 1874. The great East River suspension bridge--Connecting the cities of New York and Brooklyn. By Parsons & Atwater, del. Source: Currier & Ives. Published by Currier & Ives. Retrieved from the Library of Congress. Public Domain.

On this day in 1870, construction began on the Brooklyn Bridge, a transformative infrastructure project that reshaped New York City. Designed by engineer John A. Roebling and completed in 1883 under Washington and Emily Warren Roebling, it was the world's longest suspension bridge at the time and the first to use steel cables. Spanning the East River to connect Manhattan and Brooklyn, the bridge revolutionized transportation, supported urban expansion, and paved the way for borough unification. Its gothic arches and sweeping cables came to symbolize industrial ambition and the potential of infrastructure to shape urban identity. More than a transportation link, the Brooklyn Bridge became a civic landmark—an icon of engineering, aesthetics, and progress. It influenced generations of architects and planners, reinforcing the idea that bold design can define a city's legacy. Today, the bridge remains a celebrated monument to innovation and a powerful reminder of how visionary public works can transform the urban experience.

How can modern infrastructure projects draw inspiration from iconic structures to balance functionality with lasting cultural impact?

JANUARY 4
1884

FOUNDATION OF
THE FABIAN SOCIETY IN LONDON

"A city is the expression of the society that builds it." — Sidney Webb. British economist, social reformer, and co-founder of the Fabian Society. (Paraphrased)

Group photograph of participants in a Fabian Society summer school in the 1920s. Author unknown. Source: Image courtesy of LSE Library. Public Domain.

On this day in 1884, the Fabian Society was founded in London, emerging as a key intellectual force behind progressive urban reform and social planning in Britain. Named after the Roman general Fabius Maximus, known for his strategy of gradual, deliberate action, the society advocated for the transformation of society through democratic and incremental means rather than revolutionary upheaval. Its prominent members, including George Bernard Shaw, Sidney Webb, and Beatrice Webb, championed ideas related to housing reform, urban welfare, and the foundations of the modern welfare state. The Fabians played a significant role in shaping public policy, influencing the development of garden cities, public housing initiatives, and the broader planning movement to create healthier, more equitable urban environments. Their legacy endures in the principles of social justice embedded in urban planning practices, reflecting the belief that thoughtful design and governance can foster more inclusive and sustainable cities.

How did the Fabian Society's gradualist approach influence modern urban social policies?

NEW YORK CITY IMPLEMENTS FIRST U.S. CONGESTION PRICING PLAN

"Congestion pricing makes us confront the true cost of driving in a crowded city."
— Michael Bloomberg. American businessman and former mayor of New York City.

Rush Hour in New York City. Capturing the daily intensity of urban life, this image reflects a city where drivers lose an average of 117 hours annually to congestion—underscoring the persistent challenges of mobility in dense, global cities. By Daniel Dörfler. Licensed

On this day in 2025, New York City launched the nation's first congestion pricing program, marking a significant milestone in urban transportation policy. The plan charges vehicles entering Manhattan below 60th Street during peak hours, with tolls starting at $9. Aiming to reduce traffic congestion and greenhouse gas emissions, the program is also expected to generate significant funding for public transit improvements. After facing legal challenges and delays, its implementation reflects the growing recognition of congestion pricing as a tool for sustainable urban mobility. Advocates highlight its potential to alleviate gridlock, improve air quality, and encourage alternative transportation. However, concerns remain about economic impacts on low-income drivers and small businesses. As the first program of its kind in the U.S., New York City's initiative will serve as a test case for cities nationwide exploring solutions to address transportation challenges and environmental goals.

How can cities ensure congestion pricing policies address equity concerns while achieving environmental and mobility goals?

JANUARY 6
1907

MARIA MONTESSORI
OPENS FIRST SCHOOL

"The child is both a hope and a promise for mankind."
– Maria Montessori. Italian physician and educator.

Toddler playing with construction blocks. Early development, reflecting on the core principles of the Montessori method, which emphasizes hands-on, self-directed learning. Activities like block play foster fine motor skills, spatial awareness, and early cognitive development through tactile, purposeful engagement. By Daria_Nipot. Licensed

On this day in 1907, Maria Montessori opened her first school, the Casa dei Bambini (Children's House), in a working-class neighborhood of Rome, Italy. Established to support underprivileged children, the school introduced Montessori's groundbreaking educational philosophy, emphasizing independence, hands-on learning, and nurturing a child's natural curiosity. This innovative approach reshaped education and the design of learning spaces, prioritizing accessibility, functionality, and child-centric environments. The Casa dei Bambini became a model for integrating education into urban communities, particularly in underserved areas, creating spaces where learning could thrive alongside daily life. Montessori's methods highlighted the vital role of education in urban development, fostering social equity and empowering children to become active contributors to society. Her legacy continues to influence educational practices and the design of schools worldwide, demonstrating the transformative potential of integrating education into the urban landscape.

How can urban planning better integrate educational facilities to support underserved communities?

BIRTH OF
KEVIN LYNCH

"A good city is like a good friend—it is inviting, accessible, and memorable."
– Kevin Lynch. American urban planner and author. (Adapted)

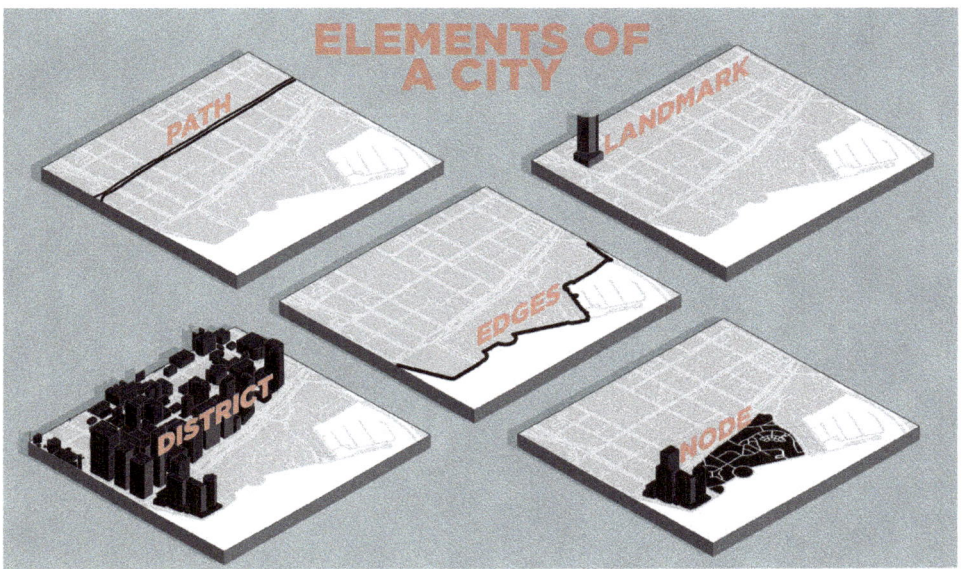

Paths, edges, districts, nodes, and landmarks—Kevin Lynch's five core elements of mental mapping—shape our understanding and experience of urban spaces. These visual and spatial cues help people navigate cities intuitively. Illustrated by Plusurbia Design, inspired by Lynch's The Image of the City. Own Work.

On this day in 1918, Kevin Andrew Lynch, a visionary urban planner and theorist, was born in Chicago, Illinois. Lynch revolutionized urban design with his seminal work, The Image of the City (1960), a landmark study that examined how people perceive and navigate urban spaces. In this influential book, Lynch introduced the concept of "imageability"—the quality of a city that makes it memorable and easy to understand—and identified five essential elements of mental maps: paths, edges, districts, nodes, and landmarks. His work highlighted the centrality of human experience in shaping urban environments, emphasizing the need for cities to be legible, navigable, and meaningful to their inhabitants. Lynch's ideas have profoundly impacted urban planning, inspiring a human-centered approach to city design that prioritizes the lived experiences of residents. His enduring legacy continues to shape the theory and practice of urban design worldwide, influencing generations of planners and designers.

How can Lynch's principles of "imageability" inform the design of cities that foster better connectivity and community identity?

JANUARY 8
1964

THE "WAR ON POVERTY"
AND THE MODEL CITIES PROGRAM

"Our aim is not only to relieve the symptom of poverty, but to cure it and, above all, to prevent it."
– Lyndon B. Johnson. 36th President of the United States.

"President Lyndon B. Johnson signs the Immigration and Nationality Act of 1965 on Liberty Island, New York, October 3, 1965. Source: LBJ Presidential Library, Photograph by Yoichi Okamoto. Courtesy of the Lyndon Baines Johnson Library and Museum. Public Domain.

On this day in 1964, President Lyndon B. Johnson declared the "War on Poverty" in his State of the Union address, a landmark initiative that profoundly impacted urban policy in the United States. As part of this effort, the Model Cities Program was introduced in 1966 to address urban poverty through comprehensive city planning. This ambitious initiative aimed to revitalize struggling neighborhoods by coordinating investments in housing, transportation, education, and public health, while emphasizing community participation. Despite facing challenges like underfunding and political resistance, the program marked a significant shift toward federal involvement in urban renewal and equitable development. It laid the groundwork for more integrated urban policies and highlighted the importance of addressing the social and economic needs of urban residents. Though its legacy is mixed, the Model Cities Program remains a critical chapter in the history of American urban planning, influencing ongoing debates about equity, neighborhood revitalization, and the role of government in city development.

What can planners learn from the Model Cities Program to tackle today's urban poverty and inequality?

JANUARY 9
2007

STEVE JOBS
DEBUTS THE IPHONE

"The ones who are crazy enough to think they can change the world are the ones who do."
— Steve Jobs. American entrepreneur and co-founder of Apple Inc.

Steve Jobs shows off iPhone 4 at the 2010 Worldwide Developers Conference. By Matthew Yohe, 2010. Via Wikipedia. CC BY-SA 3.0

On this day in 2007, Steve Jobs introduced the first iPhone at the Macworld Conference & Expo, revolutionizing communication and reshaping urban life. The iPhone sparked a global technological shift by combining a phone, internet browser, and music player into one device. Its impact on cities has been profound, enabling navigation, urban planning, and social connectivity through mobile apps and real-time data. Smartphones have become indispensable for modern urban living, powering ride-sharing services, transit tracking, and digital mapping. The iPhone also accelerated the development of smart cities, integrating technology to improve urban efficiency, inclusivity, and sustainability. Beyond transforming personal communication, it revolutionized how people interact with their urban environments, fostering a seamless, interconnected experience. Jobs' innovation continues to shape urban life, driving technological integration and paving the way for smarter, more responsive cities that adapt to the needs of their residents.

How can cities leverage smartphone technology to create more efficient, inclusive, and connected urban environments?

JANUARY 10
1927

PREMIERE OF
THE MOVIE: METROPOLIS

"The mediator between the head and the hands must be the heart."
– Metropolis film directed by Fritz Lang.

Inspired by Fritz Lang's Metropolis, this image explores the interplay between technology, architecture, and social dynamics in the city. Created by Plusurbia Design using MidJourney.

On this day in 1927, Metropolis, directed by Fritz Lang, premiered, becoming a groundbreaking science fiction film that depicted a futuristic city starkly divided between a utopian world for the elite and a dystopian underworld for exploited workers. The city's design, with its towering skyscrapers, elevated roadways, and mechanized infrastructure, reflected early 20th-century hopes and fears about urbanization, technological advancement, and social inequality. Lang's vision, heavily influenced by Art Deco and expressionist styles, resulted in a cinematic and architectural masterpiece. The film's narrative explores the conflict between the ruling elite and the working class, symbolizing the struggles of the industrial age. The upper city represents luxury and progress, while the lower city exposes the harsh realities of labor and exploitation. Metropolis remains a powerful allegory, inspiring urban and cinematic discourse while raising enduring questions about equity, sustainability, and the human cost of urban development.

How does Metropolis reflect the tension between technological progress and social equity?

BIRTH OF SHERRY ARNSTEIN

"Participation without redistribution of power is an empty and frustrating process."
— Sherry Arnstein. American urban planner and author

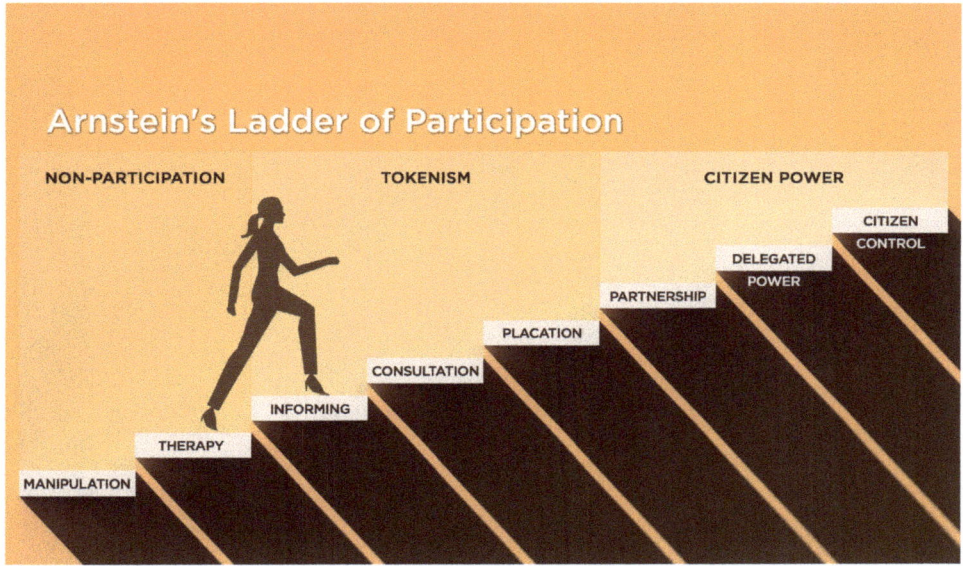

Diagram showing Sherry Arnstein's 'Ladder of citizen participation. By Plusurbia Design.

On this day in 1930, Sherry Arnstein, a transformative figure in urban planning and public policy, was born. Arnstein is best known for her influential 1969 essay, A Ladder of Citizen Participation, which introduced a powerful framework for understanding public involvement in planning processes. Her "ladder" outlined eight rungs, ranging from non-participation and tokenism to true citizen empowerment, critically examining how power imbalances can marginalize communities. Arnstein's work challenged planners to prioritize meaningful engagement, advocating for collaborative decision-making that uplifts underrepresented voices. Her ideas reshaped participatory planning, providing a lens to evaluate the inclusivity and equity of urban policies worldwide. Arnstein's insights remain vital in addressing contemporary challenges such as inequality, environmental justice, and community-led urban redevelopment. By urging planners to move beyond superficial consultation, she inspired a more democratic approach to shaping cities, leaving an enduring legacy in pursuing equitable and just urban environments.

How can planners ensure equitable participation in decision-making for marginalized communities today?

JANUARY 12
1808

ABANDONMENT OF
JOHN RENNIE'S SCHEME AT RECULVER

"It is easier to destroy than to preserve, yet in preservation lies the essence of our history and identity." – John Rennie. Scottish civil engineer. (Attributed)

Watercolor of Reculver Church, painted in 1755, depicts the historic twin towers of this medieval site on the Kent coastline, standing against the elements and erosion. The image captures a moment in time, preserving a view of the church long before its partial demolition. By L. Sullivan. Source: Wikimedia Commons. Public Domain.

On this day in 1808, plans by John Rennie to protect St Mary's Church, Reculver, from coastal erosion were officially abandoned. Originally founded in 669 CE, the church was a remarkable example of Anglo-Saxon architecture, rich in religious and cultural history. However, relentless coastal erosion threatened the structure, and despite Rennie's expertise as a pioneering civil engineer, no feasible solution emerged to save it. Authorities ultimately opted for demolition, preserving only the church's twin towers as navigational aids for sailors. This decision provoked concerns over the loss of historical architecture and sparked debates about balancing heritage conservation with environmental challenges. The fate of St Mary's Church highlights the vulnerability of cultural landmarks to natural forces and the critical need for forward-thinking strategies to protect such treasures. It serves as a poignant reminder of the intersection between environmental realities and the preservation of architectural and historical identity.

How can urban planners address environmental challenges while preserving culturally significant sites?

FOUNDING OF
THE NATIONAL GEOGRAPHIC SOCIETY

"A map is the greatest of all epic poems. Its lines and colors show the realization of great dreams." – Gilbert H. Grosvenor. American geographer and editor of National Geographic.

A National Geographic yellow frame installation in Otepää, Estonia, 2024, offers visitors a unique perspective to appreciate the natural landscape and cultural heritage of the region. By Dor Shabashewitz. CC BY 4.0

On this day in 1888, the National Geographic Society was founded in Washington, D.C., by scholars, explorers, and scientists dedicated to increasing and sharing geographic knowledge. This influential organization has profoundly shaped the global understanding of urban and natural landscapes through its pioneering work in cartography, photography, and exploration. The Society's detailed maps, captivating imagery, and in-depth studies have been instrumental in advancing urban and regional planning by providing critical geographic insights. National Geographic's contributions have emphasized the importance of sustainable development, environmental conservation, and the intricate connections between cities and ecosystems. By making complex scientific concepts accessible to a broad audience, the Society has inspired planners and policymakers worldwide to consider geography's role in urban development. Its legacy bridges science and public awareness, fostering a deeper appreciation for the interconnectedness of human settlements and the natural world.

How can the integration of geographic knowledge and storytelling shape sustainable urban planning and global environmental stewardship?

JANUARY 14
83 BCE

BIRTH OF
MARK ANTONY

"Cities are the trophies of empire, shaped by the hands of those who dare to lead."
– Mark Antony (Inspired by Mark Antony's policies).

Mark Antony shows the corpse of Julius Caesar to the citizens of Rome. Engraving by J. Kleinmichel. "El Mundo Ilustrado", 1882. Sourtce: Wikimedia Commons. Public Domain.

On this day in 83 BCE, Mark Antony, one of the most influential figures of the late Roman Republic, was born. A skilled general and politician, Antony played a key role in shaping the urban and territorial structure of the Roman world. As part of the Second Triumvirate, he oversaw land distributions to veterans, spurring the growth of new settlements and transforming rural and urban landscapes across the Republic. In the eastern provinces, cities such as Ephesus and Tarsus became important administrative and military hubs under his leadership. His alliance with Cleopatra, Queen of Egypt, further emphasized Alexandria as a cultural and economic powerhouse, blending Roman and Hellenistic traditions. This fusion of cultures left a lasting impact on the urban identity of the ancient world, illustrating how political power and alliances shaped cities and societies for generations.

How did the political and military strategies of leaders like Mark Antony shape the development and legacy of ancient cities?

CREATION OF
THE MCMILLAN PLAN FOR WASHINGTON, D.C.

"The aesthetic is as essential as the practical; beauty is as important as utility."
— Daniel Burnham. American architect and urban planner.

The McMillan Plan of 1901. The future Washington, general plan, Washington, D.C. Source: Detroit Publishing Co., courtesy of the Library of Congress Prints and Photographs Division. Public Domain.

On this day in 1902, the McMillan Plan, named after Michigan Senator James McMillan, was completed by the Senate Park Commission as a comprehensive effort to revive and update Pierre L'Enfant's original plan for Washington, D.C. Embracing the principles of the City Beautiful movement, the plan sought to enhance the city's grandeur, civic pride, and monumental character, reflecting the growing power and aspirations of the United States at the turn of the 20th century. It reimagined the National Mall as a grand, open, park-like space flanked by museums, government buildings, and formal landscapes, creating the iconic core of the nation's capital. The plan also established the locations of major landmarks like the Lincoln Memorial, Ulysses S. Grant Memorial, Union Station, and the U.S. Department of Agriculture Building, reinforcing the symbolic importance of Washington, D.C. Developed with the input of influential figures like Daniel Burnham, Frederick Law Olmsted Jr., and Charles McKim, the McMillan Plan remains the foundation of Washington, D.C.'s urban design, reflecting the enduring influence of the City Beautiful movement on American urban planning.

How does the McMillan Plan reflect City Beautiful ideals, and what can modern planners learn from it?

JANUARY 16
1556

PHILIP II
BECOMES KING OF SPAIN

"Cities are the heart of the kingdom; they must reflect the order and power of their sovereign." – Inspired by Philip II's vision for Madrid

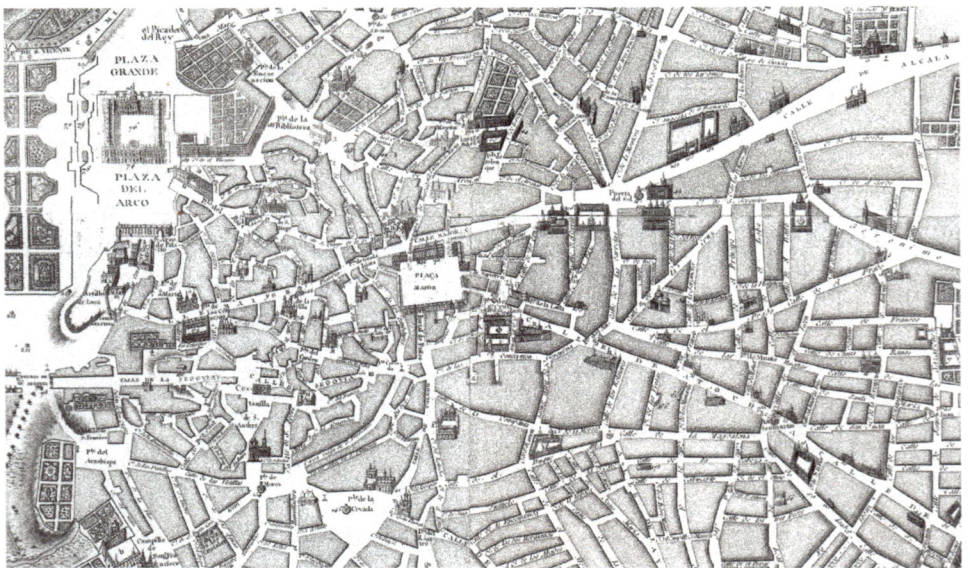

Geometric and historical plan of the town of Madrid and its surroundings, 1761. Engraved by N. Chalmandrier. Source: Bibliothèque nationale de France, département Arsenal, EST-1507 (44). Wikimedia Commons. Public Domain.

On this day in 1556, Philip II ascended the throne of Spain, marking the beginning of a reign that profoundly influenced urban development and governance across the Spanish Empire. Among his most transformative decisions was moving his court to Madrid, then a rural hunting ground. This choice established Madrid as Spain's administrative capital, catalyzing its urban growth and cementing its role as the political center of the empire. Philip II centralized governance, creating streamlined bureaucratic systems that enhanced the administration of Spain's expanding cities. His reign also oversaw monumental architectural projects, most notably El Escorial, a grand palace and monastery near Madrid. This iconic structure symbolized Spain's imperial power and religious devotion, integrating functionality, grandeur, and spirituality in its design. Philip II's urban and cultural development vision left a lasting legacy, shaping Madrid and influencing the evolution of cities throughout Spain and its colonies.

How can centralized governance and monumental architecture contribute to the identity and functionality of urban centers today?

CELEBRATION OF
BENJAMIN FRANKLIN DAY

"An investment in knowledge pays the best interest." – Benjamin Franklin.
American polymath, inventor, and Founding Father of the United States.

Commissioner Rudolph at 219 ann. of Birth of Bejamin Franklin (Sons of the Revolution) 1925. Source: National Photo Company Collection (Library of Congress). Public Domain.

On this day in 1924, Benjamin Franklin Day was first celebrated following a proclamation by President Calvin Coolidge, honoring one of America's most influential Founding Fathers. Born in 1706, Franklin left a profound mark on urban development, particularly in Philadelphia. He founded the first public library, organized the city's first volunteer fire department, and championed improvements in street lighting and sanitation—early models for civic infrastructure in American cities. His invention of the lightning rod revolutionized building safety, reflecting his belief in science-driven solutions to urban problems. Franklin also promoted public education, civic responsibility, and community welfare, values that continue to underpin modern urban planning. His work helped define what it means for a city to serve its citizens—through services, innovation, and a commitment to the public good. Today, Benjamin Franklin Day is marked by events and programs that celebrate his legacy as a visionary of urban life and a pioneer of inclusive, community-oriented city-building.

How can Benjamin Franklin's principles of civic improvement and innovation inform the development of modern urban spaces?

MARTIN LUTHER KING, JR. (MLK) DAY

"An individual has not started living until he can rise above the narrow confines of his individualistic concerns to the broader concerns of all humanity." — Martin Luther King, Jr.

Photo of Dr. Martin Luther King, Jr. being arrested in Montgomery, Alabama, for "loitering" in 1958. By the Associated Press. Source: Wikimedia Commons. Public Domain.

On this day in 1993, Martin Luther King, Jr. Day was officially observed in all 50 U.S. states for the first time, marking a historic moment in honoring the civil rights leader's enduring legacy. The holiday celebrates King's profound contributions to justice, equality, and nonviolent social change, emphasizing his vision of inclusive and equitable communities. King's work was closely tied to urban spaces, with cities such as Montgomery, Birmingham, and Washington, D.C. as pivotal stages for the civil rights movement. These urban centers became arenas for collective action, where public spaces transformed into platforms for advocating racial justice and social progress.

Observing this day nationwide highlights the critical role of cities in fostering dialogue, unity, and activism. This milestone affirmed King's vision of communities where all voices are valued and underscored the transformative potential of urban spaces in advancing social equity and justice.

How can cities continue to serve as platforms for equity and social change, honoring the legacy of leaders like Martin Luther King, Jr.?

FIRST ELECTRIC LIGHTING SYSTEM IN ROSELLE, NEW JERSEY

"What progress we are making. In the middle of the 19th century, we would have thought it impossible to illuminate cities with electricity." — Thomas Edison

Thomas Alva Edison, 1847-1931. Photo c. 1905. Source: Library of Congress Prints and Photographs Division. Public Domain.

On this day in 1883, Thomas Edison's first electric lighting system using overhead wires began operation in Roselle, New Jersey. This groundbreaking achievement marked a turning point in urban infrastructure, showcasing the transformative potential of electricity for cities. The system powered homes, businesses, and streetlights, providing a safer, more reliable, and efficient alternative to gas lamps. Edison's innovation revolutionized urban lighting and paved the way for the widespread adoption of electric power systems, soon becoming a cornerstone of modern urban life. Roselle served as a pioneering model for integrating electricity into city planning, demonstrating how technological advancements could enhance public safety, stimulate economic growth, and improve urban spaces' visual and functional quality. This milestone underscored the critical role of innovation in shaping the infrastructure and character of cities in the industrial age and beyond.

How can technological innovations like Edison's lighting system continue to shape the sustainability and functionality of modern cities?

FOUNDING OF THE 'TAULA DE CANVI,' CONSIDERED EUROPE'S FIRST PUBLIC BANK

"Commerce and finance are the lifeblood of a city, and trust is their foundation."
— Inspired by principles of the Taula de Canvi

Interior of the Saló de Contractacions (Contracts Hall) in the Gothic Quarter of Barcelona, part of the Llotja de Mar complex, a historic building that played a significant role in Catalonia's maritime and commercial history. Photograph by Carlos Delgado. CC BY-SA 2.0

On this day in 1401, the Taula de Canvi (Table of Change), widely regarded as Europe's first public bank, began operations within the Llotja de Mar in Barcelona. Created to stabilize the city's financial system and manage municipal funds, the Taula de Canvi introduced innovative practices such as issuing credit, managing deposits, and facilitating secure economic transactions. These advancements laid the groundwork for modern banking systems and significantly bolstered Barcelona's economy. By enhancing trust in financial dealings, the bank enabled large-scale public works and infrastructure projects, such as port improvements and urban expansions, reinforcing the city's role as a key Mediterranean trading hub. The Taula de Canvi was critical in supporting Barcelona's flourishing trade networks, fostering economic resilience, and ensuring its prominence during the late Middle Ages. Its legacy illustrates the profound impact of financial institutions on urban growth and economic development.

How can modern urban financial institutions draw lessons from historical innovations like the Taula de Canvi to build sustainable and equitable cities?

JANUARY 21
1801

BIRTH OF
JOHN BATMAN

"This will be the place for a village."
— John Batman, upon seeing the future site of the City of Melbourne

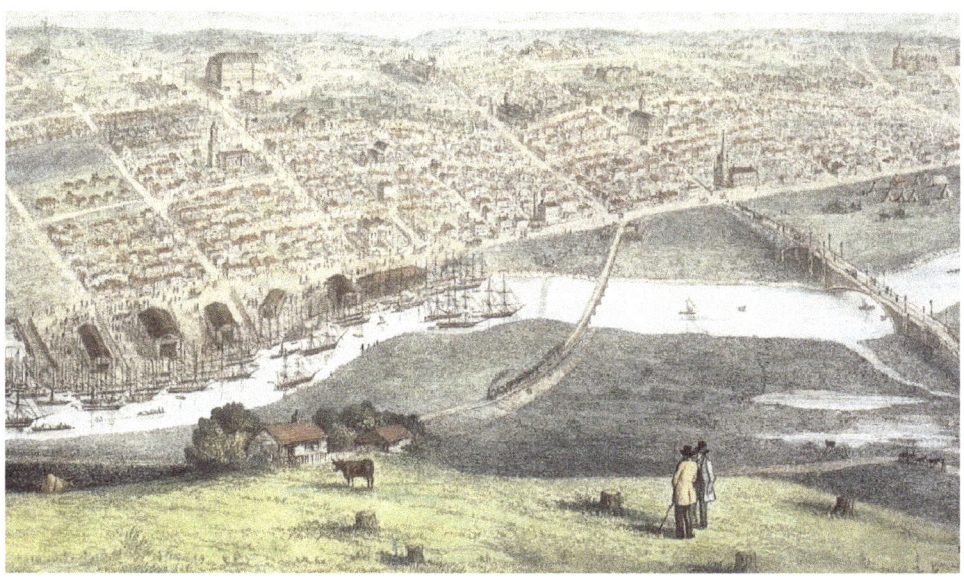

The Sandridge Bridge, 1855, one of Melbourne's earliest railway bridges, connecting the central business district to the emerging port area of Sandridge (now Port Melbourne). Drawn by Nathaniel Whittock from official surveys and sketches by G. Teale Esqr. Published by Lloyd Brothers & Co., May 9, 1855. Source: Wikimedia Commons. Public Domain.

On this day in 1801, John Batman, an Australian entrepreneur and explorer, was born. Batman is widely credited with founding Melbourne, one of Australia's most significant cities. In 1835, he negotiated what became known as Batman's Treaty with the Wurundjeri people, through which he claimed land along the Yarra River. While the treaty is now recognized as deeply unjust, it represented a pivotal moment in the colonization of Australia and the establishment of Melbourne as a major urban center. Batman's actions accelerated the growth of European settlement in the area but also contributed to the displacement and marginalization of Indigenous peoples, leaving a complex and contested legacy. Melbourne's development highlights the intersection of colonial expansion and urbanization, reflecting both the transformative impact of settlement and the enduring need to reconcile the consequences of colonization on Indigenous communities and their lands.

How can modern cities like Melbourne honor their Indigenous heritage while embracing their role as global urban centers?

JANUARY 22
1912

COMPLETION OF
HENRY FLAGLER'S OVERSEAS RAILROAD

"I prefer to let what I have done speak for me."
— Henry Flagler. American industrialist and founder of the Florida East Coast Railway.

Bahia Honda Rail Bridge before highway conversion. Circa 1920. Author unknown. Source: Florida Memory, State Library and Archives of Florida - Manuscript collection. Via Wikimedia Commons. Public Domain.

On this day in 1912, Henry Flagler's most ambitious project, the Overseas Railroad, was officially completed, connecting mainland Florida to Key West. Dubbed the "Eighth Wonder of the World," this engineering marvel stretched over 128 miles of open ocean, with bridges and viaducts linking the Florida Keys. Flagler, a co-founder of Standard Oil, transformed Florida's east coast through his visionary investments in railroads, hotels, and urban development, effectively shaping cities like Miami, West Palm Beach, and St. Augustine. His Florida East Coast Railway boosted tourism and facilitated trade and settlement, turning Florida into a thriving economic corridor. The urban growth spurred by Flagler's rail empire set the foundation for modern Florida's development, illustrating how transportation infrastructure can redefine regional identity, economic potential, and urban form—a lesson echoed in today's global cities connected by high-speed rail and transit-oriented development.

How has the development of major transportation corridors, like the Overseas Railroad, influenced the growth and identity of modern cities?

MILTON KEYNES, UK
IS ESTABLISHED AS A NEW TOWN

"Milton Keynes was planned to ensure people had the space to live, work, and play."
– Derek Walker. British architect and urban planner, chief architect and planner of Milton Keynes.

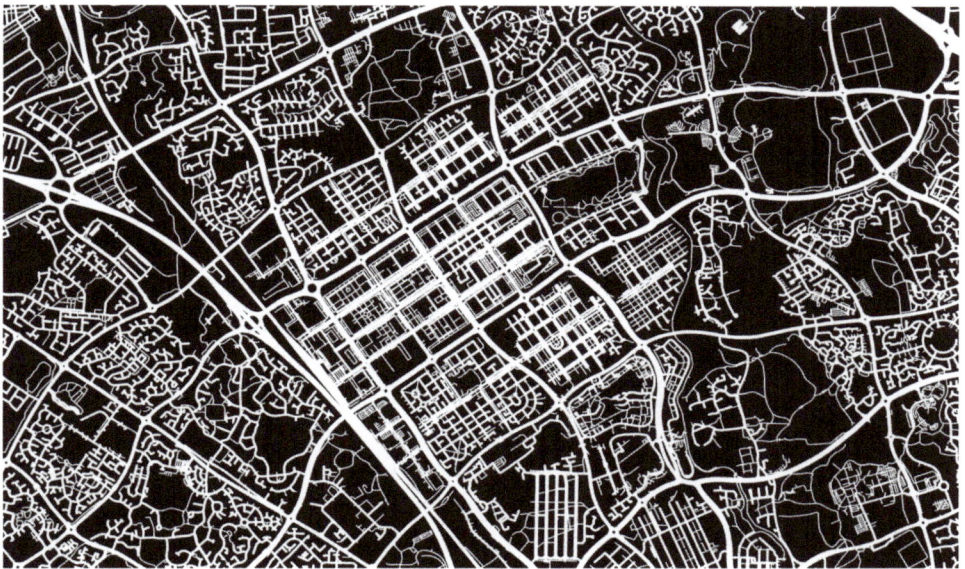

A city map of Milton Keynes, England, illustrating the town's modernist design, grid layout, and green spaces, planned in the 1960s to accommodate population overspill from London and embody new urban ideals. By Ink drop. Licensed

On this day in 1967, the UK government issued a formal order to establish Milton Keynes, a new town conceived to address the post-war housing crisis near London. Developed under the oversight of the Milton Keynes Development Corporation, the city became a flagship of the British New Towns Movement. Its plan featured a grid-based road system, generous green spaces, and a dispersed urban core—designed to foster both growth and quality of life. Prioritizing accessibility, it integrated wide roads, pedestrian paths, and cycleways to ensure seamless mobility. Unlike older urban centers, Milton Keynes embraced low-density, suburban-style living while reserving land for future expansion.

Over time, it matured into a dynamic urban hub and remains a pioneering example of modernist planning, demonstrating how deliberate urban design can reconcile rapid expansion with sustainability and livability.

What lessons can contemporary planners learn from Milton Keynes in designing suburban towns or satellite cities?

JANUARY 24
1848

DISCOVERY OF GOLD
AT SUTTER'S MILL: BIRTH OF CALIFORNIA CITIES

"Gold, like a magnet, draws men in streams to the hills, transforming the land and its cities."
– Hubert Howe Bancroft. American historian and publisher. (Paraphrased)

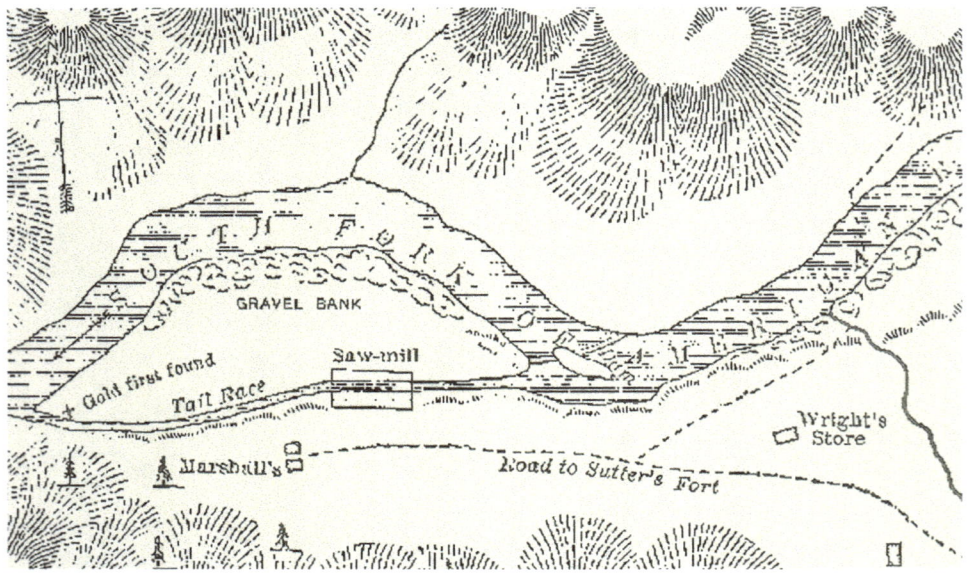

Map showing Sutter's sawmill on the south branch of the American River, 1888. Source: Hubert Howe Bancroft: History of California, vol. VI. (1848-1859), San Francisco, The History Company, Publishers. Via Wikimedia Commons. Public Domain.

On this day in 1848, James W. Marshall discovered gold at Sutter's Mill near Sacramento, California, setting off the California Gold Rush. This discovery led to one of the largest migrations in U.S. history, with hundreds of thousands of people flocking to the region in search of fortune. San Francisco, a modest settlement at the time, transformed into a booming city, its population skyrocketing from 1,000 in 1848 to over 25,000 by 1850. This rapid urban growth necessitated new infrastructure, including housing, transportation, and ports, as well as governance to manage the influx of diverse populations. The Gold Rush spurred the development of San Francisco and established California as a major economic and cultural hub, laying the foundation for the state's urbanization and influence in the modern era.

How did the California Gold Rush reshape urban development patterns in the western United States, and what lessons can modern cities draw from this transformation?

THE FOUNDING OF SÃO PAULO, BRAZIL

"In the heart of this land, we lay the foundations for a great city, guided by faith and the promise of prosperity." – José de Anchieta. Spanish Jesuit missionary, foundar of São Paulo.

Overlooking the Pátio do Colégio – the birthplace of São Paulo, where the city's first Portuguese structure was founded in 1554. By Pulsar Imagens. Licensed.

On this day in 1554, Jesuit priests Manuel da Nóbrega and José de Anchieta founded the city of São Paulo by establishing the Colégio de São Paulo de Piratininga, a Jesuit school on a plateau overlooking the Tietê River. This settlement initially focused on religious education and missionary work, became the nucleus around which São Paulo grew. Over centuries, its development was shaped by significant migration, agricultural expansion (especially coffee plantations in the 19th century), and subsequent industrialization in the 20th century. These transformations made São Paulo a magnet for workers and immigrants, contributing to its rich cultural diversity and dynamic urban landscape.

Today, São Paulo stands as a global megacity, home to over 12 million residents and a vital economic, cultural, and financial hub of South America. Its evolution from a modest mission settlement to a sprawling metropolis reflects the enduring interplay between history, economy, and urban planning.

How can modern cities balance the preservation of their historical and cultural roots while embracing rapid urban expansion and innovation?

JANUARY 26
1992

UNESCO DESIGNATION OF DUBROVNIK, CROATIA

"The destruction of history is the destruction of the soul of a city; its restoration is an act of hope." – Federico Mayor (then-Director-General of UNESCO)

Aerial view of Dubrovnik's Old Town, showcasing its well-preserved medieval walls, terracotta rooftops, and layout that hugs the Adriatic coastline. The city's historic architecture and dramatic seaside location make it one of Europe's most iconic UNESCO World Heritage sites. By Davidzfr. Licensed

On this day in 1992, UNESCO launched a major initiative to restore Dubrovnik's Old City, which had suffered extensive damage during the Siege of Dubrovnik in the Yugoslav Wars. Remarkably, during the height of the siege in late 1991, UNESCO had already declared the Old City a World Heritage Site in Danger, aiming to halt the shelling by drawing global attention to its cultural value. Dubrovnik's medieval walls, urban layout, and centuries-old buildings represent a rich legacy of urban planning and architectural continuity. The subsequent restoration campaign prioritized both structural repair and the preservation of historical authenticity, balancing heritage with the needs of a living city. Supported by international collaboration and local craftsmanship, the project became a benchmark for post-conflict urban heritage recovery. It demonstrated that even in the aftermath of war, cities can be restored with respect for their identity. Today, Dubrovnik stands as a testament to resilience and the critical role of global solidarity in protecting urban cultural landmarks.

How can cities recovering from conflict balance modernization with the preservation of cultural heritage?

EUCLID V. AMBLER REALTY CO. THE BIRTH OF ZONING

"Zoning ordinances, when reasonable, are valid exercises of the police power."
– Justice George Sutherland. Associate Justice of the U.S. Supreme Court.

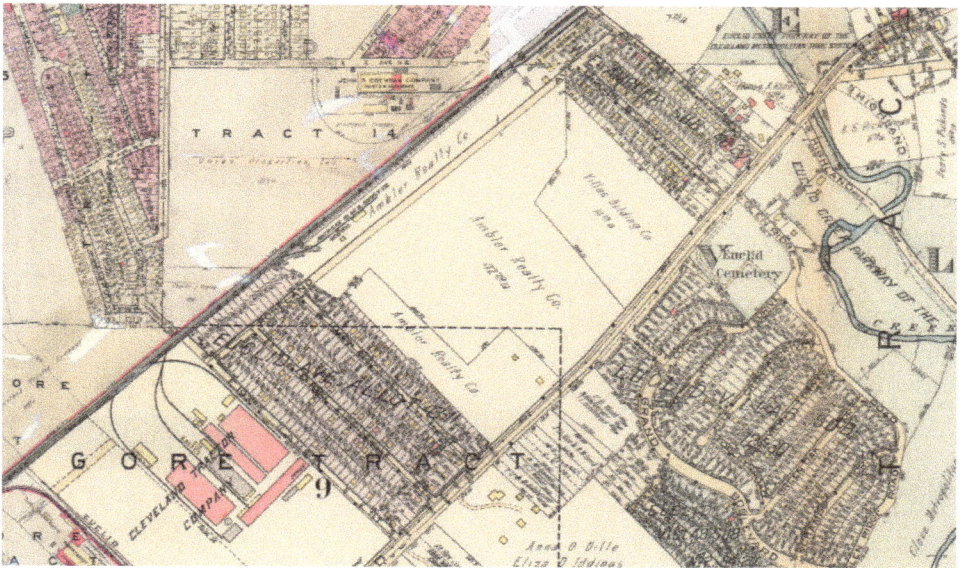

A 1920–22 map of Euclid, Ohio, featuring the Ambler property at its center. This map played a key role in the landmark 1926 Supreme Court case Village of Euclid v. Ambler Realty Co., which upheld the constitutionality of zoning laws. Source: Euclid Zoning Map. Public Domain.

On this day in 1926, the U.S. Supreme Court heard arguments in Village of Euclid v. Ambler Realty Co., a landmark case that defined the future of land-use regulation in the United States. Ambler Realty contested that Euclid, Ohio's zoning ordinance unfairly restricted the use of their property and reduced its value, challenging the extent of municipal power to regulate land use. The case posed critical questions about balancing private property rights with the public interest in promoting health, safety, and welfare. Later that year, the Court upheld zoning laws, legitimizing them as a fundamental urban planning tool. This decision provided the legal foundation for systematic land-use regulation, allowing cities to shape growth and development. However, it paved the way for exclusionary zoning practices, contributing to residential segregation and housing inequality. The case remains a cornerstone in planning history, reflecting the potential and pitfalls of zoning as a regulatory mechanism.

How can zoning laws evolve to balance community needs with resource equity?

JANUARY 28
814 CE

CHARLEMAGNE, FIRST HOLY ROMAN EMPEROR

"Right action is better than knowledge; but in order to do what is right, we must know what is right." — Charlemagne.

Aachen, also known as Aix-La-Chapelle or Aken, is a historic city in western Germany, famous for its medieval architecture, thermal springs, and as the site of Charlemagne's imperial palace and coronation church. By Engel.ac. Licensed.

On this day in 814 CE, Charlemagne, the first Holy Roman Emperor, passed away in Aachen, Germany. Known as the "Father of Europe," Charlemagne profoundly shaped the urban landscape of his empire by revitalizing key cities and establishing fortified "frontier" or mark cities to secure and expand his realm. Aachen, his capital, became a cultural and administrative hub, with its grand palace complex and chapel setting the standard for medieval urban design. Charlemagne also elevated cities like Frankfurt, Paderborn, and Regensburg as centers of governance, religion, and commerce, reinforcing their roles as imperial strongholds. Hamburg and Magdeburg defended against Viking incursions along the empire's frontiers, while Passau and Verona served as critical nodes for military and economic control. These cities fortified the empire's borders and integrated regions through trade, governance, and culture. Charlemagne's urban legacy laid the groundwork for Europe's political and architectural evolution.

How can historical leaders like Charlemagne inspire modern urban governance to create cohesive and culturally rich societies?

BIRTH OF
EBENEZER HOWARD

"A garden city is a marriage of town and country."
— Ebenezer Howard. British urban planner and founder of the Garden City movement.

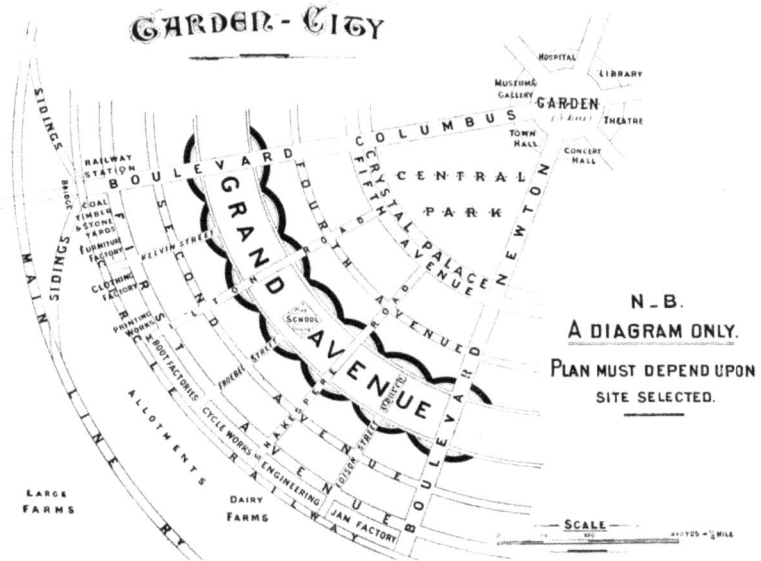

"Ward and Centre." Plate No. 3 from Ebenezer Howard's Garden Cities of Tomorrow. By Ebenezer Howard (1850-1928). Source: The Garden City Land Structure, 1902. Via Wikimedia Commons. Public Domain.

On this day in 1850, Ebenezer Howard, the visionary founder of the Garden City Movement, was born. Howard's transformative urban planning concept sought to combine the benefits of urban living with the serenity of rural life. In his seminal work, Garden Cities of To-Morrow (1898), he envisioned self-contained communities encircled by green belts with distinct residential, industrial, and agricultural zoning. His ideas were realized in the world's first garden cities: Letchworth (1903) and Welwyn Garden City (1920), pioneering sustainable and livable urban design models. Howard's approach addressed industrial cities' overcrowding, pollution, and social challenges by promoting harmonious environments where people could thrive economically, socially, and environmentally. The Garden City Movement profoundly influenced global urban planning, serving as a foundation for concepts like New Urbanism and incorporating green infrastructure into contemporary cities, ensuring Howard's legacy endures in modern urban design.

How can Howard's Garden City ideas inform sustainable suburban development today?

JANUARY 30
1914

FOUNDATION OF
THE ROYAL TOWN PLANNING INSTITUTE

"Town planning is not mere place arrangement, nor even advice upon building lines, but the direction of the growth of towns according to reason." – Raymond Unwin. Urban planner.

A view of a planned suburban community in London, showcasing typical early 20th-century garden suburb ideals—tree-lined streets, residential blocks, and green spaces integrated into the urban fabric. Such developments aimed to balance urban density with access to nature. Source: By Meoita Licensed

On this day in 1914, the Royal Town Planning Institute (RTPI) was established in the United Kingdom, marking a significant step in professionalizing urban and regional planning. Founded during a time of rapid industrialization and urban expansion, the RTPI aimed to tackle pressing issues such as overcrowding, inadequate housing, and inefficient land use. By formalizing planning as a profession, the RTPI championed systematic approaches to integrating housing, infrastructure, and green spaces into urban design. The institute played a key role in advancing transformative initiatives, including the Garden City movement, post-war reconstruction, and the development of modern planning legislation. Its impact transcended national boundaries, shaping urban design practices worldwide and emphasizing the need for sustainable and inclusive development. Over a century later, the RTPI remains at the forefront of promoting innovative, equitable, and resilient urban planning to address contemporary global challenges.

How has the formalization of urban planning as a profession shaped the development of modern cities?

FIRST MCDONALD'S RESTAURANT OPENS IN MOSCOW

"The Golden Arches have become a universal symbol, reflecting the changing face of cities in a globalizing world." – Ray Kroc. American businessman, franchising pioneer of McDonald's.

Image of a McDonald's in Moscow, reflecting the arrival of Western consumer culture in Russia after the Cold War. By Francis Bourgouin. Source: Flickr. CC BY 2.0

On this day in 1990, the first McDonald's in the Soviet Union opened in Moscow's Pushkin Square, drawing over 30,000 visitors on its first day. This historic event symbolized a profound shift in urban culture and globalization during the late Cold War. More than just a business milestone, the arrival of McDonald's reflected Moscow's gradual embrace of Western influences and commercial activity, signaling the city's transformation into a more open and interconnected urban center. The restaurant reshaped public spaces, creating new social gathering spots and introducing consumer culture that contrasted sharply with Soviet-era norms. For many Muscovites, it represented novelty and the possibility of a different, globalized future. The event also highlights broader questions faced by cities worldwide about balancing the introduction of global brands with the preservation of local culture and identity in urban commercial development.

How should cities balance embracing globalization and modern commerce while preserving their unique cultural and historical identities?

FEBRUARY 1
1960

ESTABLISHMENT OF
SINGAPORE'S HOUSING AND DEVELOPMENT BOARD

"Housing is not merely about building homes, but about building a society."
– Lee Kuan Yew. Singapore's first Prime Minister and founding father.

Singapore's transit-oriented development model creates dense, walkable neighborhoods by integrating housing, commercial centers, and public transit. It reflects a commitment to sustainable, efficient urban design. Source: By subhashpb. Licensed

On this day in 1960, the Housing and Development Board (HDB) was established in Singapore, marking the start of one of the world's most successful public housing programs. The HDB replaced the Singapore Improvement Trust (SIT), which had struggled to address the city's acute post-war housing crisis and widespread overcrowding. With the support of the newly elected People's Action Party (PAP) government, the HDB prioritized building affordable, high-quality housing for the population. The HDB constructed over 50,000 flats in its first five years, significantly transforming Singapore's urban landscape and improving living conditions. By integrating innovative urban planning with efficient land use, the HDB addressed housing needs and fostered social equity and cohesion. Today, more than 80% of Singapore's population resides in HDB flats, and the program is widely regarded as a global benchmark for sustainable urban development and effective public housing strategies.

How can cities around the world replicate Singapore's success in public housing while addressing their unique social, cultural, and economic challenges?

ADOPTION OF
THE RAMSAR CONVENTION ON WETLANDS

"Wetlands are not wastelands; they are nature's lifelines, sustaining cities and communities alike." – Luc Hoffmann. Swiss conservationist.

Image of wetlands, showcasing the rich biodiversity, flood control benefits, and ecological value of these natural habitats. Wetlands are critical to urban resilience and environmental sustainability. Source: By Creativenature. nl. Licensed

On this day in 1971, the Ramsar Convention on Wetlands of International Importance was adopted in Iran. This landmark global treaty recognized the critical role wetlands play in environmental and urban sustainability. Wetlands provide essential ecosystem services, including flood mitigation, water purification, and climate regulation, while serving as green spaces that enhance urban biodiversity. Cities such as Amsterdam, New Orleans, and Dhaka have leveraged wetland conservation to address urban challenges like rising sea levels, flooding, and habitat loss. The Ramsar Convention laid the groundwork for integrating natural ecosystems into urban planning, promoting a vision of cities that coexist harmoniously with their surrounding environments. Over 2,400 wetland sites are protected under Ramsar, underscoring a global commitment to balancing urban growth with ecological resilience and sustainability, ensuring that wetlands continue to benefit both natural systems and urban communities.

How can cities prioritize wetland preservation to enhance urban resilience against climate change and promote ecological balance?

FEBRUARY 3
2012

HUD PUBLISHES
EQUAL ACCESS RULE

"No one should be denied a home because of their sexual orientation or gender identity."
— Shaun Donovan, HUD Secretary, 2012

Equity in Diversity. By Bobboz. Licensed

On this day in 2012, the U.S. Department of Housing and Urban Development (HUD) issued the Equal Access to Housing in HUD Programs Regardless of Sexual Orientation or Gender Identity Rule, a groundbreaking policy promoting housing equality. The rule explicitly prohibited discrimination in HUD-funded housing programs based on sexual orientation or gender identity, ensuring fair access to housing opportunities for all individuals. It also extended protections to homeless assistance programs, requiring providers to offer services without making judgments based on marital status, sexual orientation, or gender identity. This landmark policy addressed long-standing housing inequities faced by LGBTQ+ individuals, a group historically marginalized in access to safe and stable housing. The rule underscored HUD's commitment to fair housing practices. It set a precedent for expanding protections for vulnerable populations in federal housing programs, marking a significant step toward greater equity and inclusivity in urban policy.

What further steps can policies take to address the challenges faced by marginalized communities in accessing safe and affordable housing?

FRANCESCO II SFORZA'S ROLE IN MILAN'S URBAN DEVELOPMENT

"A well-ordered city is the greatest legacy a ruler can leave to their people."
– Francesco II Sforza. (Paraphrased)

Aerial view of Castello Sforzesco (Sforza Castle), woven into Milan's urban fabric. Once a medieval fortress, today it anchors the city's cultural and public life, linking history with vibrant spaces and radiating out to the modern city. A testament to how historic landmarks continue to shape Milan's evolving identity. By AerialDronePics. Licensed.

On this day in 1495, Francesco II Sforza, the last Duke of Milan from the influential Sforza dynasty, was born. His leadership marked the continuation of the Sforza family's significant contributions to Milan's urban and cultural development during the Renaissance. The Sforzas were instrumental in commissioning transformative projects that shaped the city's character, including the expansion of the Sforza Castle, a symbol of Milan's power and artistic achievement, and the enhancement of the Navigli canal system, which revolutionized transportation and irrigation. These works blended functional infrastructure with artistic grandeur, reflecting the Renaissance ideals of harmony and innovation. Francesco II's tenure upheld this legacy, integrating engineering, architecture, and governance to solidify Milan's reputation as a hub of cultural and urban advancement. His contributions are a testament to how visionary leadership defined cities as centers of art, commerce, and innovation during the Renaissance.

How can modern cities balance aesthetic beauty with functional infrastructure, as exemplified in Renaissance Milan?

1754

DEATH OF NICOLAAS KRUIK

"Water is both a friend and a foe; its mastery is the key to thriving cities."
— Inspired by Nicolaas Kruik's work.

Etching of the Map of Delfland, a 1750 cartographic work by Nicolaas Cruiquius, depicting the water management systems and polders of the Dutch landscape. This map exemplifies 18th-century precision in cartography. By Nicolaas Cruiquius, 1750. Source: Rijksmuseum, Amsterdam. Via Wikimedia Commons. Public Domain.

On this day in 1754, Nicolaas Kruik, also known as Nicolaus Samuelis Cruquius, a Dutch astronomer, cartographer, and hydraulic engineer, passed away. Kruik played a crucial role in advancing water management systems in the Netherlands, a country profoundly shaped by its relationship with water. His meticulous maps and pioneering studies on tides, rivers, and flooding were instrumental in informing the design and improvement of canals, dikes, and drainage systems. These innovations protected urban and rural areas from flooding, enabling the Netherlands to reclaim and sustainably develop land. Kruik's work laid the foundation for Dutch expertise in hydraulic engineering, establishing principles that continue to influence global urban planning and water management. His legacy endures in the Netherlands' reputation as a leader in water management, exemplifying how engineering and planning can harmonize with natural systems to create resilient urban landscapes.

How can modern urban planning address the challenges of water management in the face of climate change and rising sea levels?

'OF MICE AND MEN' IS PUBLISHED

"A guy needs somebody—to be near him... A guy goes nuts if he ain't got nobody."
– John Steinbeck. American author, Nobel Prize laureate.

TV recordings of "People and Mice" by John Steinbeck. Image author: Verhoeff, Bert / Anefo. Source: Nationaal Archief. Via Wikimedia Commons. CC0.

On this day in 1937, John Steinbeck's Of Mice and Men was published, offering a poignant portrayal of social and economic struggles during the Great Depression. Although set in rural California, the novel's themes echo the broader urbanization trends of the era, as displaced rural workers migrated to cities in search of stability and opportunity. Steinbeck's narrative captures the human toll of economic upheaval, reflecting the challenges of migration, inequality, and the pursuit of the American Dream—issues that also influenced urban growth and planning during the 1930s. The influx of rural populations into cities highlighted the need for affordable housing, labor opportunities, and social services in rapidly expanding urban areas. Steinbeck's enduring work provides a lens for examining the interplay between rural hardship and urban migration, underscoring how economic and social forces shape both individual lives and the spatial organization of cities.

How can literature help us understand the social and economic forces that shape cities and migration patterns?

FEBRUARY 7
1478

BIRTH OF
SIR THOMAS MORE

"A city, if it is to be happy, must be rationally planned and equitably governed."
– Thomas More. English philosopher and author.

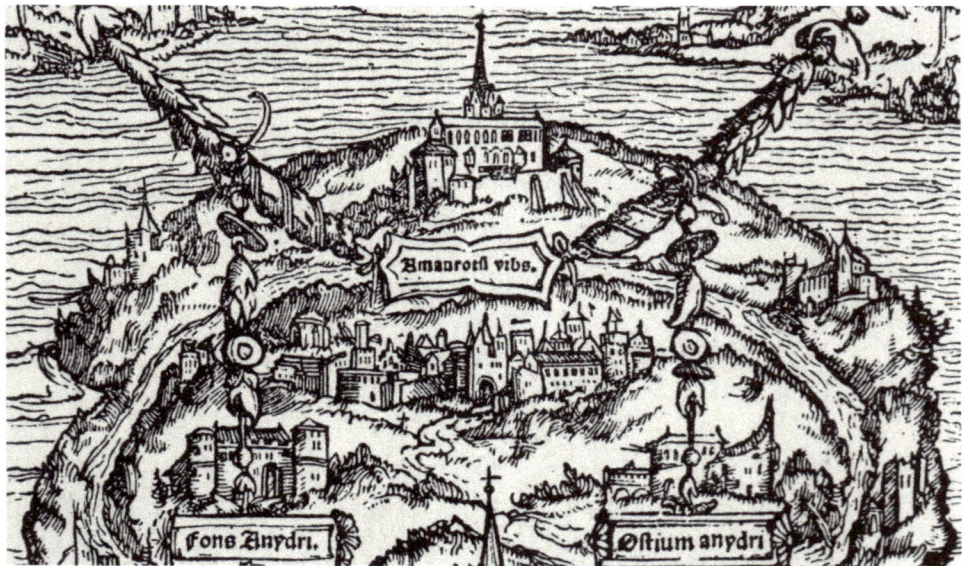

The Utopia of Sir Thomas More: in Latin from the edition of March 1518, and in English from the 1st ed. of Ralph Robynson's translation in 1551 Source: Alamy, originally published in Oxford by Clarendon Press.

On this day in 1478, Sir Thomas More, the English statesman, philosopher, and author of Utopia, was born in London. In 1516, the book was published, depicting an idealized island society characterized by shared resources, communal living, and rational urban planning. The book profoundly shaped the discourse around ideal cities, becoming a foundational text in urban utopian thought. More's vision of orderly, egalitarian cities emphasized harmony, sustainability, and the balance between human needs and the built environment. Although fictional, Utopia sparked enduring debates on governance, urban equity, and the transformative potential of planning to achieve social progress. Its influence can be seen in later movements advocating for planned communities and equitable urban development. More's legacy endures in urbanism, inspiring generations to consider how cities can embody principles of justice, efficiency, and well-being while fostering vibrant, inclusive communities.

How do utopian visions like More's challenge modern urban planners to think beyond conventional city designs?

ENACTMENT OF
THE LONDON BUILDING ACT OF 1667

"London is never finished, for it is a living, breathing organism."
– Peter Ackroyd. English historian and novelist.

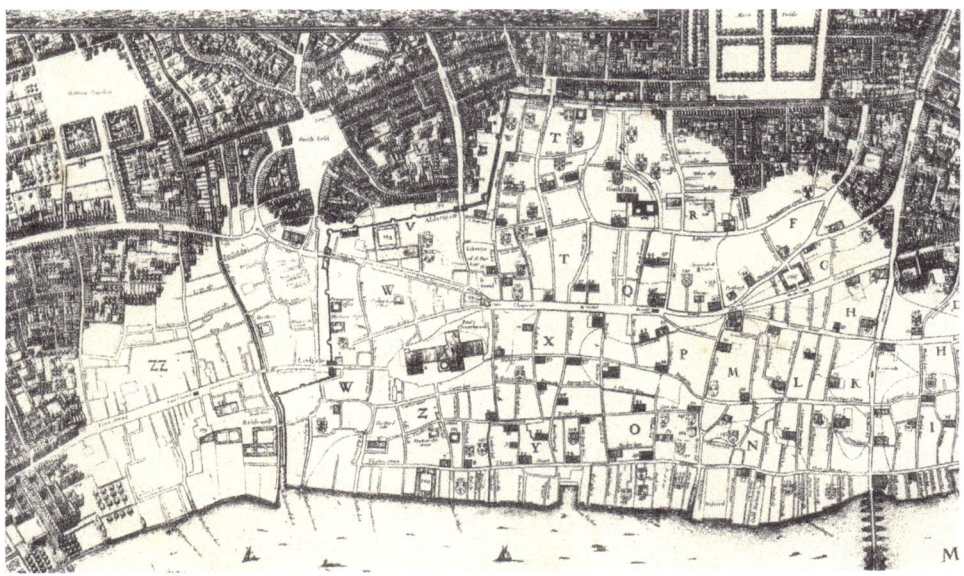

A survey of the streets, lanes, and churches contained within the ruins of London after the Fire of 1666 and described by John Leake. By Wenceslaus Hollar, 1667. Source: Alamy.

On this day in 1667, the London Building Act was enacted, marking a transformative moment in the history of urban planning and building regulation in England. Prompted by the devastating Great Fire of London in 1666, the Act introduced groundbreaking safety measures to prevent future disasters. It mandated that new buildings in the City of London be constructed using fire-resistant materials such as brick and stone, replacing the flammable timber structures that had dominated the medieval city. Additionally, the Act regulated building heights, standardized street widths, and clarified property boundaries to improve public safety and urban organization. These reforms were central to London's reconstruction, creating a more resilient and orderly urban fabric. The Act shaped the city's rebuilding and set a precedent for modern urban legislation, influencing building codes and planning practices worldwide. It remains a significant milestone in the evolution of safe and sustainable city planning.

How can the lessons from London's reconstruction after the Great Fire inspire modern cities to rebuild after disasters in a sustainable and equitable way?

FEBRUARY 9
2008

GROUNDBREAKING
OF MASDAR CITY, UAE

"We see Masdar City as a vision for sustainable living for the 21st century." – Sultan Ahmed Al Jaber. Emirati businessman and Minister of Industry and Advanced Technology.

MBZUAI Knowledge Center and other campus buildings in front of Central Park, Masdar City, 2024. By NNegm CC BY-SA 4.0

On this day in 2008, construction began in Masdar City in Abu Dhabi, which was envisioned as a groundbreaking urban utopia and a global model for sustainability. The city was designed by Foster + Partners to become the world's first zero-carbon, zero-waste urban area powered entirely by renewable energy. The master plan incorporated innovative technologies, including vast solar farms, wind towers for natural cooling, and autonomous electric vehicles for transportation. Masdar's compact, pedestrian-friendly layout emphasized resource efficiency, featuring shaded streets and energy-efficient buildings designed to combat desert heat while reducing energy use. Although the city faced significant challenges in achieving its ambitious goals, it has evolved into a testbed for green technologies and sustainable urban practices. Masdar City remains a symbol of visionary urban planning, demonstrating how advanced technology and environmental stewardship can be integrated to address urbanization and climate change, inspiring future sustainable city developments worldwide.

How can experimental urban projects like Masdar City inspire sustainable practices in cities worldwide?

3RD DRAFT OF
THE STANDARD STATE ZONING ENABLING ACT

"The physical development of a community must be directed by thoughtful zoning and planning to ensure prosperity and order."– Herbert Hoover. 31st President of the United States.

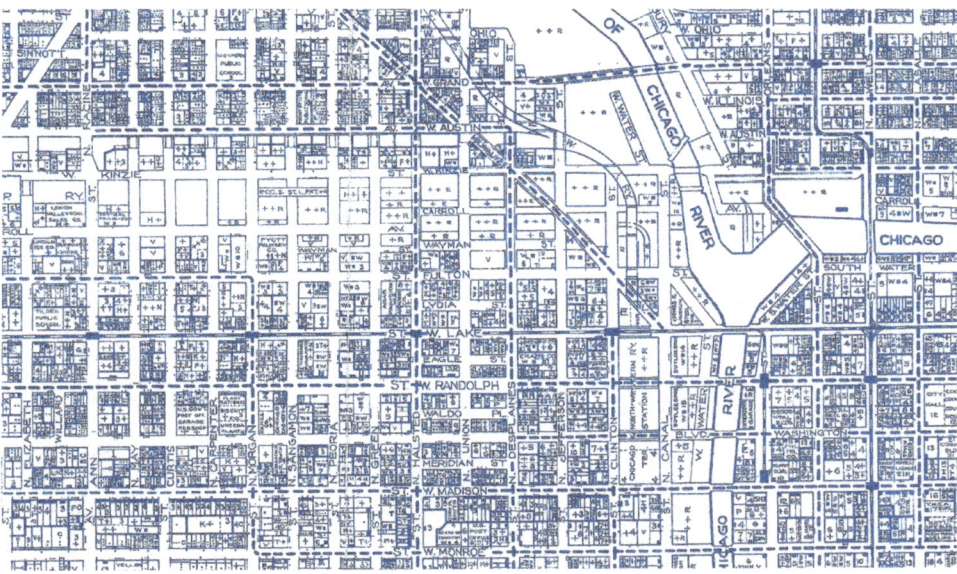

1922 Chicago zoning survey map. By Chicago (Ill.). Zoning Commission. Source: University of Chicago Visual Resources Center. Via Wikimedia Commons. Public Domain.

On this day in 1922, the U.S. Department of Commerce released the third draft of the Standard State Zoning Enabling Act (SZEA), a model law designed to guide states in establishing zoning regulations. Led by then-Secretary of Commerce Herbert Hoover, the SZEA introduced crucial provisions, such as granting zoning commissions the authority to regulate land use and mandating that zoning decisions align with a comprehensive plan. This draft marked a significant milestone in formalizing land-use regulation, empowering states to delegate zoning authority to local governments to promote orderly development. The SZEA provided the legal foundation for modern zoning practices, ensuring cities and towns could control land use to protect public health, safety, and welfare. Together with the Standard City Planning Enabling Act (1927), which addressed broader city planning issues, the SZEA created an enduring institutional framework that continues to shape land-use and urban planning practices in the United States.

What challenges and opportunities do modern zoning practices face in adapting the principles of the SZEA to address contemporary issues like equity and climate resilience?

FEBRUARY 11
1380

REDISCOVERY OF VITRUVIUS' DE ARCHITECTURA

"The human body is a model for the city's symmetry and proportion."
– Vitruvius. Roman architect and engineer.

Recto: Temple Types: in Antis and Prostyle (Vitruvius, Book 3, Chapter 2, nos. 2, 3); Verso: Temple Types: Peripteral (Vitruvius, Book 3, Chapter 2, no. 5). By Marcus Pollio Vitruvius, 1st Century BCE. Via Wikimedia Commons. Public Domain.

On this day in 1380, Gian Francesco Poggio Bracciolini, the Italian humanist credited with rediscovering Vitruvius' De Architectura, was born. This seminal Roman treatise, written in the 1st century BCE, profoundly shaped the understanding of urban planning by envisioning the city as a harmonious balance of utility, strength, and beauty. Vitruvius detailed principles of symmetry, proportion, and integrating public spaces with natural surroundings, advocating for planned streets, efficient infrastructure, and vibrant civic areas. These ideals promoted sustainable and aesthetically pleasing urban environments aligned with cultural and practical needs. The rediscovery of De Architectura during the Renaissance ignited a revival of classical urbanism, inspiring architects and planners to create orderly, human-scaled cities that balanced form and function. Its influence persists, offering timeless insights into designing cities that harmonize the needs of their inhabitants with cultural and environmental aspirations.

How can Vitruvius' principles guide modern urban planning in balancing aesthetic beauty and functional needs?

FOUNDING OF SAVANNAH, GEORGIA

"Such a settlement will not only give sustenance to its inhabitants but serve as a model for a well-regulated community." – James Oglethorpe. British general and founder of the colony of Georgia.

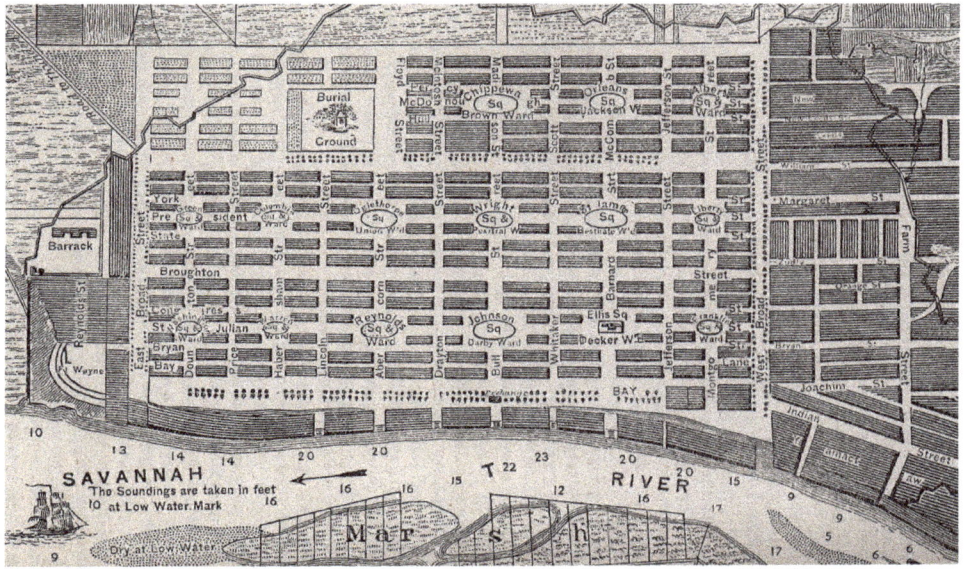

1818 map of Savannah, highlighting the city's distinctive grid and ward plan. The design features repeated modules of squares surrounded by residential and civic blocks reflecting Enlightenment ideals of order, equity, and civic life. By Moss Eng. Co., NY. Source: Wikimedia Commons. Public Domain.

On this day in 1733, General James Oglethorpe founded Savannah, Georgia, as the first settlement of the new colony of Georgia. Oglethorpe envisioned Savannah as a strategic defense outpost against Spanish Florida and a model city for equitable and orderly living. The city's innovative plan featured wards arranged in a grid pattern centered around a public square, combining practicality with community cohesion. This design encouraged social interaction, accessibility, and the integration of green spaces, reflecting Enlightenment urban planning principles. Savannah's original plan accommodated growth while maintaining harmony, a hallmark in its historic district today. Of the original 24 planned squares, 22 still exist, making Savannah a living museum of 18th-century city design. The city remains a celebrated example of how thoughtful urban planning can shape physical and social landscapes.

How did Savannah's original grid and square system influence later city planning efforts in the United States

REPORT OF
THE PUBLIC LANDS COMMISSION

"The nation behaves well if it treats its natural resources as assets which it must turn over to the next generation increased, and not impaired, in value." – Theodore Roosevelt. 26th US President.

Pisgah National Forest, NC, 2023. A historic log cabin at the Cradle of Forestry in Pisgah National Forest reflects early U.S. conservation ideals, embodying the Public Lands Commission's 1903 vision for sustainable land use, federal stewardship, and the birth of professional forest management. By Juan Mullerat. Own Work.

On this day in 1905, President Theodore Roosevelt established the Public Lands Commission to address pressing concerns about managing and conserving federal lands in the United States. The commission was tasked with assessing public land policies and recommending reforms to ensure sustainable use of natural resources. It focused on challenges like overgrazing, deforestation, and inequitable land distribution, advocating for more systematic planning and scientific resource management. The commission's findings laid the foundation for landmark conservation initiatives, including creating the U.S. Forest Service in 1905 and introducing principles that would influence urban and regional planning. Its work reflected the Progressive Era's ethos of applying science and expertise to public policy, promoting the sustainable development of both rural and urban landscapes. The commission's legacy endures in modern conservation efforts and in planning practices that balance environmental stewardship with human needs.

How can systematic land and resource planning be improved today to address challenges like climate change and urban expansion?

BIRTH OF
LEON BATTISTA ALBERTI

"The city is like a large house, and the house is in turn like a small city."
– Leon Battista Alberti. Italian Renaissance architect and theorist.

The Ideal City, attributed to Fra Carnevale c. 1480 and c. 1484, reflects Leon Battista Alberti's humanist ideals of harmony, proportion, and civic order. Source: Walters Art Museum. Acquired by Henry Walters with the Massarenti Collection, 1902. Via Wikimedia Commons. CC0.

On this day in 1404, Leon Battista Alberti, a foundational figure in Renaissance architecture and urban planning, was born in Genoa, Italy. Alberti's influential writings, particularly De Re Aedificatoria (On the Art of Building), revolutionized architectural theory by emphasizing harmony, proportion, and functionality in urban and building design. Melding classical ideals with innovative approaches, Alberti advanced the concept of a city as an interconnected entity where architecture, infrastructure, and societal needs worked in balance. His principles guided the design of urban layouts, public spaces, and iconic structures, including his contributions to the Basilica of Santa Maria Novella in Florence. Alberti's vision extended beyond individual buildings to embrace the city as a unified organism, shaping Renaissance urban thought. His legacy endures in modern architecture and urban planning, inspiring a holistic approach that integrates aesthetic beauty with practical and social purpose in city design.

How can Alberti's principles of harmony and functionality be applied to contemporary urban planning to create more livable and aesthetically pleasing cities?

FEBRUARY 15
438 CE

THEODOSIUS II
PUBLISHES: CODEX THEODOSIANUS

"The strength of a city lies in the order of its laws and the equity of its governance."
— Inspired by Theodosius II's legislative efforts

Cicero Denounces Catilina. By Cesare Maccari, 1889. A fresco at Maccari Hall, Italian Senate, Palazzo Madama, Rome, capturing Cicero's famous speech exposing Catiline's conspiracy, symbolizing civic duty, oratory, and the defense of the Roman Republic. Via Wikimedia Commons. Public Domain.

On this day in 438 CE, Roman Emperor Theodosius II issued the Codex Theodosianus, a monumental compilation of Roman laws enacted since 312 CE. This legal codex standardized legislation across the empire, significantly shaping urban governance, property rights, and city planning. It addressed critical urban issues, including regulating public works, zoning laws, taxation, and maintaining essential infrastructure such as aqueducts, roads, and bridges. By ensuring a consistent legal framework, the codex reinforced the role of cities as administrative, economic, and social centers of the Roman Empire. Its influence extended beyond antiquity, serving as a foundational text for medieval European legal traditions. The Codex Theodosianus not only preserved Roman legal thought but also provided enduring principles for the governance and development of cities, leaving a lasting impact on urban management and the evolution of legal systems throughout Europe.

How can the principles of uniformity and equity in historical legal codes inform modern urban governance and legislative reforms?

KYOTO PROTOCOL
COMES INTO FORCE

"The time for action is now. It is never too late to do something."
— Carl Sandburg. American poet and historian.

Flood-affected village in Northern Bangladesh, showing submerged homes and disrupted infrastructure, highlighting the vulnerability of rural settlements to climate change and extreme weather events. By Abdul Momin. Licensed.

On this day in 2005, the Kyoto Protocol officially came into force after being ratified by Russia, marking a milestone in global efforts to combat climate change. This landmark international treaty set binding targets for reducing greenhouse gas emissions, emphasizing the need for sustainable practices. The protocol significantly influenced urban planning, inspiring cities to adopt greener infrastructure, renewable energy solutions, and enhanced public transportation systems to lower emissions. Its principles also encouraged energy-efficient building designs, waste reduction strategies, and the integration of green spaces to improve urban resilience against climate impacts. The Kyoto Protocol fostered a global shift toward sustainability and carbon neutrality by recognizing cities as key players in addressing environmental challenges. Its legacy continues to shape urban development, demonstrating the critical role of cities in leading innovative climate action and building a more sustainable future.

How can urban planners build on the legacy of the Kyoto Protocol to create cities that are resilient to climate change and committed to sustainability?

FEBRUARY 17
2003

LONDON INTRODUCES CONGESTION CHARGE ZONE

"The Congestion Charge has transformed central London into a cleaner, quieter, and more accessible space for everyone." – Ken Livingstone. Former Mayor of London.

London Traffic, showcasing the density and dynamism of urban life in the capital, highlighting challenges in mobility, congestion, and the balance of people and cars in modern cities. By CL-Medien Licensed

On this day in 2003, London introduced its pioneering Congestion Charge Zone, a groundbreaking policy designed to reduce car traffic in the city center. Drivers entering the designated zone were required to pay a daily fee, encouraging alternatives such as public transport, cycling, and walking. Spearheaded by Mayor Ken Livingstone, the initiative achieved immediate success, reducing car traffic by 15% and significantly increasing bus ridership. The policy also contributed to lower air pollution levels and generated substantial revenue for improving public transit infrastructure. Over time, the Congestion Charge Zone has evolved, adopting technologies like automatic number plate recognition and introducing ultra-low emission zones (ULEZ) to target high-polluting vehicles. London's innovative approach has become a global model for traffic management, inspiring cities worldwide to implement similar strategies and underscoring the importance of sustainable urban mobility in creating more livable, efficient urban environments.

How can cities strike a balance between traffic management, equitable access to urban centers, and reducing environmental impacts from car use?

PASSING OF JOHN NOLEN

"The city is the home of man. It should be planned for the comfort, convenience, and health of all its inhabitants." — John Nolen. American landscape architect and city planner.

View of San Diego, CA. By John Nolen 1908. Source: A comprehensive plan for its improvement. Boston: Geo. H. Ellis Co. 1908, and Ford, G. B, Ed. City planning progress in the United States, 1917. Committee on Town Planning, American Association of Architects. 1917. Source: Wikimedia Commons. Public Domain.

On this day in 1937, John Nolen, a pioneering American landscape architect and urban planner, passed away. Nolen was a visionary in early 20th-century city planning, advocating for the integration of green spaces, efficient transportation systems, and sustainable land use. His influential work included plans for cities such as Madison, Wisconsin, and Mariemont, Ohio, where he crafted livable communities designed to promote health, well-being, and social connection. Nolen's approach seamlessly blended aesthetics with functionality, emphasizing public parks, walkable neighborhoods, and carefully planned roadways to create balanced and harmonious urban environments. His work laid the groundwork for modern urban planning principles, particularly prioritizing human-centric design and the interplay between nature and the built environment. Nolen's legacy endures in cities that continue to embody his ideals of thoughtful, people-focused development and his enduring commitment to quality of life in urban spaces.

How can modern cities draw inspiration from John Nolen's vision to create healthier, more sustainable urban environments?

EUGÈNE HÉNARD'S LEGACY: INVENTOR OF THE ROUNDABOUT

"The city of the future must be conceived as a whole, with its circulation systems harmoniously integrated to serve both movement and repose." – Eugène Hénard. French architect and urban planner.

Aerial view of the Summerlin neighborhood, Las Vegas, Nevada. A master-planned community developed in the late 20th century, Summerlin integrates residential zones, commercial centers, and recreational areas within a structured urban layout. Photo by Trekandphoto. Licensed.

On this day in 1923, Eugène Hénard, the French architect and urban planner credited with inventing the modern roundabout, passed away in Paris. First implemented in 1907 at Place de l'Étoile (now home to the Arc de Triomphe), Hénard's roundabout addressed the growing problem of urban congestion caused by the rise of automobiles. His innovative traffic design allowed vehicles to flow continuously in a circular motion, reducing delays and improving safety at busy intersections. This concept revolutionized urban traffic management and has since become a standard feature in cities worldwide, with over 40,000 roundabouts now operating in the United States alone.

Hénard's vision for efficient, harmonious urban circulation has left an enduring legacy, influencing city layouts and transportation planning for over a century.

How has the roundabout shaped the way cities manage traffic flow, and what lessons can modern planners draw from this century-old innovation?

PUBLICATION OF
THE FUTURIST MANIFESTO

"We declare that the splendor of the world has been enriched by a new beauty: the beauty of speed." – Filippo Tommaso Marinetti. Italian poet and founder of the Futurist movement.

Filippo Tommaso Marinetti, Italian poet and founder of the Futurist movement. Known for the 1909 Manifesto of Futurism, which advocated for modernity, speed, and industrialization in art and urbanism. Author unknown. Source: Wikimedia Commons. Public Domain.

On this day in 1909, Filippo Tommaso Marinetti's Futurist Manifesto was published in the French journal Le Figaro, heralding a bold vision for modernity that rejected tradition in favor of speed, technology, and industrial progress. This groundbreaking document profoundly influenced architecture and urban design, imagining cities as dynamic, machine-driven environments that embodied the energy of the modern age. Futurist ideals inspired architects like Antonio Sant'Elia, whose visionary designs proposed vertical cities, efficient transportation systems, and functional structures emphasizing movement and innovation. Although the movement was controversial and short-lived, its radical embrace of transformation and its challenge to conventional urban forms pushed designers to reconsider the potential of cities in a rapidly industrializing world. The Futurist Manifesto remains a milestone in the history of urbanism, reflecting the optimism and upheaval of early 20th-century modernity.

How can the principles of bold innovation and progress balance with preserving the cultural and historical identity of cities?

FEBRUARY 21
1936

BIRTH OF
BARBARA JORDAN

"What the people want is simple. They want an America as good as its promise."
– Barbara Jordan. American lawyer, educator, and politician. (Paraphrased from speeches).

Barbara Jordan, member of the U.S. House of Representatives (D-Texas). 1976. By Thomas J. O'Halloran. Source: Library of Congress, Prints and Photographs Division. CC0.

On this day in 1936, Barbara Jordan, a trailblazing African American lawyer, politician, and civil rights advocate, was born in Houston, Texas. Jordan broke barriers as the first Black woman elected to the Texas Senate and later as a U.S. House of Representatives member. She was a powerful voice for justice and equity, championing legislation that addressed urban inequalities, promoted fair housing, and fought against systemic discrimination. Her work underscored the importance of equitable access to public resources and reshaped policies to dismantle barriers faced by marginalized communities. Jordan's leadership extended beyond legislation, inspiring more inclusive approaches to city planning and governance that emphasized equality, accessibility, and fairness. Her legacy continues to guide efforts to create urban environments that reflect the principles of social justice and sustainability, ensuring that all residents can thrive within their communities.

How can urban planners and policymakers ensure equitable representation and resource distribution in contemporary cities?

GALILEO'S DIALOGUE
PRESENTED TO FERDINANDO II

"The sun, with all those planets revolving around it... can still ripen a bunch of grapes as if it had nothing else in the universe to do." – Galileo Galilei. Italian astronomer, physicist, and engineer.

The trial of Galileo Galilei before the Inquisition, 1633. A pivotal clash between scientific discovery and institutional power, captured in this dramatic painting. Attributed to Joseph-Nicolas Robert-Fleury. Source: Wikimedia Commons. Public Domain.

On this day in 1632, Ferdinando II de' Medici, Grand Duke of Tuscany, received the first printed copy of Galileo Galilei's Dialogue Concerning the Two Chief World Systems. This seminal work defended Copernicus's heliocentric theory against the traditional geocentric view, marking a pivotal moment in the Scientific Revolution. Under Ferdinando's patronage, Florence thrived as a Renaissance hub of intellectual exchange, where scholars and artists challenged established norms and advanced new ideas. Galileo's Dialogue exemplified the transformative role of urban centers in fostering innovation, serving as crucibles for groundbreaking scientific and cultural progress. Beyond its impact on astronomy, the book embodied the broader shift toward empirical evidence and questioning traditional authority. This moment underscores how cities have historically provided the resources, networks, and environment necessary for revolutionary ideas to emerge, shaping the trajectory of global thought and progress.

How can cities today create spaces that promote innovation while challenging existing paradigms?

FEBRUARY 23
1455

PUBLICATION OF THE GUTENBERG BIBLE

"Give me 26 soldiers of lead, and I will conquer the world."
— Commonly attributed to Johannes Gutenberg. German inventor of the printing press.

Print of Johannes Gutenberg's house in Mainz, Germany, 1450. By Karl Fasol. Source: Österreichische Nationalbibliothek - Austrian National Library. Via Wikimedia Commons. Public Domain.

On this day in 1455, the Gutenberg Bible, the first major book printed using movable type, was traditionally completed in Mainz, Germany, by Johannes Gutenberg. This revolutionary achievement transformed communication and democratized access to knowledge, catalyzing the spread of literacy and ideas across Europe. The Gutenberg Bible marked the dawn of the information age, profoundly influencing urban centers by positioning them as hubs of learning, culture, and commerce. The printing press spurred the growth of universities, libraries, and publishing industries within cities, fostering intellectual exchange and innovation. By enabling the mass production of books, Gutenberg's invention shifted the dynamics of knowledge distribution, shaping urban societies as engines of cultural and educational progress. The legacy of the Gutenberg Bible underscores the enduring impact of technological advancements on urban development and their role in shaping cities' intellectual and cultural foundations.

How can modern urban centers continue to innovate in the dissemination and democratization of knowledge?

THE LANTERN FESTIVAL CELEBRATIONS IN HAN CHINA

"The city is not merely a repository of culture but the instrument of culture."
– Lewis Mumford. American historian and urban theorist.

Stone-paved street lined with traditional storefronts in Lijiang Old Town, Yunnan, China. Red lanterns overhead highlight the area's rich cultural heritage. By toa555. Licensed.

On this day, in 206 BCE, the Han Dynasty was established. During this period, the first recorded celebrations of what is now known as the Chinese Lantern Festival took place. Emperor Hanmingdi, an advocate of Buddhism, introduced the lighting of lanterns in temples to honor Buddha. Over time, the festival evolved into a grand urban celebration, particularly in major cities like Chang'an. During the Tang Dynasty (618–907 CE), the Lantern Festival became a centerpiece of urban life, with streets adorned by intricate lanterns, cultural performances, and community gatherings. These public events transformed city centers into vibrant hubs of social and cultural interaction, fostering a sense of unity among diverse populations. Today, the festival highlights the importance of urban spaces as venues for cultural continuity, creating communal bonds that transcend generations.

How can modern cities use public spaces to preserve and celebrate cultural traditions while fostering inclusivity and unity?

FEBRUARY 25
1969

PUBLICATION OF
ROGER TOMLINSON'S SEMINAL GIS PAPER

"GIS is the technology of integration, where everything can be linked to a place."
— Roger Tomlinson. British geographer and "father of GIS."

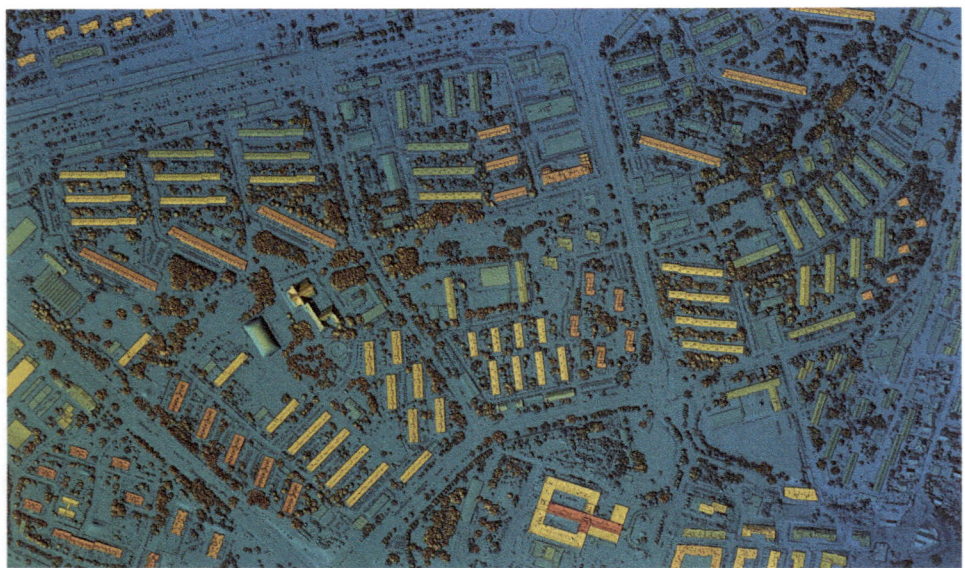

Digital elevation model (DEM) produced through GIS analysis of drone imagery. The model visualizes topography, roads, and suburban development patterns within the urban landscape. By Ungrim. Licensed.

On this day in 1969, Roger Tomlinson, widely recognized as the "Father of GIS," published his landmark paper, A Geographic Information System for Regional Planning. Building on his pioneering work with the Canada Land Inventory (CLI) in 1963, Tomlinson's paper formally introduced Geographic Information Systems (GIS) principles and applications. This groundbreaking innovation enabled the integration of spatial data with geographic analysis, revolutionizing urban and regional planning, environmental conservation, and land management. GIS gave planners powerful tools to visualize, analyze, and model complex data, transforming fields such as transportation planning, zoning, environmental science, and public health. Tomlinson's visionary approach laid the foundation for GIS technology to become a cornerstone of modern planning, shaping decision-making processes and fostering more sustainable, data-driven urban development worldwide. His work continues to influence how cities and regions are planned, managed, and understood today.

How has GIS evolved since its inception, and what new challenges and opportunities does it present for urban and regional planning today?

ESTABLISHMENT OF
GRAND CANYON NATIONAL PARK

"The wonders of the Grand Canyon cannot be adequately represented in symbols of speech, nor by speech itself." – John Wesley Powell. American explorer and geologist.

The Lookout, Grand Canyon National Park. By Fred Harvey, 1905-1949. Source: Detroit Publishing Company Collection. The Newberry Library. Via Wikimedia Commons. Public Domain.

On this day in 1919, the U.S. Congress passed an act establishing Grand Canyon National Park in Arizona, preserving one of the world's most remarkable natural wonders. Encompassing over 1 million acres, the park protects the Grand Canyon, a 277-mile-long chasm carved by the Colorado River over millions of years. The area is rich in cultural heritage and is home to Indigenous tribes such as the Hopi, Navajo, Zuni, Paiute, Havasupai, and Hualapai, who have lived in and around the canyon for over 2,000 years. Designated as a UNESCO World Heritage Site, the park is celebrated for its unparalleled geological features, biodiversity, and cultural significance. Its creation was a milestone in the American conservation movement, emphasizing the importance of safeguarding natural treasures for future generations. Today, Grand Canyon National Park remains an iconic symbol of environmental preservation and a major global destination, drawing millions of visitors annually.

How can modern urban planning and conservation balance tourism, development, and the preservation of cultural and natural heritage?

FEBRUARY 27
1908

FINAL PREPARATIONS FOR
THE NEW YORK CONGESTION EXHIBIT

"Congestion in our cities is not simply a housing problem, it is a problem of humanity."
— Benjamin Marsh, Executive Secretary, Committee on Congestion

Block of Old Style Tenements, NY (Congestion Exhibit). Source: Bain News Service photograph collection via the Library of Congress Prints and Photographs Division. Public Domain.

On this day in 1908, preparations were finalized for the New York Congestion Exhibit at the American Museum of Natural History in Manhattan, marking a pivotal moment in the history of urban reform. Organized by the Committee on Congestion of Population, the exhibit highlighted the dire living conditions in New York City's overcrowded tenements, particularly in immigrant neighborhoods. Through maps, charts, photographs, and models, it illustrated issues such as poor sanitation, inadequate light and air, and the health and social impacts of extreme density. The exhibit attracted over 6,000 visitors, including policymakers, civic leaders, and the public, sparking discussions on improving urban living conditions. It catalyzed reform, influencing the development of zoning laws, public housing programs, and new approaches to urban planning. By emphasizing data-driven analysis and visual storytelling, the exhibit underscored the role of urban planning in addressing social inequities and creating healthier, more equitable cities.

How can data visualization and public exhibits be used to raise awareness and drive action on contemporary urban challenges?

BIRTH OF
GUILLAUME DELISLE

"Accuracy is the soul of cartography, for only through precision can we truly understand and shape the world around us." – Guillaume Delisle. French cartographer.

Map of the City and Faubourgs of Paris, 1720. Created by Guillaume Del'Isle, a prominent French cartographer. The map illustrates the urban morphology and expansion of Paris in the early 18th century. 1716. Source: David Rumsey Historical Map Collection. Public Domain.

On this day in 1675, Guillaume Delisle, a pioneering French cartographer, was born. Renowned for his meticulous and scientifically accurate maps, Delisle revolutionized cartography during the Enlightenment, establishing standards that profoundly influenced urban planning. His detailed maps of Paris and other urban centers became essential tools for land use planning, infrastructure development, and city layout design. Delisle's work prioritized geographic precision and reliability, enabling planners to visualize urban spaces with unprecedented clarity and to design cities more systematically. By combining technical accuracy with artistic presentation, Delisle bridged the gap between science and urban design, shaping city development across Europe. His legacy endures in modern cartographic principles, underscoring the critical role of maps in understanding, organizing, and managing urban growth and infrastructure. Delisle's contributions remain foundational to integrating geography into urban planning and design.

How can cartographic advancements today, such as GIS, transform urban planning and create smarter, more sustainable cities?

MARCH 1
1872

FOUNDING OF YELLOWSTONE AS THE WORLD'S FIRST NATIONAL PARK

"For the benefit and enjoyment of the people."
– Inscription on the Roosevelt Arch at Yellowstone's north entrance.

President Roosevelt speaking of Yellowstone Park, Gardiner, Montana. From Illus. in: Frank Leslie's illustrated newspaper, v. 36, no. 911 (1873 March 15), p. 12. Underwood & Underwood, publisher.. Source: Library of Congress Prints and Photographs Division. Via Wikimedia Commons. Public Domain.

On this day in 1872, President Ulysses S. Grant signed the Yellowstone National Park Protection Act, establishing the world's first national park. Spanning Wyoming, Montana, and Idaho, Yellowstone was created to protect its extraordinary geothermal features, diverse ecosystems, and iconic landscapes, including geysers, hot springs, and the Grand Canyon of Yellowstone. This landmark decision marked the birth of the global conservation movement, setting a precedent that natural wonders should be preserved for public benefit rather than private exploitation. Yellowstone's founding inspired the creation of national parks worldwide, establishing a model for environmental stewardship and sustainable land management. As a natural and cultural treasure, Yellowstone exemplifies the delicate balance between preservation, tourism, and ecosystem management, serving as a lasting symbol of humanity's commitment to safeguarding the planet's most extraordinary places for future generations.

How did the establishment of Yellowstone as a national park shape the global conversation about conservation and public access to natural landscapes?

PASSING OF
MESTRE VALENTIM

"Public spaces are the heart of a city, where art and nature unite to enrich the lives of its people." – Mestre Valentim. Brazilian sculptor and architect.

XV de Novembro Square, with the Mestre Valentim Fountain in the foreground. By Marc Ferrez. Source: Courtesy of Coleção Gilberto Ferrez/Acervo Instituto Moreira Salles. With Permission.

On this day in 1813, Valentim da Fonseca e Silva, widely known as Mestre Valentim, passed away, leaving an enduring legacy as one of Brazil's most influential artists and urban planners of the colonial era. Mestre Valentim is celebrated for his transformative contributions to Rio de Janeiro's urban landscape, most notably the design of the Passeio Público, completed in 1783. As one of the earliest public parks in the Americas, the Passeio Público blended European neoclassical influences with Brazilian aesthetics, establishing a model for integrating public spaces into city planning. Beyond the park, Valentim's work included fountains, sculptures, and urban features that combined artistic beauty with practicality, reflecting Enlightenment ideals of civic improvement and accessibility. His vision helped reshape Rio de Janeiro into a city that valued cultural refinement and public engagement, making him a pioneer in the evolution of urban design in the Americas.

How can modern urban planners draw inspiration from historical figures like Mestre Valentim to create enduring public spaces that reflect cultural identity?

MARCH 3
1879

ESTABLISHMENT OF
THE UNITED STATES GEOLOGICAL SURVEY

"The objective of the USGS is to provide impartial information on the condition of the land, water, and resources essential for national progress." – USGS Mission Statement

Geodetic survey marker at Acadia National Park, used for precise measurement and mapping of the Earth's surface. Survey markers are critical for geospatial data accuracy and infrastructure planning. By Nikki. Licensed.

On this day in 1879, Congress established the United States Geological Survey (USGS) to map, survey, and analyze the nation's natural resources. Created within the Department of the Interior, the USGS became an essential urban and regional planning resource, providing critical data on land use, water resources, and geological conditions. Its early efforts supported city expansion, transportation planning, and resource management, laying the groundwork for modern urban development. Over time, the agency's mission expanded to include studying natural hazards such as earthquakes, floods, and landslides, enabling planners to design safer and more resilient cities. The USGS's impartial scientific research has been instrumental in bridging environmental knowledge with sustainable urban growth, influencing infrastructure design, disaster preparedness, and climate change adaptation. From mapping the western frontier to advancing modern ecological monitoring, the USGS has played a pivotal role in shaping how cities interact with and adapt to their natural landscapes.

How can urban planners and policymakers use geological data to design more resilient and sustainable cities in the face of climate change and natural disasters?

HERBERT HOOVER DELIVERS INAUGURAL ADDRESS ON PROSPERITY

"Given the chance to go forward with the policies of the last eight years, we shall soon... be in sight of the day when poverty will be banished from this nation." — Herbert Hoover. 31st US President.

President Hoover's Inauguration, 1929. Bird's-eye view of Capitol grounds and inaugural crowds, taken from the roof of the Capitol, looking north. Author unknown. Source: Library of Congress Prints and Photographs Division. Public Domain.

On this day in 1929, Herbert Hoover delivered his inaugural address as the 31st President of the United States, promoting optimism, technological progress, and economic prosperity. Hoover's vision emphasized improving living standards through suburban growth, homeownership, and car ownership, reflecting the transformative ethos of the 1920s. The mass production of automobiles reshaped urban and suburban life, with cars becoming symbols of freedom and upward mobility. Suburban housing developments increasingly featured driveways and garages, embedding the car into daily life and suburban design. While the Great Depression soon overshadowed Hoover's presidency, his ideals left a lasting legacy. The connection between cars, suburbanization, and the American Dream profoundly influenced urban planning and development, driving the expansion of car-centric infrastructure and shaping the spatial organization of cities and suburbs. This trend continues to impact urban landscapes today.

How did the optimism of the late 1920s shape the built environment of suburban America, and what lessons can modern planners draw from this era of car-dependent development?

MARCH 5
1766

ANTONIO DE ULLOA
ARRIVES IN NEW ORLEANS

"Cities evolve through the hands of those who govern them, blending resilience with the vision of a new era." – Antonio de Ulloa. Spanish explorer and colonial administrator.

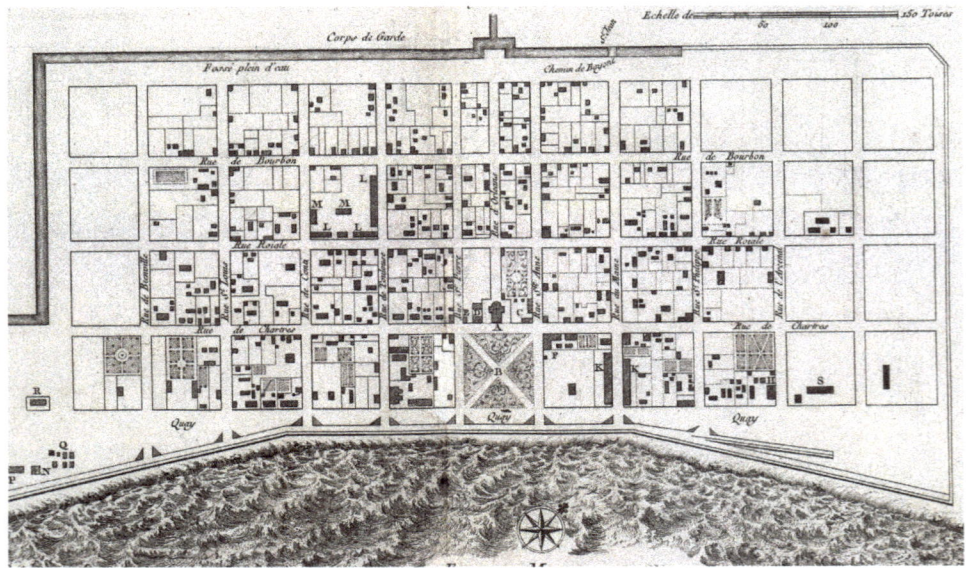

Plan de la Nouvelle Orleans. By Bellin, Jacques Nicolas, 1703-1772. Source: Library of Congress, Geography and Map Division, Louisiana: European Explorations and the Louisiana Purchase. Public Domain.

On this day in 1766, Antonio de Ulloa, the first Spanish governor of Louisiana, arrived in New Orleans to assume control of the colony, marking its transition from French to Spanish rule under the Treaty of Fontainebleau (1762). Spanish governance significantly changed the city, particularly in urban planning and architecture. Following devastating fires in 1788 and 1794, Spanish authorities enforced fire-resistant building codes, leading to the construction of the brick and stucco buildings that define the French Quarter today. These policies transformed New Orleans' urban fabric, creating a more resilient and distinctive architectural character. Additionally, the Spanish administration improved governance and trade regulations, fostering the city's growth into a bustling port and cultural hub. Although met with resistance from the French-speaking population, Spanish rule left an indelible mark on New Orleans, solidifying its reputation as a unique crossroads of culture, commerce, and history.

How can cities with complex colonial histories balance preserving their heritage while addressing the challenges of modern urban development?

DEATH OF
HENRY PELHAM, LONDON'S URBAN GROWTH

"Commerce is the beating heart of a thriving city, driving its growth and shaping its future."
— Inspired by the era of Henry Pelham. British Prime Minister and financier.

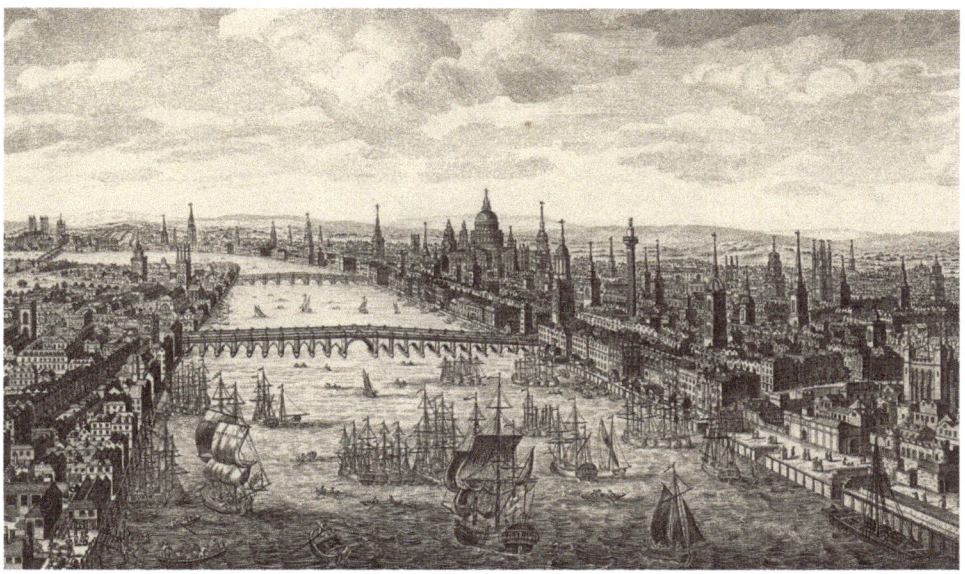

A General view of London, 1760s. Source: The Miriam and Ira D. Wallach Division of Art, Prints, and Photographs: Print Collectio. New York Public Library. Via Wikimedia Commons. Public Domain.

On this day in 1754, Henry Pelham, who served as Prime Minister of Great Britain from 1743 to 1754, died. Pelham significantly influenced policies that shaped London's growth during the mid-18th century. His administration prioritized fiscal reforms that stabilized Britain's economy, enabling investments in urban infrastructure and supporting the city's transformation into a global trade center. These economic measures indirectly fostered improvements in transportation, sanitation, and public spaces, addressing the challenges posed by London's rapidly expanding population. While not directly involved in urban planning, Pelham's governance laid the groundwork for London's evolution into a modern metropolis. His leadership during a substantial urban and economic growth period highlights the interconnectedness of governance and urban development in shaping vibrant, functional cities. Pelham's legacy underscores the critical role of political stability and financial innovation in fostering urban progress.

How can modern cities balance economic expansion with the need for sustainable and equitable urban development?

MARCH 7
1876

ALEXANDER GRAHAM BELL PATENTS THE TELEPHONE

"Mr. Watson, come here—I want to see you."
— Alexander Graham Bell, first words spoken over the telephone

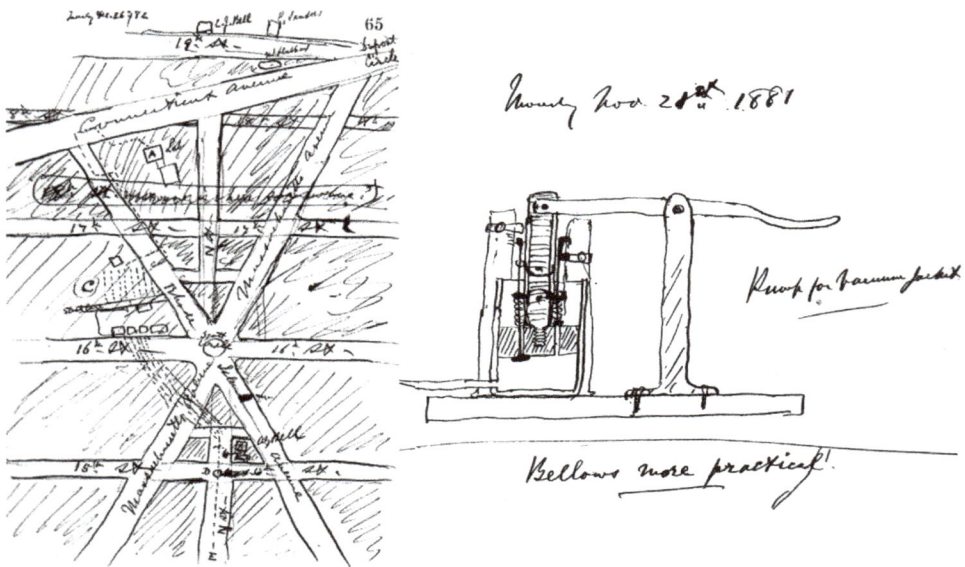

Experimental sketches by Alexander Graham Bell, dated between June 25, 1881, and December 26, 1882. These drawings reflect Bell's explorations into telegraphy, artificial respiration, radiation, and optical instruments. Images 3 and 13. Source: Library of Congress, Manuscript Division, Alexander Graham Bell Family Papers. Via Wikimedia Commons. Public Domain.

On this day in 1876, Alexander Graham Bell was granted a patent for the telephone, a groundbreaking invention that revolutionized urban communication and connectivity. The telephone transformed how cities functioned during the Industrial Revolution by enabling real-time voice communication over long distances. It enhanced the efficiency of business operations, governance, and daily urban life, allowing for faster decision-making and coordination across growing metropolitan areas. Beyond convenience, the telephone fostered the creation of new industries and infrastructures, such as switchboards, telecommunication networks, and service providers, which became integral to the development of modern cities. This innovation connected people and contributed to the evolution of urban economies, enabling the rise of centralized offices and new forms of urban organization. Bell's invention remains a cornerstone of urban technology, influencing how cities operate and grow in an increasingly interconnected world.

How can cities leverage advancements in communication technology to promote inclusivity and efficiency in urban life?

VOLKSWAGEN BEGINS PRODUCTION OF THE MICROBUS

"The car of the future must connect people, not just places." – Ben Pon. Dutch businessman and early advocate for the Volkswagen Microbus. (Paraphrased).

Baden-Württemberg, Germany, 1960. By Willem van de Poll. Source: Nationaal Archief. CC0 1.0

On this day in 1950, Volkswagen expanded its product line by unveiling the Microbus, officially known as the Volkswagen Type 2. Designed as a versatile vehicle for commercial and personal use, the Microbus became a post-war symbol of mobility, practicality, and freedom. Its compact size, affordability, and adaptability made it well-suited for navigating urban environments, helping transform city transportation. Beyond its functionality, the Microbus became a cultural icon, embraced by countercultural movements in the 1960s and 1970s, symbolizing community, creativity, and adventure. Its design influenced the development of multipurpose urban vehicles, laying the groundwork for the modern minivan. Today, the legacy of the Microbus endures, with Volkswagen reimagining the iconic vehicle as an electric model to meet the demands of sustainable urban mobility, blending nostalgia with innovation while addressing the transportation needs of contemporary cities.

How do iconic vehicles like the Volkswagen Microbus shape urban transportation and cultural identity in cities?

MARCH 9
1776

PUBLICATION OF
THE WEALTH OF NATIONS

"The division of labor, so far as it can be introduced, occasions, in every art, a proportionable increase of the productive powers of labor." – Adam Smith. Scottish economist and philosopher.

Cartoon showing Cyrus Field, Jay Gould, Cornelius Vanderbilt, and Russell Sage, seated on bags of "millions" on a large raft and being carried by workers of various professions. By N.Y. : Published by Keppler & Schwarzmann, 1883 February 7. Source: Library of Congress Prints and Photographs Division. CC0

On this day in 1776, Adam Smith's An Inquiry into the Nature and Causes of the Wealth of Nations was published, revolutionizing economic thought and shaping the development of cities and industries. Smith's analysis of market dynamics, specialization, and the division of labor explained the economic forces fueling urbanization during the Industrial Revolution. His emphasis on efficiency in production and exchange influenced the structure of industrial cities, driving their growth and organization. Smith also touched on the importance of public goods, suggesting the necessity of shared urban infrastructure to support economic and social activity. While focused on economics, the book provided a framework for understanding urban growth, trade networks, and the interdependence of cities within broader economic systems. Smith's ideas continue to influence discussions on the balance between market forces and public welfare, offering insights into modern urban development principles.

How can principles of economic specialization and market forces be used to create more equitable and sustainable urban economies today?

EMPEROR MAXIMIAN'S TRIUMPHAL ENTRY INTO CARTHAGE

"A city's strength lies not only in its walls but in the loyalty it inspires among its people."
– Ancient Roman saying.

Antonine Baths in Carthage, Tunisia. This grand Roman bath complex, built in the 2nd century CE, highlights the scale and sophistication of Roman public architecture in what was once the heart of the Carthaginian world. By Jkraft5. Licensed.

In 298 CE, Roman Emperor Maximian concluded a successful military campaign in North Africa. He made a triumphant entry into the city of Carthage, underscoring the Roman Empire's profound influence on cities in the region. Once a Punic stronghold, Carthage had been transformed into a key Roman urban and administrative hub, symbolizing the empire's dominance. The city was renowned for its sophisticated infrastructure, including aqueducts, baths, basilicas, and an amphitheater, reflecting Roman priorities of civic pride and public utility. Similar Roman influences were seen across North Africa in cities such as Leptis Magna, known for its grand forum, and the Severan Basilica, and Timgad, celebrated for its perfectly planned grid layout and impressive public spaces. Maximian's triumph in Carthage showcased Roman military and political power and emphasized the role of urban centers in integrating North Africa into the empire through architecture, trade, and culture.

How did cities like Carthage serve as focal points for projecting imperial power and fostering civic identity in ancient empires?

MARCH 11
1779

ESTABLISHMENT OF
THE U.S. ARMY CORPS OF ENGINEERS

"Engineers build not just structures, but the foundations of a nation's progress."
– Henry P. Johnston. American historian. (Paraphrased).

Everglades National Park Restoration by the Army Corps of Engineers, 1972. By Fred Ward. Source: National Archives at College Park. Still Picture Records Section, Special Media Archives Services Division (NWCS-S), and the U.S. National Archives and Records Administration. CC0

On this day in 1779, the Continental Congress formally established the U.S. Army Corps of Engineers to oversee the planning, design, and construction of military environmental and structural facilities. Composed initially of Continental Army soldiers, French officers, and civilian workers, the Corps played a pivotal role in Revolutionary War battles, including Bunker Hill, Saratoga, and Yorktown, where their expertise in fortifications and infrastructure was critical. Following the war, the Corps expanded its mission to support the nation's development, spearheading projects such as canals, harbors, bridges, and roadways, laying the groundwork for modern urban planning and infrastructure.

Over time, their role evolved to include flood management, environmental conservation, and public works, addressing the challenges of urban growth and climate adaptation. Today, the U.S. Army Corps of Engineers continues to shape cities and landscapes, showcasing its enduring legacy in building resilient and sustainable urban environments.

How has the U.S. Army Corps of Engineers influenced the design and resilience of modern cities through its historical and contemporary work?

W.H.O. PRESENTS
COVID-19 AS A GLOBAL PANDEMIC

"COVID-19 has made it abundantly clear: our health is interconnected with the health of our cities." – Paraphrased from speeches by WHO Director-General Tedros Adhanom Ghebreyesus.

Empty streets and sidewalks of Soho are eerily quiet during the 2020 coronavirus pandemic lockdown in New York City. By Deberarr. Licensed

On this day in 2020, the Director-General of the World Health Organization (WHO) addressed a mission briefing on COVID-19, following WHO's official declaration the day before—on March 11—that the outbreak constituted a global pandemic. This announcement marked a pivotal moment that profoundly transformed urban life worldwide. The virus spread rapidly through interconnected urban centers, exposing vulnerabilities in densely populated areas. Cities implemented unprecedented measures such as lockdowns, social distancing, and remote work to curb the virus's spread, fundamentally altering transportation, housing, public spaces, and healthcare systems. The pandemic highlighted the critical role of urban planning in public health and resilience, prompting a reevaluation of urban density, green spaces, and infrastructure. It also accelerated adoption of digital technologies, with cities employing smart systems for contact tracing and service delivery. The crisis reshaped how cities prepare for global health challenges, fostering a renewed focus on sustainability, equity, and adaptive planning to create healthier, more resilient urban environments. COVID-19's impact continues to influence urban development strategies worldwide.

How can cities build resilient systems to respond effectively to future public health crises while enhancing urban livability?

MARCH 13
1325

FOUNDING OF TENOCHTITLÁN

"Tenochtitlán was a city of wonders, where ingenuity turned water into land and vision built an empire." – Inspired by Spanish missionary Bernardino de Sahagún's writings on the Mexica.

Mural by Diego Rivera of the Aztec city of Tenochtitlan and life in Aztec times. 1945. By Diego Rivera, Muralist. Source: Miguel Aguilar Moreno and Erika Cabrera, Diego Rivera: A Biography, Greenwood, 2011, p.82. Mural at the Palacio Nacional, Mexico City. Public Domain.

On this day in 1325, the founding of Tenochtitlán is commemorated, although the exact date remains uncertain. In 1925, March 13 was officially chosen to celebrate the city's 600th anniversary. Established by the Mexica people on an island in Lake Texcoco, Tenochtitlán was founded based on a prophecy involving an eagle perched on a cactus while devouring a serpent. Over time, the city became the capital of the Aztec Empire and a symbol of advanced urban planning, featuring aqueducts, chinampas (floating gardens), causeways, and bustling marketplaces. Tenochtitlán's innovative infrastructure supported a large population, demonstrating remarkable ingenuity in water management and urban design. Today, the anniversary highlights the enduring legacy of Tenochtitlán as modern Mexico City stands atop its ruins, blending ancient Indigenous heritage with contemporary urban life. The commemoration underscores the cultural and historical importance of Tenochtitlán in shaping Mexico's identity.

How can cities celebrate their historical roots while adapting to the demands of modern urban life?

BIRTH OF
ALBERT EINSTEIN

"The important thing is not to stop questioning. Curiosity has its own reason for existing."
– Albert Einstein. German-born theoretical physicist.

Aerial view of Ulm, Germany, showing the city's urban layout, historical core, and post-war reconstruction. By luchschenF. Licensed

On this day in 1879, Albert Einstein, one of history's most influential scientists, was born in Ulm, Germany. Einstein's groundbreaking theories, including the theory of relativity, revolutionized modern science and technology, indirectly shaping urban infrastructure development. His work laid the foundation for advancements in energy, such as nuclear power, and innovations in communications and transportation that transformed cities and improved global connectivity. Beyond his scientific achievements, Einstein's advocacy for peace, education, and humanitarian causes underscored intellectuals' vital role in addressing urban and societal challenges.

Cities worldwide have honored his legacy with institutions, museums, and public spaces celebrating his contributions to science and humanity. Einstein's life and work continue to inspire innovation and progress as a reminder of how transformative ideas can shape science and the cities and societies in which we live.

How do intellectual figures like Albert Einstein influence the evolution of urban environments and inspire innovation in city planning?

MARCH 15
2019

GLOBAL YOUTH CLIMATE STRIKE

"We deserve a safe future. And we demand a safe future. Is that really too much to ask?"
– Greta Thunberg. Swedish climate activist.

Global Climate Strike, UK 2019. Source: Global Climate Strike 20/09/2019. By Garry Knight. Source: Flickr - Global Climate Strike. CC0 1.0

On this day in 2019, an estimated 1.4 million young people from 123 countries participated in a global climate strike, demanding urgent action to combat climate change. Inspired by activist Greta Thunberg's Fridays for Future movement, the strikes emphasized implementing sustainable policies to address the climate crisis. As major contributors to greenhouse gas emissions, urban areas were a focal point of the demands, with calls for green infrastructure, renewable energy transitions, and enhanced public transit systems to reduce dependency on fossil fuels. The coordinated demonstrations showcased the power of youth-led advocacy in influencing public discourse and policy-making. By spotlighting the need for sustainable urban development, the climate strikes reinforced the importance of integrating environmental responsibility into urban planning. This historic day highlighted the vital role of younger generations in shaping a more sustainable and resilient future for cities and the planet.

How can cities integrate youth voices into urban planning to create sustainable and climate-resilient communities?

DEMOLITION OF
THE PRUITT-IGOE HOUSING COMPLEX

"Pruitt-Igoe became the icon of urban renewal's failure."
— Peter Hall, Cities of Tomorrow. British urbanist and historian.

Demolition of Pruitt–Igoe. By U.S. Department of Housing and Urban Development Office of Policy Development and Research Source: Creating Defensible Space. Via Wikimedia Commons. Public Domain.

On this day in 1972, the first building of the Pruitt-Igoe housing complex in St. Louis, Missouri, was demolished with explosives, marking the symbolic failure of a highly ambitious public housing project. Designed by architect Minoru Yamasaki and completed in 1954, Pruitt-Igoe was initially celebrated as a modernist solution to urban poverty, featuring 33 high-rise buildings to house thousands of low-income residents. However, systemic underfunding, poor maintenance, racial segregation, and concentrated poverty led to social and physical deterioration. By the late 1960s, the complex became synonymous with crime, vacancy, and urban decline. The demolition of Pruitt-Igoe, which continued through 1976, became a powerful symbol in urban planning history, signifying the shortcomings of mid-20th-century public housing policies. It also sparked debates about urban renewal, social equity, and the role of government in addressing housing needs.

What lessons can the failure of Pruitt-Igoe teach us about the design and management of public housing, and how can planners avoid similar mistakes in addressing affordable housing today?

MARCH 17
1992

SOUTH AFRICAN
REFERENDUM ON ENDING APARTHEID

"The vote we cast today is the first step in a journey towards a new South Africa."
– F.W. de Klerk, former President of South Africa

Photograph of Doornfontein train station at rush hour, showing the effects of apartheid. By Ernest Cole. Published in 1967 in the book House of Bondage. Via Wikimedia Commons. Public Domain.

On this day in 1992, South Africa held a historic referendum in which 68.7% of white voters chose to end apartheid, a system of institutionalized racial segregation that had profoundly shaped the nation's urban and social landscapes. This landmark decision began South Africa's transition toward inclusive governance and equality, profoundly impacting its cities. The dismantling of apartheid-era policies led to efforts to desegregate urban areas, ensuring more equitable access to housing, education, and public services. Cities that had long been divided by racial and economic barriers began to evolve into spaces better reflecting the country's diverse population.

This transformative event highlights how legislative and democratic actions can drive significant urban planning and governance changes, fostering social justice and inclusivity. The referendum's outcome remains a defining moment in the struggle to create equitable and integrated urban environments in South Africa.

How can urban planners ensure that cities continue to evolve toward greater inclusivity and equity in the aftermath of systemic segregation?

BEGINNING OF
THE PARIS COMMUNE

"We are fighting for the future city, where the people themselves shape their destiny."
– Louise Michel. French anarchist and revolutionary.

Paris Commune. Photo taken on May 29, 1871, after the "Semaine sanglante" (Bloody Week). Author unknown. Source: Published in L'Histoire, July-August 2006. Via Wikimedia Commons. Public Domain.

On this day in 1871, the Paris Commune was established after an uprising in Paris against the French government. This revolutionary socialist government represented one of the earliest examples of a workers' movement seizing power in an urban context. The Commune implemented progressive reforms to foster a more equitable urban society, including free education, gender equality in the workforce, and local self-governance. These measures addressed long-standing inequalities and empowered citizens to shape their urban environment. Although the Commune lasted only two months before being violently suppressed, it became a powerful symbol of urban resistance and the struggle for social justice. Its legacy continues to inspire debates on governance, housing, and the role of cities in advancing social rights. The Paris Commune highlights the transformative potential of urban movements to challenge existing systems and reimagine more inclusive and equitable societies.

How can cities balance progressive social reforms with stability to create inclusive and equitable urban environments?

MARCH 19
1277

BYZANTINE–VENETIAN TREATY OF 1277

"Commerce is the lifeblood of cities, weaving connections that transcend borders and empires." – Inspired by Venetian civic ideals during Doge Lorenzo Tiepolo's reign.

Byzantine architecture, St Mark's Cathedral (Basilica di San Marco), Venice, Italy. The structure exemplifies the synthesis of Eastern and Western architectural styles, featuring domes, mosaics, and a Greek cross plan. By Dario Lo Presti. Licensed.

On this day in 1277, the Byzantine Empire and the Republic of Venice signed a treaty establishing a two-year truce and renewing Venice's commercial privileges within Byzantine territories. This agreement was crucial for maintaining Venice's dominance over Mediterranean trade routes, allowing the free movement of goods, people, and ideas between Europe and Asia. The treaty strengthened the economic and urban connections between Venetian cities, such as Venice, and Byzantine hubs, like Constantinople, by securing access to Byzantine markets and ports. These ties facilitated urban growth on both sides, fostering architectural influence, cultural exchange, and robust economic systems. The treaty underscores the importance of diplomacy in shaping urban development and international trade during the medieval period, illustrating how strategic alliances ensured prosperity and influenced the cultural and structural character of interconnected cities across regions.

How can modern cities draw from historical trade agreements to promote peaceful economic collaboration and shared urban prosperity?

MARCH 20
1602

ESTABLISHMENT OF
THE DUTCH EAST INDIA COMPANY

"Trade is the architect of cities, forging them from the tides of ambition and enterprise." – Reflecting on views by Jan Pieterszoon Coen. Dutch administrator and founder of Batavia (Jakarta).

Dutch colonies, East-Indies, Dutch East India Company, Asia 18th C. Source: Rijksmuseum. Public Domain.

On this day in 1602, the Dutch East India Company (VOC) was founded, becoming the world's first multinational corporation and a major force in shaping urban development through global trade. The VOC established key port cities such as Batavia (modern-day Jakarta) and Cape Town, which became critical hubs for commerce, governance, and cultural exchange. These cities were meticulously designed to facilitate trading operations, featuring infrastructure like harbors, warehouses, and fortifications that prioritized the needs of colonial commerce. While the VOC drove economic growth and urban expansion, its activities were also marked by exploitation, cultural displacement, and the enforcement of colonial rule, leaving a complex legacy. The company's impact illustrates how global trade networks influenced the formation and growth of urban centers, underscoring the interplay between economic power, colonialism, and urbanization during the early modern era.

How can cities with colonial histories reconcile their past while promoting equitable and sustainable urban futures?

MARCH 21
1994

U.N. FRAMEWORK
CONVENTION ON CLIMATE CHANGE

"The climate crisis is a challenge for our cities, but it is also an opportunity to build a sustainable future." – Christiana Figueres. Former Executive Secretary of the UNFCCC. (Adapted)

Cracked soil with a plant emerging in an arid landscape, symbolizing resilience in the face of climate change and desertification. The image highlights environmental challenges and the adaptation of ecosystems to global climate shifts. By Piyaset. Licensed.

On this day in 1994, the United Nations Framework Convention on Climate Change (UNFCCC) officially entered into force, signaling a global commitment to addressing climate change and its impact on cities and the environment. The UNFCCC established a framework for international cooperation, paving the way for agreements like the Kyoto Protocol and the Paris Agreement. Its objectives include stabilizing greenhouse gas concentrations, promoting sustainable development, and mitigating the effects of climate change, such as rising sea levels and extreme weather. Urban areas, as significant sources of emissions and hubs of innovation, are central to implementing the convention's goals. To meet these challenges, cities worldwide have adopted policies supporting renewable energy, green infrastructure, and climate resilience. The UNFCCC continues to guide efforts toward sustainable and adaptive urban development, emphasizing the critical role of cities in creating a more climate-resilient future.

How can urban areas balance economic growth with sustainability to meet global climate goals?

PASSAGE OF THE STAMP ACT

*"The cause of liberty is the cause of the cities; in their streets lies the pulse of revolution."
– Samuel Adams. American revolutionary leader and political philosopher. (Paraphrased)*

Funeral procession of the Miss Americ-Stamp, British Cartoon Print, 1765. Published in: The American Revolution in drawings and prints. Source: Library of Congress Prints and Photographs Division. Public Domain.

On this day in 1765, the British Parliament enacted the Stamp Act, imposing a tax on printed materials in the American colonies, including legal documents, newspapers, and playing cards. This marked the first direct tax levied by Britain on its colonies, sparking widespread dissent. Urban centers like Boston and New York became epicenters of resistance, with protests, boycotts, and public demonstrations. The colonists viewed the tax as violating their rights, rallying under the slogan "no taxation without representation." The act's unpopularity led to the creation of the Stamp Act Congress, where representatives from nine colonies united to draft petitions against the tax. These efforts galvanized colonial opposition to British rule and set the stage for the American Revolution. The Stamp Act exemplifies the power of urban activism in challenging systemic injustice and catalyzing transformative political change.

How can lessons from urban protests like those against the Stamp Act inform contemporary movements for social justice?

MARCH 23
1857

INSTALLATION OF
THE FIRST SAFETY ELEVATOR BY ELISHA OTIS

"The elevator broke the barrier of height, enabling cities to grow upward."
– Elisha Otis's legacy. American inventor and founder of the Otis Elevator Company.

Broadway: The Store of Messrs. E.V. Haughwout and Co. Illus. in: The Illustrated London News, 1859. Source: Library of Congress Prints and Photographs Division. Public Domain.

On this day in 1857, Elisha Otis installed the first passenger safety elevator at the E.V. Haughwout Building in New York City, marking a milestone in urban development. The elevator featured a revolutionary safety mechanism that prevented it from falling if the hoisting cable failed, alleviating a major public fear and paving the way for widespread adoption. Although the Haughwout Building was only five stories tall, the elevator's success demonstrated the feasibility of vertical transportation, enabling the construction of taller buildings and transforming urban skylines. Otis's invention revolutionized architectural possibilities and enhanced accessibility and the functionality of urban spaces. By making upper floors viable for residential and commercial use, the elevator contributed to the densification of cities, facilitating the rise of skyscrapers and modern urban environments. Otis's legacy endures as a cornerstone of urban architecture and design.

How can technological innovations in building design continue to shape the future of cities and their sustainability?

NEW JERSEY SUPREME COURT
ISSUES LANDMARK MOUNT LAUREL DECISION

"Municipalities must not use the zoning power to shut out the living accommodations of any but the affluent." — New Jersey Supreme Court, Mount Laurel Decision

Zoning (land use) map displaying typical color-coded classifications used in urban planning. The image illustrates the composition of different landuse zones within a city's urban fabric. By Olivier-Tuffé. Licensed.

On this day in 1975, the New Jersey Supreme Court issued its decision in Southern Burlington County N.A.A.C.P. v. Mount Laurel Township, a landmark ruling that prohibited exclusionary zoning practices and required municipalities to provide a "fair share" of affordable housing for low- and moderate-income residents and workers. The court found that Mount Laurel Township's zoning ordinances, which effectively excluded affordable housing development, violated the New Jersey State Constitution's guarantees of fairness and equal protection. This case marked the first legal challenge to exclusionary zoning in the United States and established a precedent that municipalities must proactively address housing equity. However, weak enforcement led to a second ruling in 1983, known as Mount Laurel II, which strengthened compliance mechanisms by creating a formula for determining fair share obligations and granting developers the ability to challenge non-compliant municipalities.

How can the lessons of the Mount Laurel decision inform modern efforts to combat exclusionary zoning and address the nationwide affordable housing crisis?

MARCH 25
421 CE

FOUNDATION OF VENICE, ITALY

"Venice is built not on land, but on the strength of its people and the ingenuity of their vision." – Marin Sanudo. Venetian historian and diarist.

Aerial view of Venice, Italy, showcasing the Grand Canal and the city's historical urban morphology, characterized by a dense network of canals, narrow streets, and historic architecture. By a_medvedkov. Licensed.

On this day in 421 CE, Venice was traditionally founded by refugees fleeing Roman cities to escape barbarian invasions, seeking safety in the marshy Venetian Lagoon. Over the centuries, the settlement evolved from a modest fishing community into a thriving maritime republic renowned for its strategic trade routes connecting Europe and the East. Venice's unique urban form, shaped by its aquatic environment, replaced streets with canals and relied on bridges to connect its scattered islands. Ingenious engineering, including wooden piles driven into the lagoon's sediment, supported its iconic architecture, exemplified by St. Mark's Basilica and the Doge's Palace. This blend of practicality and grandeur enabled Venice to become a cultural and economic powerhouse, celebrated for its resilience and innovation. Today, Venice remains an enduring symbol of how human ingenuity can adapt to and thrive in challenging environments, leaving an indelible mark on global urban and architectural history.

How has Venice's unique geography influenced its urban form and cultural identity throughout history?

BAKER V. CARR
EMPOWERING CITIES

"Legislators represent people, not trees or acres."
— Chief Justice Earl Warren. American jurist and 14th Chief Justice of the United States.

Street Sign Urban versus Rural. By Thomas Reimer. Licensed

On this day in 1962, the U.S. Supreme Court issued its landmark decision in Baker v. Carr, ruling that federal courts have the authority to review legislative district apportionment. The case challenged Tennessee's unequal representation, where rural districts held disproportionate power compared to rapidly growing urban areas, violating the Equal Protection Clause of the Fourteenth Amendment. The Court's decision established the principle of "one person, one vote," requiring legislative districts to have roughly equal populations. This ruling shifted political power toward urban centers, giving cities and residents a stronger voice in state legislatures. As a result, issues critical to urban areas—such as mass transit, civil rights, housing, and infrastructure—gained greater legislative focus. Baker v. Carr profoundly impacted urban planning and policy, ensuring more equitable representation and highlighting the role of fair governance in shaping vibrant, responsive cities.

How did the Baker v. Carr ruling influence the prioritization of urban issues in state legislatures, and what lessons does it offer for equitable representation today?

MARCH 27
1886

BIRTH OF
MIES VAN DER ROHE

"Architecture starts when you carefully put two bricks together. There it begins."
– Ludwig Mies van der Rohe. German-American architect and pioneer of modernist architecture.

The Chicago Federal Center designed by Mies van der Rohe includes the John Kluczynski Federal Building, Everett McKinley Dirksen United States Courthouse, and Alexander Calder's sculpture "Flamingo". By Carol M. Highsmith. Source: Library of Congress Prints and Photographs Division. Public Domain.

On this day in 1886, Ludwig Mies van der Rohe was born in Aachen, Germany, becoming one of the most influential figures in modernist architecture and urban design. Renowned for his "less is more" philosophy, Mies championed simplicity, functionality, and elegance in design, reshaping the architectural and urban landscape of the 20th century. His iconic works, including the Barcelona Pavilion, the Seagram Building in New York, and Chicago's Lake Shore Drive Apartments, embody minimalism while prioritizing structure and material innovation. Mies's vision extended to urban planning, advocating for open spaces, transparency, and a harmonious relationship between buildings and their surroundings. His approach to architecture and design inspires contemporary urbanism, reflecting a balance between aesthetic clarity and practical utility. Mies's legacy highlights the potential of architecture to shape not only individual structures but also the broader fabric of modern cities.

How can modern urban design balance simplicity with the complexities of contemporary urban life?

STARS IN
THE HOLLYWOOD WALK OF FAME

"Hollywood is a place where they'll pay you a thousand dollars for a kiss and fifty cents for your soul." — Marilyn Monroe. American actress and cultural icon.

Sidewalk of Hollywood Boulevard, Los Angeles, California, USA. The image depicts the Hollywood Walk of Fame, an iconic feature of the boulevard, with embedded stars honoring notable figures in the entertainment industry. By Travelview. Licensed.

On this day in 1960, the first star on the Hollywood Walk of Fame was unveiled on Hollywood Boulevard, honoring actress Joanne Woodward. Conceived as a tribute to the entertainment industry, the Walk of Fame quickly became a symbol of Los Angeles' cultural identity and a major tourist attraction. Stretching along Hollywood Boulevard and Vine Street, the project was also an urban renewal initiative designed to revitalize a struggling district by drawing visitors and boosting local commerce. The stars, embedded in pink terrazzo and brass, recognize contributions to film, television, music, theater, and radio, connecting Hollywood's glamour with the city's vibrancy.

Now boasting over 2,700 stars, the Walk of Fame blends cultural preservation with economic development. It continues to celebrate the entertainment industry while serving as an enduring example of how urban planning can integrate heritage and commerce to sustain city life.

How do cultural landmarks like the Hollywood Walk of Fame contribute to the urban identity and economic vitality of cities?

MARCH 29
1918

BIRTH OF
SAM WALTON, FOUNDER OF WALMART

"If we work together, we'll lower the cost of living for everyone... we'll give the world an opportunity to see what it's like to save and have a better life." – Sam Walton

Sam Walton's original Walton's Five and Dime, now the Wal-Mart Visitor's Center, Bentonville. By Walmart from Bentonville, USA. CC BY 2.0

On this day in 1918, Sam Walton, the founder of Walmart and Sam's Club, was born, revolutionizing the retail industry with his innovative approach to large-scale discount stores. Walton's strategies prioritized centralized logistics, efficient supply chains, and competitive pricing, creating a model that reshaped suburban shopping centers and revitalized commerce in small towns and cities. Walmart's rapid expansion into urban and rural areas influenced the development of commercial hubs, often serving as anchors for new retail districts. While the company's growth provided affordable goods and economic opportunities, it also sparked debates about the impact of large retailers on local businesses, employment, and community identities. Walton's legacy highlights the profound influence of commerce on urban planning and social dynamics, demonstrating how retail innovations can drive economic growth while raising critical questions about sustainability and community cohesion in cities and towns worldwide.

How can cities balance the benefits of large-scale retailers with the need to preserve local businesses and community character?

BIRTH OF
MEHMED THE CONQUEROR

"Istanbul shall be the heart of empires, where worlds converge and civilizations thrive." – Mehmed II

Panorama of Constantinople in the early Ottoman period. By Giovanni Andreas Vavassore, circa 1535. Source: Germanisches Nationalmuseum, Nuremberg, via the University of California Press. Via Wikimedia Commons. Public Domain.

On this day in 1432, Mehmed II, later known as "Mehmed the Conqueror," was born. As Ottoman Sultan, Mehmed is renowned for capturing Constantinople in 1453, which ended the Byzantine Empire and marked the city's transformation into the Ottoman capital, Istanbul. Under Mehmed's leadership, the city underwent sweeping urban renewal, with restored infrastructure, the construction of grand mosques like the Fatih Mosque, and policies encouraging diverse populations— Greeks, Armenians, Jews, and others— to settle within its walls. These efforts revitalized trade routes and fostered cultural exchange, establishing Istanbul as a cosmopolitan center straddling Europe and Asia. Mehmed's vision laid the groundwork for Istanbul's enduring role as a global metropolis, celebrated for its architectural splendor, commercial vitality, and cultural diversity. His legacy underscores the profound impact of strategic urban planning and inclusive governance on shaping a city's identity and global significance.

How can modern cities preserve the legacies of historical transformations while continuing to evolve as inclusive, modern urban centers?

MARCH 31
1889

COMPLETION OF
THE EIFFEL TOWER

"I believe the Tower will have its own beauty—a monumental pillar, unique in the world, whose strong design gives it distinct character." – Gustave Eiffel. French civil engineer and architect.

Vintage postcard view of the Eiffel Tower, Paris, France, circa 1900. The image captures the tower's role as a global icon of engineering and urban modernity during the Belle Époque period. By Denys Kuvaiev. Licensed.

On this day in 1889, the Eiffel Tower was officially completed and inaugurated in Paris as the centerpiece of the 1889 World's Fair (Exposition Universelle). Designed by Gustave Eiffel and his team, the 300-meter iron structure was a groundbreaking achievement in engineering, symbolizing France's embrace of modernity and progress. At the time, it was the tallest man-made structure in the world and a bold demonstration of iron's potential as a material for monumental architecture. Although initially met with criticism from artists and intellectuals who deemed it an eyesore, the tower quickly became a celebrated icon of innovation and a defining feature of Paris' skyline. Its completion marked a turning point in urban design, showcasing how engineering and aesthetics could converge to create enduring landmarks. Today, the Eiffel Tower remains a global symbol of Paris and a testament to the transformative vision of 19th-century urban planning and architecture.

How do iconic structures contribute to the identity of cities, and what modern equivalents echo the Eiffel Tower's impact?

FOUNDATION FOR THE FIRST COMPREHENSIVE PLAN

"City planning is not merely for today, but for generations to come."
– Alfred Bettman. American city planner and legal pioneer of zoning.

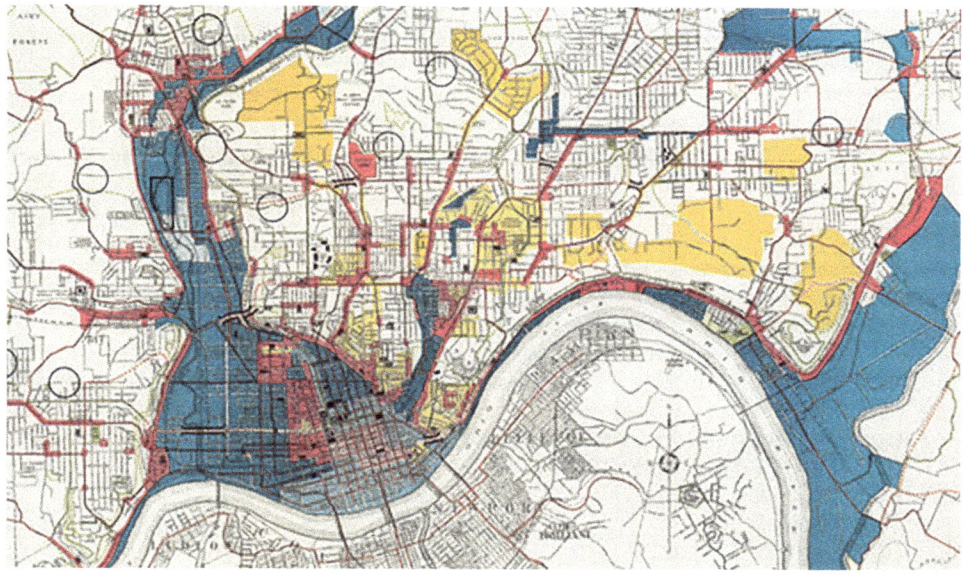

Official City Plan Map - Cincinnati 1925. Source: City of Cincinnati, Planning Department. Public Domain.

On this day in 1924, Cincinnati unanimously adopted its Building Zone Ordinance, a critical step that paved the way for the city's landmark comprehensive plan of 1925. Recognized as one of the first truly integrated city plans in the United States, the Cincinnati Plan was shaped by Alfred Bettman and Ladislas Segoe and set a national precedent for coordinated urban development. The 1924 ordinance established zoning as a central planning tool, enabling the comprehensive plan to align land use with transportation, public infrastructure, and open space. This strategic layering of legal and planning mechanisms positioned Cincinnati as a model for cities nationwide. The plan's legal validation in court further affirmed the legitimacy of comprehensive planning as a function of municipal governance. By anchoring long-term growth in regulation and foresight, Cincinnati's planning efforts helped launch the era of modern urban planning in America, illustrating how thoughtful frameworks can support sustainable and equitable urban futures.

How did Cincinnati's 1925 Comprehensive Plan shape the legal and professional foundations of modern urban planning?

APRIL 2
1962

LONDON INSTALLS
THE FIRST PANDA CROSSING

"The city is what it is because our citizens are what they are."
– Plato. Ancient Greek philosopher.

Ernest Marples, Minister of Transport, and A. C. Dennis, Mayor of Lambeth, are the first to use the new Panda pedestrian crossing at York Road, outside Waterloo Station. The Panda crossings, to be tried for an experimental 12 month period, have flashing warning lights operated by push-button controls. Source: Source: PA Images via Alamy.

On this day in 1962, London introduced the first "Panda crossing," an experimental pedestrian crossing system designed to enhance road safety. Installed outside Waterloo Station, the Panda crossing featured black-and-white stripes, accompanied by a "WAIT" signal and flashing lights to guide pedestrians across the road. The concept aimed to reduce accidents and improve traffic flow by providing a clearer system for both pedestrians and drivers. However, the crossing faced significant challenges, as many pedestrians found its operation confusing. Within a few years, the Panda Crossing was replaced by more intuitive systems like Zebra and, later, Pelican Crossings, which incorporated push buttons and timed lights for better usability. Despite its short-lived implementation, the Panda Crossing demonstrated London's willingness to innovate in urban transportation. This trial-and-error approach highlights the city's ongoing efforts to adapt infrastructure to meet public needs and improve urban mobility and safety.

How can urban transportation experiments contribute to long-term improvements in pedestrian safety and city planning?

FRENCH TGV SETS WORLD SPEED RECORD ON CONVENTIONAL TRACKS

"A high-speed train doesn't just connect cities—it transforms them."
— French National Railways (SNCF)

SNCF 82 (TGV PSE) & SNCF 542 (TGV Réseau) high-speed trains, illustrating French advancements in railway technology and the role of high-speed rail in regional and national connectivity. By Alf van Beem. Source: Via Wikimedia Commons. CC0 1.0.

On this day in 2007, a French TGV (Train à Grande Vitesse) set a world speed record for conventional trains, reaching 574.8 km/h (357 mph) on the LGV Est high-speed line. The specially modified train, known as V150, showcased cutting-edge rail engineering and highlighted the future of high-speed transportation. The achievement was more than a technical milestone—it underscored the role of high-speed rail in reshaping urban and regional development. By linking cities with unprecedented speed, the TGV reduced travel times, boosted local economies, and offered a sustainable alternative to air and car travel. Since its launch, the TGV has been central to France's integrated transportation strategy, promoting balanced urban growth and reducing environmental impacts. The record-breaking run of the V150 continues to symbolize the potential of rail innovation in building more connected and sustainable cities worldwide.

How can high-speed rail shape the future of urban development and reduce the environmental impact of transportation?

BIRTH OF ZÉNOBE GRAMME, INVENTOR OF THE GRAMME DYNAMO

"Electricity is the lifeblood of modern cities, illuminating streets and powering progress."
– Zénobe Gramme. (Paraphrased)

Dynamo used by the American Red Cross, 1914. Source: Library of Congress. Public Domain.

On this day in 1826, Belgian engineer Zénobe Gramme was born, a pioneer whose invention of the Gramme dynamo revolutionized the generation of direct current (DC) electricity. His dynamo, the first practical generator capable of producing continuous DC power, was a critical innovation that made urban electrification feasible. Gramme's invention powered streetlights, factories, and early public transportation systems, fundamentally transforming urban infrastructure and daily life. By enabling the development of electrical grids, his work reshaped cities, providing reliable energy to homes and businesses and enhancing safety, productivity, and overall quality of life. Gramme's contributions highlight the pivotal role of technological innovation in urban evolution, laying the groundwork for the electrified cities of the late 19th and early 20th centuries. His legacy endures in the energy systems that sustain modern urban environments, underscoring the profound impact of engineering on the development of vibrant, functional, and interconnected cities.

How can cities continue to harness technological innovation to improve infrastructure and enhance the quality of urban life while addressing environmental sustainability?

CHARLES V'S
ROYAL ENTRY INTO ROME

"Let us restore the grandeur of Rome, for in it lies the glory of the empire."
– Attributed to Charles V. Holy Roman Emperor and King of Spain.

The City of Rome taken by Constable of Bourbon from the Triumphs of Charles V. By Cornelis Boel (Netherlandish, Antwerp ca. 1576–after 1621). Source: Metropolitan Museum of Art. Public Domain.

On this day in 1536, Holy Roman Emperor Charles V made a triumphant entry into Rome, staging an elaborate procession to affirm his authority and evoke the grandeur of ancient Rome. To prepare for the event, significant portions of the city were demolished to create a ceremonial route reminiscent of a Roman triumph. This urban transformation served practical and symbolic purposes, showcasing the emperor's power while linking his reign to Rome's imperial past. The procession underscored Charles V's role as the defender of Christendom and reinforced Rome's historical and political significance. The alterations to the city's landscape highlight how rulers used urban design to project authority, aligning the built environment with their cultural and political ambitions. Charles V's entry into Rome remains a striking example of how leaders have reshaped cities to serve as stages for power and spectacle throughout history.

How can cities honor their historical identities while adapting to contemporary urban demands?

APRIL 6
1652

FOUNDING OF CAPE TOWN

"A city is born where the world converges, shaped by its geography and its history."
– Jan van Riebeeck. Dutch colonial administrator and founder of Cape Town. (Paraphrased).

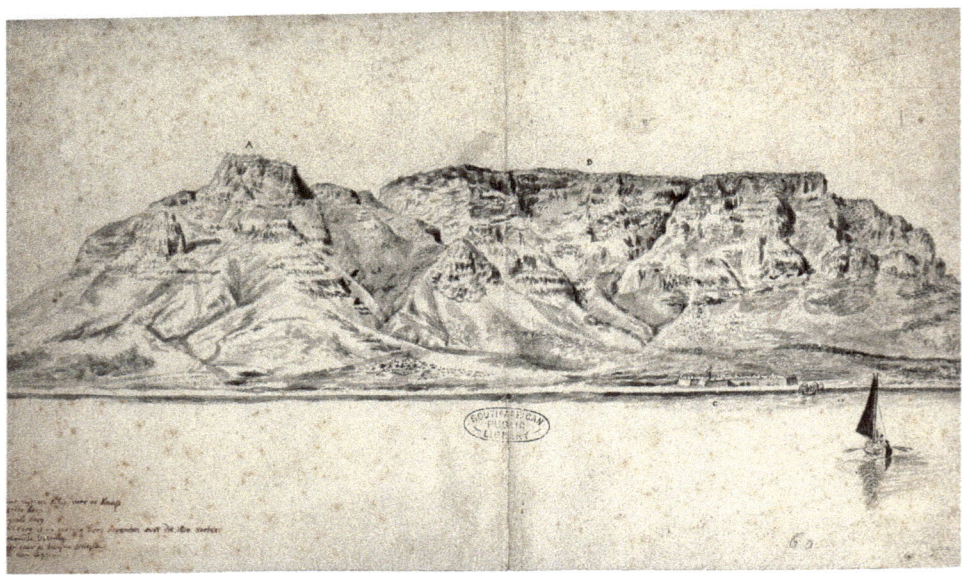

Cape of Good Hope; Forts and fortifications. Netherlands Colonies; Table Bay (South Africa) Circa 1700. Source: The Khoikhoi at the Cape of Good Hope, World Digital Library, Courtesy of the World Digital Library and the Library of Congress. Public Domain.

On this day in 1652, Dutch sailor Jan van Riebeeck established a resupply camp at the Cape of Good Hope for the Dutch East India Company, marking the beginning of Cape Town. Initially intended as a strategic waypoint on the maritime route between Europe and Asia, the settlement gradually expanded into one of Africa's earliest European colonial cities. Cape Town's location shaped its urban development, fostering cultural diversity through trade and migration. However, its growth also underscored the darker aspects of colonialism, including the displacement of indigenous Khoikhoi communities and the establishment of racially segregated urban spaces that persisted into the apartheid era. Today, Cape Town is celebrated for its cultural vibrancy and natural beauty while grappling with challenges of inequality and reconciliation, striving to balance its colonial legacy with aspirations for an inclusive urban future.

How can cities like Cape Town address their colonial past while building inclusive, equitable urban environments for the future?

BIRTH OF LEON KRIER, ADVOCATE OF TRADITIONAL URBANISM

"The modern city is not a machine; it is a living organism that must serve its people."
— Leon Krier. Luxembourgish architect and urban theorist.

Ciudad Cayalá, Guatemala City, Guatemala, master planned by Leon Krier, 2003. By Vicente Aguirre. Via Wikimedia Commons. CC BY-SA 4.0

On this day in 1946, Leon Krier, a prominent architect and urban theorist, was born. Krier is celebrated for his critique of modernist planning and his advocacy for traditional urbanism, emphasizing compact, walkable, and human-scaled urban forms. Rejecting sprawling, car-dependent environments, he champions the revival of mixed-use neighborhoods, classical design principles, and vibrant public spaces that foster community and sustainability. His influential writings, such as Rational Architecture and the Density of Urban Form (1984) and The Architecture of Community (2009), have shaped urban planning discourse worldwide. Krier's master plan for Poundbury, a model town in England commissioned by King Charles III (then Prince of Wales), demonstrates how traditional urbanist ideals can adapt to contemporary needs, blending timeless aesthetics with sustainable design. As a key figure in the New Urbanism movement, Krier's work inspires efforts to create livable, resilient communities prioritizing human connection and environmental balance.

How can Krier's focus on traditional urbanism guide the retrofitting of sprawling modern cities into more sustainable and human-centered environments?

APRIL 8
1904

LONGACRE SQUARE
RENAMED TO TIMES SQUARE

"Times Square is a monument to the rhythm of the city, where the world comes to see itself reflected." – Adolph S. Ochs, Publisher of The New York Times.

Times Square, New York, circa 1908—A bustling crossroads that shaped New York City's cultural and commercial identity. Photo by Detroit Publishing Co. Source: The Library of Congress, Prints and Photographs Division. Public Domain.

On this day in 1904, New York City's Longacre Square was officially renamed Times Square in honor of The New York Times, which had announced plans to move its headquarters to the area. The newspaper's publisher, Adolph S. Ochs, persuaded the city's Board of Aldermen to approve the name change, reflecting the paper's significant influence on the city's cultural and urban landscape. The Times Tower, located at the intersection of Broadway and Seventh Avenue, became a focal point of the newly named square. This renaming began Times Square's transformation into a vibrant entertainment, commerce, and media hub. The area soon attracted theaters, hotels, and restaurants, evolving into the bustling intersection known today for its dazzling billboards and as the epicenter of New York's theater district. The annual New Year's Eve ball drop tradition, initiated by Ochs in 1907, further cemented Times Square's reputation as "The Crossroads of the World."

How do the naming and branding of urban spaces influence their development and the cultural identity of a city?

PHILIP III ISSUES THE DECREE FOR THE EXPULSION OF THE MORISCOS

"Granada is the most beautiful and serene city in the world."
– Ibn Battuta. 14th-Century Moroccan Explorer and Chronicler of Cities

Granada. Spain. Landscape. By Svetlana. Licensed

On this day in 1609, Philip III of Spain issued the decree of the "Expulsion of the Moriscos," descendants of Spain's Muslim population who had profoundly shaped the country's cities and infrastructure. During their centuries of influence, the Moors introduced groundbreaking urban technologies, including sophisticated water management systems with aqueducts, irrigation canals, and fountains that supplied cities and transformed agriculture. They developed advanced sewer systems and well-planned streets, improving sanitation and urban organization. Cities like Córdoba, Granada, and Seville became innovation centers, showcasing architectural and engineering marvels such as the Alhambra and the Great Mosque of Córdoba. The Moorish legacy didn't just transform Spain—it spread throughout Europe, influencing urban planning, engineering, and architecture far beyond the Iberian Peninsula. While the expulsion ended the Moriscos' presence, their technological and cultural contributions remain an enduring foundation of modern urbanism and a testament to the value of cultural exchange.

How does the cultural and technological legacy of displaced populations, such as the Moriscos, continue to influence cities and urban life today?

APRIL 10
1964

RESTON, VIRGINIA, FOUNDED AS A VISIONARY NEW TOWN

"The idea was to create a place where people could live, work, and play in harmony with nature." – Robert E. Simon, Jr. American urban planner and founder of Reston, Virginia.

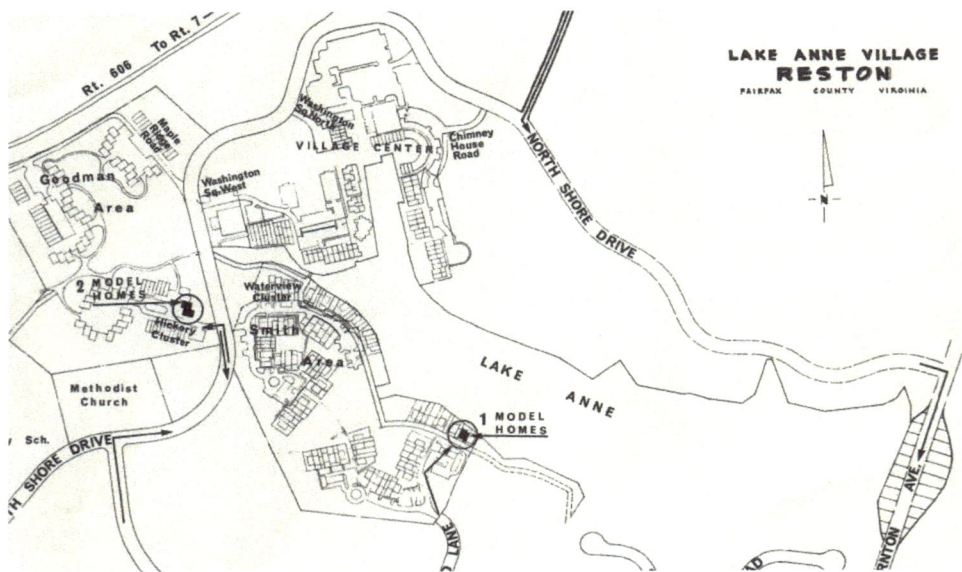

Plan of Reston VA, New Town. By: Simon Enterprises. Courtesy of The Reston Historic Trust. and Reston Museum, with permission.

On this day in 1964, Robert E. Simon, Jr. founded Reston, Virginia, a 6,750-acre new town designed as an innovative model for suburban development. Simon envisioned Reston based on seven principles, emphasizing walkability, higher-density housing, access to nature and green space, and racial and economic diversity—revolutionary ideas for the time. Reston's design featured village centers, each with its architectural style, central plaza, local services, and a larger town center for the community. Simon's plans required Fairfax County to create a new zoning designation, the Planned Residential Community (PRC), to accommodate the mixed-use, mixed-density vision. However, escalating costs led Simon to bring in Gulf Oil as a financial backer in 1967, and the company ultimately removed him from the project. Despite this, Reston's pioneering principles influenced urban planning and remain a celebrated example of new town design.

How did Reston's design challenge traditional suburban planning of its time, and what lessons can modern planners draw from its successes and setbacks?

APRIL 11
1968

FAIR HOUSING ACT
SIGNED INTO LAW

"We have come some of the way, not near all of it. There is much yet to do."
— President Lyndon B. Johnson. 36th President of the United States.

FHA Low Income Project, Holyoke, Massachusetts. By John Collier. Source: Library of Congress Prints and Photographs Division. Public Domain.

On this day in 1968, President Lyndon B. Johnson signed the Fair Housing Act, a landmark legislation prohibiting housing discrimination based on race, color, religion, or national origin. Subsequent amendments expanded protections to include gender (1974), disability, and familial status (1988). Enacted during the Civil Rights Movement, the act aimed to dismantle systemic housing discrimination and segregation, providing marginalized groups with fair access to housing. Its passage, heavily debated in Congress, gained urgency following Dr. Martin Luther King Jr.'s assassination, with President Johnson urging lawmakers to act decisively. While the Fair Housing Act marked a pivotal step toward addressing inequality, studies show that significant racial and economic disparities in housing and community integration remain, underscoring the ongoing need for enforcement and reform. The act's legacy continues to shape discussions on equity and inclusion in urban planning and housing policy.

How can planners and policymakers build on the legacy of the Fair Housing Act to address persistent housing inequality and segregation today?

APRIL 12
1901

NEW YORK STATE ENACTS THE TENEMENT HOUSE LAW

"The very essence of tenement house reform is the improvement of the living conditions of the poor." — Lawrence Veiller. American housing reformer and social worker.

Yard of Tenement at Park Ave. and 107th Street, New York. c. 1900s. Source: Detroit Publishing Company photograph collection, Library of Congress Prints and Photographs Division. Public Domain.

On this day in 1901, the New York State Tenement House Law, or the New Law, was enacted, revolutionizing housing standards to address the unsafe and unsanitary conditions in overcrowded tenements. These buildings, home to many immigrant and working-class families, were notorious for poor ventilation, inadequate lighting, and shared outdoor toilets. The New Law introduced stricter regulations for new buildings, mandating improvements such as better ventilation, windows in every room, indoor plumbing, and fire safety features like fire escapes. It also prohibited the construction of "dumbbell tenements," whose cramped layouts had become emblematic of unhealthy urban living. Advocated by reformers like Lawrence Veiller and supported by the Tenement House Committee, the legislation set a precedent for urban housing reform. Its influence extended nationwide, shaping building codes and emphasizing the role of government in ensuring safe and humane living conditions for urban residents.

How can the principles of the Tenement House Law inform current efforts to ensure safe, affordable, and equitable housing in modern cities?

SOVIET URBAN PLANNING REFORMS

"Cities must serve the collective good, reflecting the ideals and needs of the people."
– Vladimir Lenin. Russian revolutionary and political theorist. (Paraphrased).

Kuibyshev (Samara), housing, Architects: Matveyev, Bosin, 1936. By Academy of Architecture publication, unsigned photograph. Source: Years of Architecture in Soviet Russia, M, 1950. Via Wikimedia Commons. Public Domain.

On this day in 1925, the Soviet government enacted the Statute on Urban Land Management. This transformative policy abolished private land ownership in cities and transferred all urban land to municipal control. This legislation gave city councils authority over urban planning, land use, and construction rights to address critical housing shortages and support rapid industrialization. By prioritizing state-managed housing and infrastructure, the statute sought to improve living conditions and align urban development with the Soviet Union's collectivist ideology. While the policy enabled significant urban growth, it also led to standardized, utilitarian designs and inefficiencies in planning. Despite its challenges, the statute marked a radical departure from traditional urban governance, embedding state control into the foundation of Soviet city design. Its legacy shaped Soviet urban landscapes for decades and continues to influence debates on centralized planning and equitable land management in urban development today.

How can lessons from Soviet urban planning, both successes and failures, inform modern efforts to create equitable and efficient urban environments?

APRIL 14
1900

OPENING OF
THE 1900 EXPOSITION UNIVERSELLE IN PARIS

"The 20th century belongs to the city. It is the century of light and transformation."
– Inspired by the vision of the Exposition Universelle

Panoramic View of the Exposition Universelle of 1900. By Lucien Baylac (1851–1913). Via Wikimedia Commons. Public Domain.

On this day in 1900, the Exposition Universelle (World's Fair) opened in Paris, celebrating the achievements of the 19th century while heralding the innovations of the 20th. The event introduced groundbreaking technologies, including escalators, diesel engines, and early cinematic films, highlighting the transformative potential of modern industry and design. It showcased the role of cities as global centers of cultural and technological exchange, illustrating how urban spaces foster collaboration and innovation. Iconic structures like the Grand Palais and Petit Palais were built for the exposition, blending Beaux-Arts elegance with practicality and leaving a lasting architectural legacy in Paris. Attracting millions of visitors, the fair inspired ideas about urbanism, infrastructure, and global interconnectedness, shaping the narrative of modern cities. The Exposition Universelle symbolized a new era of progress and exchange, influencing city planning and the design of international exhibitions for decades to come.

How can modern world fairs or similar events be designed to inspire urban transformation and innovation while ensuring sustainability and inclusivity?

FRANK LLOYD WRIGHT'S
BROADACRE CITY

"No longer was the city to be an overgrown village—it was to be a new thing, essentially different." — Frank Lloyd Wright. American architect and urban planner.

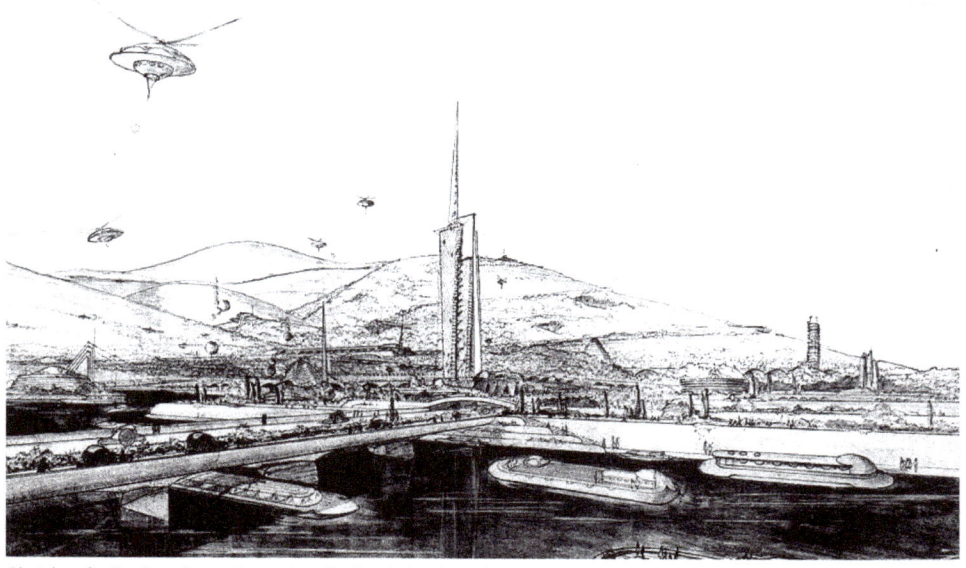

Sketches for the Broadacre City project. By Frank Lloyd Wright. Source: Scanned by Kjell Olsen. Via Wikimedia Commons. CC BY-SA 2.0

On this day in 1935, Frank Lloyd Wright's model of Broadacre City was unveiled to the public at the Industrial Arts Exposition in the Forum at Rockefeller Center, bringing to life the radical urban vision first outlined in his 1932 book The Disappearing City. Broadacre City proposed a decentralized, anti-urban model where each family would live on a one-acre plot, blending rural and urban elements. Wright rejected the dense, industrialized metropolis in favor of green space, personal autonomy, and automobile-centered mobility. The physical model showcased a vast, low-density landscape integrating homes, farms, workplaces, and civic spaces, all designed to promote self-sufficiency and individual freedom. It was a direct critique of centralized urban planning, offering a utopian vision that emphasized harmony with nature and technological advancement. Though never built, Broadacre City significantly shaped suburban thinking and continues to provoke debate about sprawl, sustainability, and the role of decentralization in contemporary urban planning.

How can elements of Wright's Broadacre City concept inspire sustainable planning in today's suburban and rural communities?

APRIL 16
1853

INDIA'S FIRST
PASSENGER TRAIN JOURNEY

"The introduction of railways has been one of the most powerful levers of civilization and progress." – George Stephenson. English engineer and "Father of Railways."

A refugee special train at Ambala Station. The carriages are full and the refugees seek room on top. Author unknown. Photo Division, Government of India. Via Wikimedia Commons. Public Domain.

On this day in 1853, the Great Indian Peninsula Railway launched India's first passenger train service, connecting Bori Bunder in Bombay (now Mumbai) to Thane. Covering 34 kilometers (21 miles) in just 57 minutes, the journey marked the dawn of a transformative era in Indian transportation. This milestone revolutionized travel and catalyzed urbanization, laying the foundation for modern India's interconnected cities. Railways quickly became the lifeblood of urban centers like Bombay, Calcutta, and Delhi, enabling the efficient movement of goods, people, and raw materials while driving economic growth and industrialization. Rail network expansion spurred industrial city development, reshaping the urban landscape and fostering a new sense of connectivity across vast regions. Witnessed by crowds celebrating progress, the inaugural train journey symbolized the power of infrastructure to redefine cities, bridge distances, and propel a nation toward modernization.

How can historical transportation milestones, like India's first railway, inspire modern approaches to sustainable and equitable urban mobility?

BIRTH OF CAMILLO SITTE

"The art of building cities is not just about practicality, but about creating spaces that move the human soul." — Camillo Sitte. Austrian architect and urban theorist.

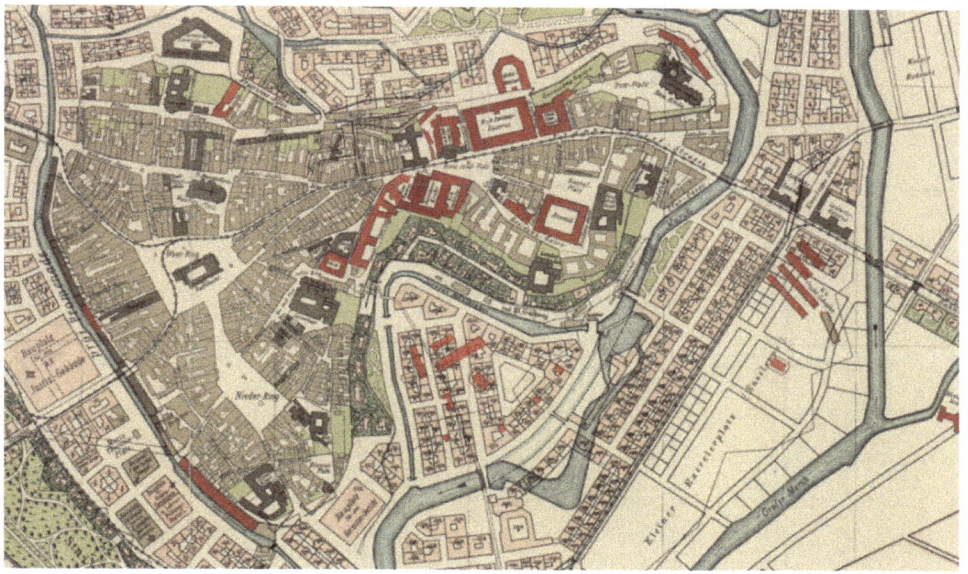

Plan of the Royal Capital City of Olomouc / Expansion of the City according to Camillo Sittes Project. By Camillo Sitte, 1895. Source: Muzeum um_ní Olomouc. Via Wikimedia Commons. CC BY-SA 3.0 CZ

On this day in 1843, Camillo Sitte, one of the most influential urban theorists of the 19th century, was born in Vienna, Austria. An architect, painter, and city planner, Sitte became renowned for his landmark 1889 book, Der Städtebau nach seinen künstlerischen Grundsätzen (The Art of Building Cities), which reshaped urban planning by emphasizing the aesthetic and human aspects of city design. Sitte criticized the rigid, geometric layouts of industrial cities, arguing for a return to the organic forms of medieval and Renaissance towns, where public squares and streets fostered vibrant social and cultural life. His ideas influenced many 20th-century urban design movements, including New Urbanism, by championing the integration of beauty, functionality, and livability in urban environments. Sitte's legacy remains a cornerstone of debates on how cities should balance modern needs with timeless design principles.

How can Camillo Sitte's emphasis on aesthetic and human-centered design guide the development of inclusive and vibrant urban spaces today?

APRIL 18
1923

FORMATION OF THE REGIONAL PLANNING ASSOCIATION OF AMERICA

"The city must be an expression of the life of its people."
— Lewis Mumford. American historian and urban theorist.

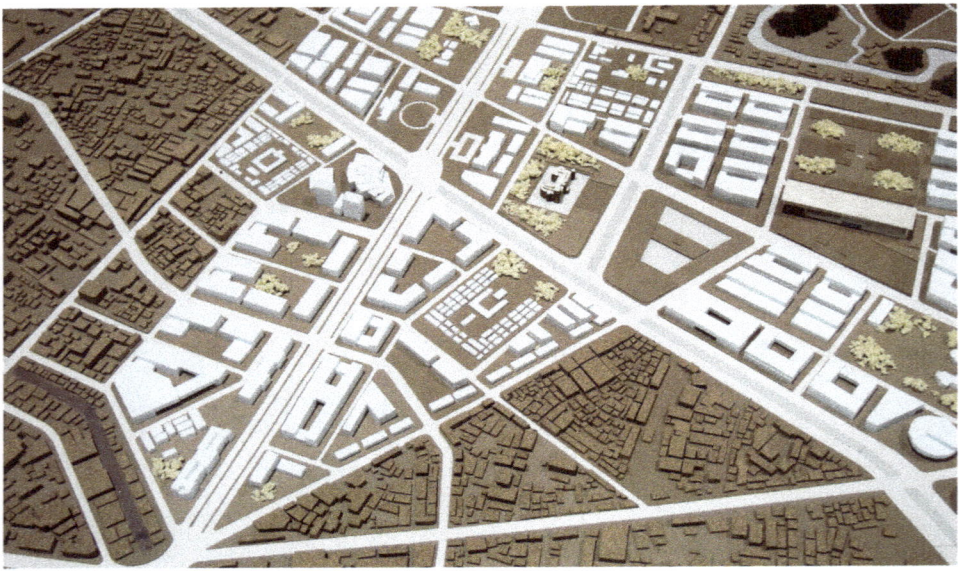

Generic City model. By Chatchai. Licensed

On this day in 1923, the first official meeting of the Regional Planning Association of America (RPAA) was held, bringing together planners, architects, writers, and reformers to rethink urban and regional development in the United States. Prominent members such as Lewis Mumford, Clarence Stein, Henry Wright, and Catherine Bauer advocated integrating urban planning, housing reform, and environmental conservation. The RPAA sought to address challenges like suburban sprawl, social inequality, and unsustainable land use by promoting planned communities, regionalism, and the inclusion of green spaces. Their work led to influential projects like Radburn, New Jersey, a pioneering garden city model that emphasized walkability, green spaces, and innovative traffic designs. The RPAA played a critical role in shaping the modern planning movement, blending practical solutions with utopian ideals to balance urban growth with societal and environmental needs, leaving a lasting legacy on urban and regional planning.

How did the RPAA's advocacy for regionalism and planned communities influence contemporary urban planning and environmental design?

FIRST BOSTON MARATHON HELD

"A marathon weaves a city together, turning its streets into a path of perseverance and celebration." – John Graham. American marathon founder and race director. (Paraphrased).

A sketch from the Boston Globe of the events of the first Boston Marathon in 1897, which John McDermott won, 1897. Author unknown. Source: The Boston Globe, Tuesday, April 20, 1897, page 9. Via Wikimedia Commons. Public Domain.

On this day in 1897, the first Boston Marathon took place, inspired by the marathon race in the 1896 Summer Olympics in Athens. Starting with just 15 runners on a course from Ashland to Boston, the event has since evolved into the world's oldest annual marathon, attracting thousands of participants and millions of spectators each year. The Boston Marathon has become a cornerstone of the city's urban culture, using public streets and infrastructure to celebrate athletic achievement and community spirit. The race underscores the role of urban planning in facilitating large-scale events that unite diverse communities and foster local pride. Its integration into Boston's urban fabric highlights how recreational activities can enrich city life while promoting health and international connection. Today, the Boston Marathon stands as a symbol of endurance, unity, and the power of urban spaces to bring people together on a global stage.

How can urban planners design cities to host large public events while ensuring accessibility, sustainability, and community engagement?

APRIL 20
1974

VOLUNTEER RECOGNITION DAY ESTABLISHED

"Cities have the capability of providing something for everybody, only because, and only when, they are created by everybody." – Jane Jacobs. American-Canadian journalist and urban activist.

American Red Cross. Croix Rouge Americaine. Magasin No. 1. Between 1918 and 1920. Source: American National Red Cross photograph collection, Library of Congress. Public Domain.

On this day in 1974, Volunteer Recognition Day was officially established to celebrate the individuals who dedicate their time and talents to improving communities. Volunteers have long played a vital role in shaping urban environments, contributing to everything from city planning and public engagement to environmental stewardship and crisis response. Their efforts range from organizing neighborhood cleanups and leading grassroots advocacy to serving on advisory boards and participating in design processes. These acts of civic engagement help foster stronger social ties, promote sustainability, and improve quality of life, particularly in underserved communities.

During critical moments—such as wartime or natural disasters—volunteer organizations like the American Red Cross have mobilized to provide essential services and support. Volunteer Recognition Day highlights the profound impact that collective action and civic participation have on urban transformation. It serves as a reminder that inclusive, resilient, and vibrant cities are often built not just by professionals, but by the many hands and voices of citizens.

How can cities better involve volunteers in inclusive urban planning?

FOUNDING OF ROME

"Rome was not built in a day, but its foundations were laid for eternity."
— Modern proverb reflecting Rome's enduring legacy.

Historical map of ancient Rome, 1st century CE, as imagined by Renaissance cartographers and published in Italy in 1570. This map reflects early modern interpretations of classical urbanism and Roman grandeur. Published in Italy by Pyrrhus Ligorious, 1570. Source: Wikimedia Commons. Public Domain.

On this day in 753 BCE, according to legend, Romulus founded the city of Rome, becoming its first king after defeating his twin brother, Remus. The site, strategically located on the Tiber River and surrounded by the Seven Hills, offered defensibility and access to vital trade routes. What began as a modest settlement of shepherds and farmers evolved into one of history's most influential cities, shaping urban planning for millennia. Rome introduced innovations such as aqueducts, roads, and public spaces like forums and amphitheaters, setting a foundation for the urban infrastructure of future civilizations. The city's founding, blending mythology with practical considerations, began the Roman Empire's lasting impact on governance, engineering, and city-building. Today, April 21st, is the "Natale di Roma," the "Birthday of Rome," honoring the city's legendary origins and enduring legacy as a model of urban ingenuity and cultural resilience.

How did the myths and early planning principles of Rome influence the city's evolution into one of the most enduring urban models in history?

APRIL 22
1970

FIRST CELEBRATION OF EARTH DAY, USA

"The ultimate test of man's conscience may be his willingness to sacrifice something today for future generations whose words of thanks will not be heard." – Gaylord Nelson. Founder of Earth Day. (Adapted)

Climate Change Rally. By Xavier Lorenzo. Licensed

On this day in 1970, the first Earth Day was celebrated across the United States, with millions participating in rallies, teach-ins, and community events advocating for environmental protection. Organized by Senator Gaylord Nelson and activist Denis Hayes, Earth Day united diverse groups to address issues such as pollution, deforestation, urban sprawl, and ecological degradation. This historic event marked the birth of the modern environmental movement and influenced landmark U.S. legislation, including the Clean Air Act, the Clean Water Act, and the Endangered Species Act. Earth Day's call to action inspired urban planners and architects to integrate sustainability into city development through green spaces, renewable energy initiatives, and eco-friendly design. Now celebrated globally, Earth Day raises awareness and drives action on critical environmental challenges, reminding us of the shared responsibility to create a more sustainable and resilient future for our cities and planet.

How has Earth Day influenced the global conversation about sustainability, and what role do cities play in leading the fight against climate change?

COLUMBIA UNIVERSITY STUDENT PROTESTS

"To rebel is justified." — Mark Rudd. American student activist and leader of Columbia University's Students for a Democratic Society (SDS).

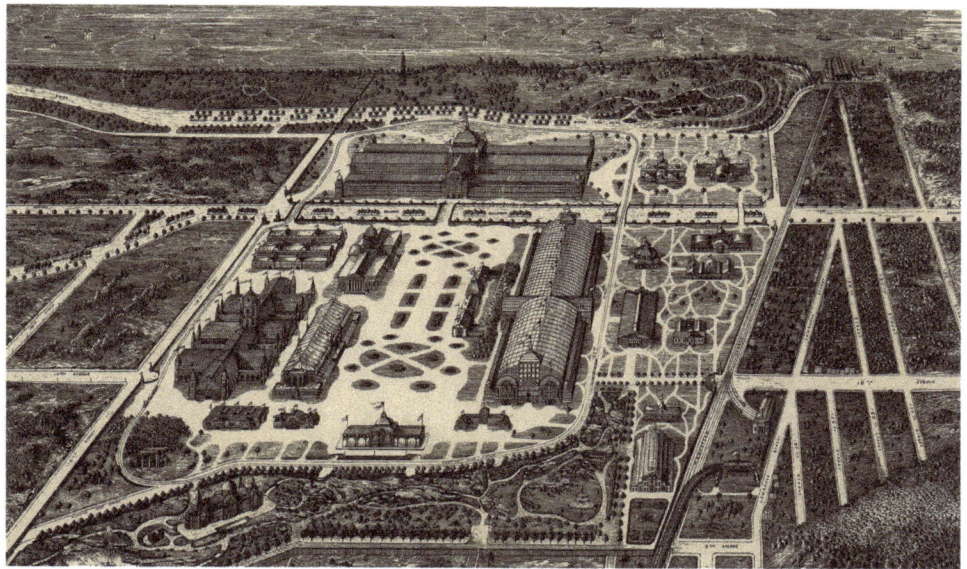

Proposed site for World's Fair in: between 110th and 125th Streets, Morning Side and River Side Parks, N.Y. Area 300 acres. By Stranders, W. (1879). Published in New York: Demorest's Illustrated Monthly Magazine. Source: Library of Congress Prints and Photographs Division. Public Domain.

On this day in 1968, students at Columbia University in New York City occupied administration buildings in protest of the university's military research ties and controversial plans to build a gymnasium in Morningside Park, a project seen disregarding the needs of neighboring Harlem. The protests, organized mainly by student activists, brought attention to social equity, urban development, and institutional accountability issues. Youth-led movements like this highlight students' critical role in questioning urban policies and advocating for inclusive development. The Columbia protests were a turning point in emphasizing the importance of community collaboration in shaping urban spaces. They set a precedent for student engagement in broader urban and social issues. This event underscores the power of youth to influence policy and the built environment through advocacy and activism.

How can cities better engage youth and students in urban planning to ensure that development reflects the needs of future generations?

APRIL 24
1913

OPENING OF
THE WOOLWORTH BUILDING

"A skyscraper is a machine that makes the land pay."
– Cass Gilbert. American architect.

The Woolworth Building and City Hall Park, New York City.

Glossy color postcard of "The Woolworth Building and City Hall Park, New York City." Published by The American Art Publishing Co., New York city. Source: H. Finkelstein & Son - scanned. Via Wikimedia Commons. Public Domain.

On this day in 1913, the Woolworth Building in New York City officially opened as the tallest building in the world at the time, standing at 792 feet (241 meters) with 60 stories. Designed by architect Cass Gilbert, this neo-Gothic skyscraper symbolized the rise of urban density, vertical development, and the evolving role of cities as centers of commerce and innovation. The Woolworth Building introduced innovative technologies, including fireproofing, high-speed elevators, and steel-frame construction, paving the way for future skyscrapers. Its vertical scale allowed for efficient land use in an increasingly crowded Manhattan, reinforcing the shift toward high-density urban environments. While high-rises optimize land use and create iconic skylines, they can raise questions about livability, accessibility, and environmental sustainability compared to low-rise, human-scale urban design. Balancing density with livability remains a central challenge for modern cities, reflecting the lessons of early skyscrapers like the Woolworth Building.

How can cities balance the benefits of high-rise development with the human-scale advantages of low-rise urban environments, particularly in addressing density and sustainability?

GROUND BROKEN
FOR THE SUEZ CANAL

"To dig a canal is to reshape the map of the world and the destiny of its cities."
– Ferdinand de Lesseps. (Paraphrased)

Suez Canal and Lake Timsah 1909. Source: Library of Congress Source: National Photo Company Collection, Library of Congress Prints and Photographs Division. Via Wikimedia Commons. Public Domain.

On this day in 1859, construction began on the Suez Canal in Port Said, Egypt, a groundbreaking project led by French engineer Ferdinand de Lesseps and funded by international investors. Designed to connect the Mediterranean Sea to the Red Sea, the canal transformed global trade by drastically reducing travel distances between Europe and Asia, eliminating the need to sail around Africa. Completed in 1869, the 163-kilometer canal was a monumental feat of engineering and labor that significantly influenced the urban growth of Port Said, Suez, and surrounding areas. Its completion elevated the region's geopolitical importance, cementing Egypt's status as a global trade hub and boosting regional economic activity. Today, the Suez Canal remains one of the world's most critical maritime routes, exemplifying the transformative power of infrastructure in shaping urban centers, fostering global connectivity, and driving international commerce on an unprecedented scale.

How do large-scale infrastructure projects shape the economic and urban landscapes of their surrounding regions?

APRIL 26
1822

BIRTH OF
FREDERICK LAW OLMSTED

"The enjoyment of scenery employs the mind without fatigue."
— Frederick Law Olmsted. American landscape architect.

A young Frederick Law Olmstead (Center Image), Manual and industrial training, 1885. By Norfolk House Centre (Roxbury and Boston, Mass.). Source: Boston Public Library via Flickr Commons. Public Domain.

On this day in 1822, Frederick Law Olmsted, often called the father of American landscape architecture, was born. A visionary designer, reformer, and environmentalist, Olmsted championed the transformative power of green spaces in urban settings. Collaborating with Calvert Vaux, he co-designed New York's Central Park (1858), a pioneering urban oasis that blended recreation, aesthetics, and public health. Olmsted's philosophy centered on creating accessible, naturalistic landscapes to enhance city residents' physical and mental well-being. His portfolio includes landmark projects such as Brooklyn's Prospect Park, Boston's Emerald Necklace, and the grounds of the U.S. Capitol. Beyond individual parks, Olmsted advocated for integrating green spaces into broader urban networks, laying the foundation for modern green infrastructure. His innovative ideas and enduring designs continue to influence the creation of sustainable, equitable, and restorative urban environments worldwide, solidifying his legacy as a transformative figure in urban planning and design.

How can urban parks be designed to serve as spaces of respite and inclusion in modern cities

FOUNDING OF
ROBERT OWEN'S NEW HARMONY

"Eight hours labour, eight hours recreation, eight hours rest."
– Robert Owen. Welsh social reformer and industrialist.

A bird's eye view of a community in New Harmony, Indiana, 1838. Drawn and engraved by F. Bate. Published by "The Association of all Classes of all Nations," at their institution, 69, Great Queen Street. Lincoln's Inn Fields, London. Via Wikimedia Commons. Public Domain.

On this day in 1825, British industrialist and social reformer Robert Owen purchased the town of New Harmony, Indiana, from a religious community with the aim of establishing what he called 'a new moral world.' Conceived as a utopian experiment in communal living, New Harmony was designed to demonstrate how education, equality, and cooperative economics could form the foundation of a just society. The settlement featured shared resources, equitable housing, and institutions dedicated to science, learning, and cultural advancement. It attracted a remarkable array of intellectuals, educators, and reformers, briefly transforming the town into a hub for progressive thought. Yet, practical challenges—ranging from resource allocation to ideological disputes—led to its collapse by 1829. Though short-lived, New Harmony's bold vision left a lasting imprint, influencing future cooperative movements and urban planning models centered on social reform, inclusivity, and collective welfare. It endures as a symbol of the 19th-century utopian spirit and the enduring aspiration to shape more equitable urban futures.

How do utopian experiments like New Harmony influence modern urban planning and community design?

APRIL 28
1925

LE CORBUSIER
PRESENTS PLAN VOISIN AT PARIS EXPOSITION

"A city made for speed is a city made for success."
– Le Corbusier. French-Swiss architect and urban planner.

Model of the Plan Voisin for Paris by Le Corbusier displayed at the Nouveau Esprit Pavilion (1925). By Le Corbusier. Source: SiefkinDR. Via Wikimedia Commons. CC BY-SA 4.0

On this day in 1925, the Exposition Internationale des Arts Décoratifs et Industriels Modernes was inaugurated in a private ceremony by the President of France, one day before its grand public opening. At this landmark event in Paris, Le Corbusier presented his provocative Plan Voisin, a radical proposal to transform the historic Marais district. The plan envisioned demolishing much of the old urban fabric to construct a modernist core of 18 cruciform skyscrapers set amid vast green spaces and wide boulevards. Rooted in his concept of the 'Radiant City,' it emphasized functional zoning, automobile mobility, and architectural uniformity. Though never implemented, Plan Voisin became one of the most influential and contentious urban visions of the 20th century. It ignited debates over modernism, heritage preservation, and the social consequences of top-down urban renewal. Its legacy continues to inform contemporary urban discourse, highlighting the tensions between modernization and cultural continuity in city planning.

How can planners balance the need for modernization with preserving the cultural and historic fabric of cities?

LOS ANGELES RIOTS: A TURNING POINT IN URBAN JUSTICE

"Why can't we all just get along?"
– Rodney King, American construction worker and figure central to the 1992 Los Angeles riots.

LA Riots aftermath, 1992. The image captures the destruction of commercial buildings and urban infrastructure following the civil unrest in Los Angeles, highlighting issues of social inequality, racial tension, and urban resilience. By Mick Taylor. Via Wikimedia Commons. CC BY-SA 2.0.

On this day in 1992, the Los Angeles Riots erupted after the acquittal of four police officers in the beating of Rodney King, despite video evidence of excessive force. The unrest, which lasted six days, resulted in over 60 deaths, thousands of injuries, and nearly $1 billion in property damage, with South Central Los Angeles bearing the brunt of the destruction. The riots laid bare systemic inequalities, including racial segregation, economic disinvestment, and strained community-police relations, that had long plagued urban communities. In the aftermath, rebuilding efforts focused on community-based urban planning, economic revitalization, and initiatives to address racial and economic disparities. While these efforts brought some improvements, the riots remain a stark reminder of the deep-seated issues that cities face, highlighting the urgent need for equitable development, justice, and inclusive urban policies to prevent such crises in the future.

How can cities use moments of social unrest as catalysts for long-term change, creating equitable and inclusive urban environments for all residents?

APRIL 30
1914

CARRYING OUT
THE CITY PLAN

"Plans without legal frameworks are dreams; implementation is the measure of success."
— Flavel Shurtleff. American planning theorist.

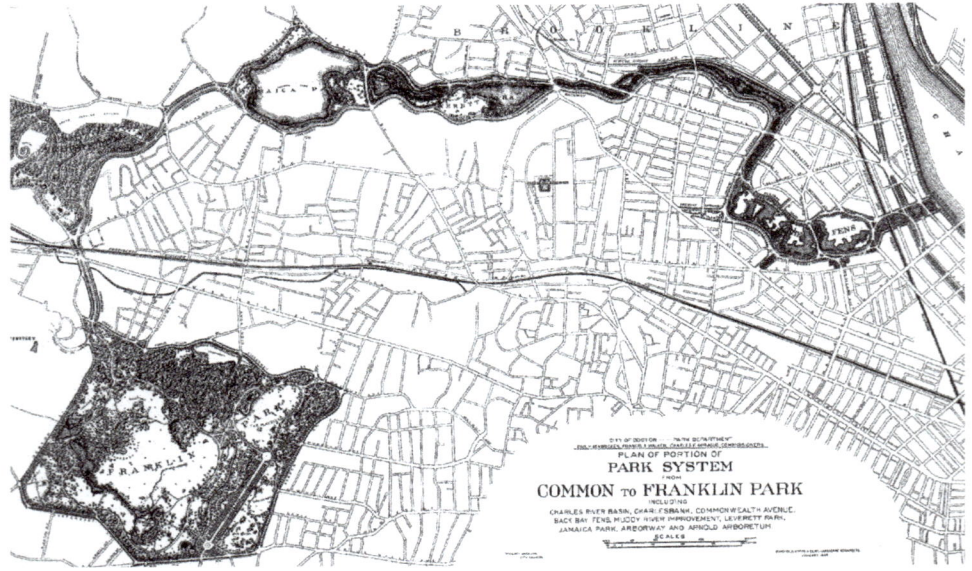

Olmsted Park System. One of the first park systems created in the United States, Boston's Olmsted Park System, was a model for metropolitan open space planning initiatives elsewhere. By Boston Parks Department & Olmsted Architects, NPS Olmsted Archives. Public Domain.

On this day in 1914, Flavel Shurtleff and Frederick Law Olmsted Jr. finalized the introduction to Carrying Out the City Plan, a pioneering text that became the first major treatise on the legal and administrative foundations of city planning in the United States. Drawing from two years of in-depth research into American and European planning practices, the book laid out a framework for implementing urban plans through formal governance structures. Shurtleff, a lawyer and planner, brought technical precision, while Olmsted—already a respected voice in landscape and city planning—strengthened the book's authority and public reach. The authors emphasized the necessity of

planning commissions, zoning ordinances, and intergovernmental cooperation to translate visionary plans into enduring urban form. By advocating for legal mechanisms to support comprehensive planning, the book helped legitimize planning as a profession and influenced policy for decades. Its legacy persists in today's planning institutions and remains a cornerstone in the history of American urbanism.

How can strong legal frameworks and governance structures support the long-term success of city planning initiatives today?

CREATION OF
THE RESETTLEMENT ADMINISTRATION

"A decent home, a suitable living environment, and a fair chance to work are the birthrights of every American." — Rexford G. Tugwell. American economist. (Paraphrased).

Suburban Resettlement Administration poster, 1935. Source: Farm Security Administration - Office of War Information Photograph Collection. Library of Congress. Public Domain.

On this day in 1935, President Franklin D. Roosevelt established the Resettlement Administration (RA) as part of the New Deal to combat rural poverty, unemployment, and substandard living conditions during the Great Depression. Led by Rexford G. Tugwell, the RA aimed to relocate struggling families to planned communities with improved housing and infrastructure. Among its most notable projects were the Greenbelt Towns— Greenbelt, Maryland; Greenhills, Ohio; and Greendale, Wisconsin—which became pioneering sustainable and cooperative living models. These towns featured green spaces, efficient layouts, and community-oriented designs that balanced urban and rural qualities. Despite criticism for its cost and experimental nature, the RA left a lasting legacy in urban planning and housing policy. Its emphasis on federal involvement in creating livable, equitable communities influenced later initiatives, marking a significant moment in the evolution of planned communities and sustainable urban development in the United States.

How did the Resettlement Administration's planned communities shape modern ideas about sustainable, equitable housing and urban design?

MAY 2
1910

BIRTH OF EDMUND BACON

"A city is the physical form of a society's aspirations and values."
– Edmund Bacon. American architect and urban planner.

Street in Society Hill, Philadelphia, Pennsylvania, showcasing a historic neighborhood characterized by its 18th-century row houses, cobblestone streets, and preservation of early American urban form. By Jonbilous. Licensed.

On this day in 1910, Edmund Bacon, the visionary urban planner who reshaped mid-20th century Philadelphia, was born. Serving as the executive director of the Philadelphia City Planning Commission from 1949 to 1970, Bacon spearheaded transformative redevelopment projects that revitalized the city's urban core. His influential work included Society Hill, which blended historic preservation with modern housing, the corporate hub of Penn Center, and the culturally significant Independence Mall. Bacon's approach emphasized walkability, public spaces, and a cohesive urban fabric, balancing modernity with respect for the past. His seminal book, Design of Cities (1967), became a cornerstone of urban planning literature. While his legacy is debated due to the displacement caused by urban renewal policies, Bacon's impact underscores both the opportunities and complexities of reshaping cities, leaving a lasting influence on Philadelphia and the broader field of urban design.

How can contemporary urban planning learn from both the successes and criticisms of Edmund Bacon's large-scale urban renewal projects in Philadelphia

MAY 3
1948

RACIALLY RESTRICTIVE COVENANTS BANNED

"Equal protection of the laws is not achieved through indiscriminate imposition of inequalities." — U.S. Supreme Court, Shelley v. Kraemer

Fair housing protest in Lake City, 1964. This photograph captures a pivotal moment in the American civil rights movement, highlighting the struggle for housing equality. Photograph by Seattle Municipal Archives. CC BY 2.0

On this day in 1948, the U.S. Supreme Court issued its landmark decision in Shelley v. Kraemer, ruling that the courts could not enforce racially restrictive covenants in property deeds, effectively prohibiting their use in housing discrimination. These covenants, widely employed in the early 20th century, barred selling or renting homes to individuals based on race, fostering segregation in urban and suburban neighborhoods. While the decision rendered such covenants legally unenforceable, they remained in property records for decades, perpetuating racial inequalities and shaping patterns of segregation. The ruling was pivotal in the struggle for housing equality,

signaling a shift toward addressing systemic discrimination. It laid the foundation for subsequent legislation, including the Fair Housing Act of 1968, which sought to combat discriminatory practices and promote more equitable access to housing across the United States.

How can urban planners address the lingering effects of racially restrictive covenants on housing equity and community development?

MAY 4
1916

BIRTH OF
JANE JACOBS

"Cities have the capability of providing something for everybody, only because, and only when, they are created by everybody." – Jane Jacobs. Journalist and urban activist.

Image of a typical New York Brownstone, based on Jane Jacob's descriptions in her book: "The Death and Life of Great American Cities." By Plusurbia Design. Created using MidJourney.

On this day in 1916, Jane Jacobs, a transformative urban thinker and activist, was born. Her groundbreaking book, The Death and Life of Great American Cities (1961), revolutionized urban planning by challenging the dominant, top-down approaches of the time, which often prioritized large-scale redevelopment and freeway construction at the expense of local communities. Jacobs championed vibrant, diverse neighborhoods, mixed-use development, and the organic rhythms of city life, arguing that the vitality of cities stems from their complexity and social interactions. Her grassroots activism, including her successful opposition to New York's Lower Manhattan Expressway,

protected historic neighborhoods and underscored the importance of resident involvement in urban decision-making. Jacobs' advocacy for walkability, density, and community-centered planning reshaped the field, influencing generations of planners and activists. Her legacy endures as a cornerstone of contemporary discussions about sustainable, livable cities that prioritize human connection and the needs of residents.

How can Jacobs' advocacy for community-based planning shape cities facing rapid redevelopment today?

INAUGURATION OF
PUBLIC SERVICE RECOGNITION WEEK

"The best way to find yourself is to lose yourself in the service of others."
– Mahatma Gandhi. Indian independence leader and advocate for non-violence.

CIVIC DUTY	PUBLIC OUTREACH	COMMUNITY SUPPORT	SOCIAL SERVICES	PUBLIC WELFARE	GOVERNMENT ASSISTANCE
PUBLIC SAFETY	SOCIAL WELFARE	GOVERNMENT RESOURCES	CIVIC RESPONSIBILITY	PUBLIC SECTOR	COMMUNITY CARE
PUBLIC ADMINISTRATION	PUBLIC POLICY	PUBLIC AWARENESS	GOVERNMENT SERVICES	CITIZEN SERVICES	PUBLIC ADVOCACY

Public Service. By Santricon. Licensed

On this day in 1985, the United States celebrated the first Public Service Recognition Week (PSRW), honoring the contributions of public servants at federal, state, and local levels. Held annually during the first week of May, PSRW shines a spotlight on the essential role of government employees in shaping and sustaining communities. The inaugural event featured outreach programs, award ceremonies, and public awareness campaigns, emphasizing the impact of public service in areas like education, public safety, health, and infrastructure. In urban areas, public servants are vital to city governance, managing transportation systems, maintaining infrastructure, and delivering critical citizen services. PSRW not only fosters appreciation for these efforts but also inspires younger generations to pursue careers in public service. By celebrating the dedication of public employees, the week underscores their role in building thriving, resilient, and well-functioning cities and communities.

How can cities foster greater public appreciation and recognition of the work performed by government employees?

MAY 6
1935

CREATION OF
THE WORKS PROGRESS ADMINISTRATION

"The only thing we have to fear is fear itself."
– Franklin D. Roosevelt. 32nd President of the United States.

William Boellhoeff, Supervisor of the Wood Carving Department, showing visitors the new eagle carving for the Boston City Hall. Federal Art Project, Work Projects Administration for Massachusetts. By Works Progress Administration, United States. Source: Boston Public Library. Via Wikimedia Commons. Public Domain.

On this day in 1935, President Franklin D. Roosevelt issued Executive Order 7034, creating the Works Progress Administration (WPA) as part of the New Deal. Designed to combat the economic devastation of the Great Depression, the WPA provided millions of jobs through public works projects that reshaped urban landscapes across the United States. The program built roads, bridges, schools, parks, and libraries, revitalizing infrastructure and enhancing urban environments. Beyond construction, the WPA supported cultural initiatives like the Federal Art Project, funding murals, performances, and public art that enriched city life. This unprecedented investment demonstrated the transformative potential of government intervention, fostering economic recovery while improving the quality of life in cities. The WPA's legacy highlights the power of large-scale public works to address urban challenges, promote community well-being, and leave lasting contributions to the nation's built environment.

How can cities today draw lessons from the WPA in addressing unemployment and investing in infrastructure to create resilient and equitable urban environments?

DEVELOPMENT OF LEVITTOWN, NEW YORK, BEGINS

*"No man who owns his own house and lot can be a Communist. He has too much to do."
— William Levitt. Real estate developer, known as the "father of modern American suburbia."*

Aerial view of suburban Levittown, Pennsylvania. Circa 1959. Source: The College of New Jersey. Via Wikimedia Commons. Public Domain.

On this day in 1947, Levitt & Sons officially announced the creation of Levittown, New York, the first large-scale, mass-produced suburban community in the United States. Situated on Long Island, Levittown was designed to address the postwar housing shortage by offering affordable, efficiently built homes to returning World War II veterans and their families. Using assembly-line construction techniques, the developers built nearly 17,500 homes within four years, each featuring standardized designs and modern amenities like central heating and kitchen appliances. Levittown quickly became a symbol of suburbanization and the American Dream of homeownership, influencing suburban development models across the country. However, it also institutionalized racial exclusion through restrictive covenants that barred non-white buyers, revealing the deep racial inequities in postwar housing policy. Despite its contradictions, Levittown marked a transformative moment in urban planning and suburban growth, leaving a lasting imprint on the built environment and social landscape of postwar America.

What lessons can be learned from Levittown's successes and shortcomings in shaping equitable and sustainable suburban development today?

BIRTH OF
ROBERTO ROSSELLINI, PIONEER OF NEOREALISM

"The real world is far more fascinating than any fiction."
– Roberto Rossellini. Italian film director and screenwriter.

From right. Roberto Rossellini, Renzo Rossellini and Carlo Carlini on Set. 1964 By Patrizia Mannajuolo. Via Wikimedia Commons. Public Domain.

On this day in 1906, Italian filmmaker Roberto Rossellini was born in Rome. A pioneer of the Neorealist movement, Rossellini redefined how cities were portrayed on film by using real urban environments and non-professional actors to depict life's raw realities. His landmark film Rome, Open City (1945) captures the hardships of ordinary Romans under Nazi occupation, blending documentary-style realism with narrative drama. Shot on location in war-torn Rome, the film serves as both a cinematic masterpiece and a visual archive of the city's streets, ruins, and resilience. Rossellini's work emphasized the complexity of urban life, portraying cities not as backdrops but as living, breathing characters in their own right. His approach influenced filmmakers worldwide, inspiring a more authentic depiction of cities and cementing the idea of urban spaces as dynamic, evolving places shaped by history and human experience.

How did Rossellini's films change the way cities are represented in visual media and influence global perceptions of urban life?

COMPLETION OF
ONE WORLD TRADE CENTER

"As we rise, we honor the past and build the future."
– David Childs, American architect.

Aerial view of Manhattan, New York City, prominently showcasing One World Trade Center, the tallest building in the Western Hemisphere, symbolizing urban resilience and renewal in the post-9/11 era. By Christian Horras. Licensed.

On this day in 2013, the final pieces of the 408-foot spire were being lifted into place atop One World Trade Center in New York City, completing its ascent to a symbolic height of 1,776 feet and making it the tallest building in the Western Hemisphere. Designed by architect David Childs, the tower stands as a powerful emblem of resilience, renewal, and unity following the September 11, 2001 attacks. Its height intentionally references the year of American independence, linking the nation's founding ideals with its contemporary spirit. Combining cutting-edge engineering with sustainable design, One World Trade Center serves both as a commercial powerhouse and a cultural landmark. The completion of the spire marked a major milestone in the rebuilding of Lower Manhattan and reinforced the city's role as a beacon of perseverance and progress, honoring the past while looking confidently toward the future.

How do iconic structures like One World Trade Center shape a city's identity and inspire collective resilience?

MAY 10
1869

COMPLETION OF
THE FIRST U.S. TRANSCONTINENTAL RAILROAD

"The completion of the Pacific Railroad...is the most important achievement of the age."
– The New York Times, May 11, 1869

Print showing an allegory of linking of the Trans-Continental railroad at Promontory Summit, Utah, 1869. By Frank Beard, 1869. Source: Library of Congress Prints and Photographs Division. Public Domain.

On this day in 1869, the Union Pacific and Central Pacific railroads met at Promontory Summit, Utah Territory, completing the first U.S. transcontinental railroad. This monumental achievement revolutionized transportation, connecting the East and West coasts and reducing travel time from months to days. The railroad transformed the nation's economy by enabling the rapid movement of people, goods, and ideas, fostering trade, immigration, and industrial growth. It played a pivotal role in westward expansion, facilitating the settlement of vast territories and the emergence of new towns and cities along its route. The railroad symbolized national unity following the Civil War and underscored the U.S.'s ambition to grow into a global economic power. However, its construction came at a significant human cost, particularly for Chinese immigrant laborers who faced dangerous conditions and discrimination. The transcontinental railroad remains a 19th-century innovation, ambition, and transformative infrastructure legacy.

How did the transcontinental railroad reshape urban development patterns in the United States during the late 19th century?

CONSTANTINE DEDICATES BYZANTIUM AS NEW ROME

"Thus Constantine built a city that should last as long as the world itself."
– Edward Gibbon, The Decline and Fall of the Roman Empire

Aerial view of Istanbul, Turkey, showcasing the city's historical and modern urban landscape, including its dense neighborhoods, waterways, and prominent landmarks such as the Bosphorus Strait. By a_medvedkov. Licensed.

On this day in 330 CE, Emperor Constantine the Great officially dedicated the rebuilt city of Byzantium as Nova Roma (New Rome), later renamed Constantinople in his honor. This event marked the establishment of the Eastern Roman Empire's new capital, strategically located on the Bosporus Strait to control trade routes between Europe and Asia. Constantine transformed the city with grand public buildings, Christian basilicas, and formidable fortifications, reshaping it into a monumental urban center. The dedication symbolized a blend of Roman engineering, Hellenistic culture, and emerging Christian influences, making Constantinople a beacon of cultural and political power for centuries.

The city's elevation as the new imperial capital reinforced the division of the Roman Empire into eastern and western halves, ensuring the continuity of Roman governance, culture, and urban planning principles in the East for over a millennium. Constantinople remains a landmark in the history of urbanization and empire building.

How did the establishment of Constantinople influence the development of other major urban centers in the medieval and modern eras?

MAY 12
1551

FOUNDING OF
THE NATIONAL UNIVERSITY OF SAN MARCOS

"The strength of a city lies in the enlightenment of its people."
– Francisco Pizarro. Spanish conquistador and founder of Lima, Peru. (Paraphrased).

Postcard of the Universidad Mayor de San Marcos - Lima, Perú, 1930-1945. Published by Tichnor Bros., Inc., Boston, Massachusetts. Courtesy of the Boston Public Library, Tichnor Brothers Collection. Public Domain.

On this day in 1551, the National University of San Marcos was established in Lima, Peru, making it the oldest university in the Americas. Founded during Spanish colonial rule, it quickly became a vital center of intellectual, cultural, and scientific development in the New World. Located in Lima, the administrative and cultural hub of the Spanish Empire in South America, the university reinforced the city's prominence as a center for education and innovation. Over the centuries, it significantly advanced academic thought, scientific research, and political movements in Peru and beyond. The university's enduring presence underscores the transformative role of higher education institutions in shaping urban identity, driving progress, and fostering cultural and intellectual growth. As a cornerstone of Lima's historical and academic landscape, it remains a symbol of the city's legacy as a cradle of learning in the Americas.

How can cities today leverage the presence of historic universities like San Marcos to promote education, innovation, and cultural heritage in urban development?

DEATH OF JOHN NASH

"Architecture aims to establish a balance between the city's past and its aspirations for the future." – John Nash. British architect and urban planner.

View of the East side of Regent Street as originally constructed under John Nash, between Tenison Court and Beak Street. Source: Image extracted from page 267 of Metropolitan Improvements, or London in the Nineteenth Century, by James Elmes. The original was held and digitized by the British Library and copied from Flickr. Public Domain.

On this day in 1835, John Nash, one of Britain's most influential architects and urban planners, passed away. Nash played a pivotal role in shaping Regency-era London, leaving a profound legacy through iconic projects such as Regent Street, Regent's Park, St. James's Park, and the remodeling of Buckingham Palace. His designs exemplified neoclassical elegance while introducing practical urban layouts that integrated green spaces with architectural grandeur, significantly enhancing the city's livability. Nash's vision set new benchmarks for harmonious urban design, blending beauty and functionality to create vibrant public spaces. His work transformed London into a global urban planning model, influencing the aesthetics and structure of modern cities. Nash's innovative approach to integrating public parks, promenades, and grand architecture inspires contemporary urban designers, underscoring his enduring impact on the evolution of urban spaces worldwide.

How can cities preserve and adapt historical urban layouts to meet the demands of modern sustainability and inclusivity?

MAY 14
1973

SKYLAB, THE UNITED STATES' FIRST SPACE STATION, IS LAUNCHED

"From space, cities appear as networks of light, reminding us of our shared responsibility to the Earth." – Wernher von Braun. German-American aerospace engineer. (Paraphrased).

The unmanned Skylab 1/ Saturn V Space Vehicle is launched from Pad A, Launch Complex 39, 12:00 noon EDT, 05/29/1973. Source: NASA. Via Wikimedia Commons. Public Domain.

On this day in 1973, Skylab, the first U.S. space station, was launched from the Kennedy Space Center, marking a significant milestone in space exploration and scientific research. Designed for experiments in microgravity, Skylab provided valuable insights into living and working in confined, resource-limited environments, offering parallels to urban challenges such as efficient space utilization and resource management. The station's Earth observation capabilities advanced understanding of atmospheric and environmental systems, enabling satellite monitoring of urban growth, ecosystems, and disaster impacts. Skylab's data supported urban planning efforts by improving models for sustainable development and resilience. Its legacy highlights the synergy between space exploration and urban science, demonstrating how technology designed for space can enhance the management and sustainability of cities on Earth. Skylab paved the way for future innovations in satellite monitoring and integrating space-based technologies in urban development strategies.

How can satellite technology and space exploration inform sustainable urban development and climate resilience strategies?

FELIPE GUAMAN POMA DE AYALA INTRODUCED TO THE KING

"Inca cities were built to honor both the heavens and the earth, respecting all that came before." — Inspired by Ayala's chronicles on Inca urban life.

Drawings from Guaman Poma, Nueva corónica y buen gobierno c. 1615. Pages 1013 (Villa de Riobamba), 1039 (Ciudad de Lima), 1043 (Ciudad de Cuzco). Source: Royal Danish Library, GKS 2232 kvart. With Permission

On this day in 1587, Don Martín Guaman Mallque de Ayala introduced his son Felipe Guaman Poma de Ayala's work to King Philip III of Spain through a formal letter, establishing his son's noble Inca lineage and legitimizing the forthcoming manuscript. This introduction served as a crucial endorsement for El primer nueva corónica y buen gobierno (The First New Chronicle and Good Government), which Felipe would complete around 1615. The manuscript, spanning over 1,180 pages with nearly 400 illustrations, presents a detailed Indigenous account of Inca history, urban organization, and governance, while offering a forceful critique of Spanish colonial rule. Guaman Poma emphasized the harmony, sustainability, and social order of Inca urban systems, contrasting them with the corruption and inequality of colonial administration. Though the manuscript never reached the king, its rediscovery in 1908 affirmed it as one of the most significant historical sources on Andean civilization and the urban consequences of colonialism.

How can modern urban planning honor Indigenous perspectives and preserve the cultural heritage of historically colonized regions?

MAY 16
1888

NIKOLA TESLA'S
LECTURE ON ALTERNATING CURRENT

"The day when we shall know exactly what electricity is will chronicle an event probably greater than any other recorded in human history." – From interviews attributed to Nikola Tesla.

Nikola Tesla with his experimental equipment, c.1899. The photograph captures Tesla's pioneering work in electricity and engineering, laying the foundations for modern urban electrification. By Dickenson V. Alley. Via Wikimedia Commons. CC-BY-4.0.

On this day in 1888, Nikola Tesla delivered a groundbreaking lecture to the American Institute of Electrical Engineers in New York City, unveiling his alternating current (AC) systems innovations. Tesla's work revolutionized urban electrification by efficiently generating and transmitting power over long distances, overcoming the limitations of direct current (DC) systems. His AC technology transformed urban infrastructure, enabling widespread street lighting, powering industries, and improving the quality of life in cities. This breakthrough allowed urban areas to expand and modernize, laying the foundation for the electrically powered cities of the 20th and 21st centuries. Tesla's contributions remain central to modern electrical grids, influencing sustainable and efficient energy distribution systems worldwide. His vision continues to inspire advancements in renewable energy and urban electrification, highlighting the enduring impact of his work on the evolution of cities.

How can modern cities honor Tesla's legacy by innovating and expanding sustainable energy systems for the future?

FOUNDING OF
VILLE MARIE DE MONTRÉAL

"It is not necessary to hope in order to undertake, nor to succeed in order to persevere."
– Paul de Chomedey, Sieur de Maisonneuve. Military officer and founder of Montreal.

Map of Ville-Marie (modern-day Montreal) as it appeared in 1704, illustrating the early fortifications and settlement patterns along the St. Lawrence River. This map reflects the strategic importance of Montreal as a hub for trade and military defense in New France. By Jacques Levasseur de Néré. Courtesy of Wikimedia Commons. Public Domain.

On this day in 1642, Paul de Chomedey, Sieur de Maisonneuve, officially founded Ville-Marie on the banks of the Saint Lawrence River, laying the foundation for modern-day Montreal. Established as a mission to convert Indigenous peoples to Christianity and serve as a fur trade hub, Ville-Marie's strategic location encouraged both cultural exchange and economic activity between French settlers and Indigenous communities. The settlement's design—featuring a fortified layout and communal public spaces—reflected European urban planning ideals, adapted to the realities of the North American frontier. Over time, Ville-Marie evolved into Montreal, a vibrant metropolis known for its multicultural identity, economic significance, and distinctive blend of historic and modern architecture. The founding of Ville-Marie was a pivotal moment in North American urban development, influencing regional settlement patterns and early colonial city-building. It also laid the groundwork for Montreal's enduring role as one of Canada's most dynamic and globally recognized cities.

How did European colonial urban planning influence the development of cities in North America, and what lessons can be learned from their evolution?

MAY 18
1883

BIRTH OF
WALTER GROPIUS AND THE BAUHAUS

"Let us together create the new building of the future."
– Walter Gropius. German architect and founder of the Bauhaus School.

Bauhaus Dessau, view from Gropiusallee, showcasing the iconic modernist architecture designed by Walter Gropius, which became a symbol of functional design, innovation, and the integration of art and technology. By M_H.DE. Via Wikimedia Commons. CC-BY-3.0.

On this day in 1883, Walter Gropius, a visionary architect and founder of the Bauhaus School, was born in Berlin, Germany. Gropius revolutionized modern design by integrating art, craft, and technology to meet the challenges of urbanization and industrialization. Established in 1919, the Bauhaus School introduced a groundbreaking curriculum that combined fine arts, craftsmanship, and modern technology, prioritizing functionality, simplicity, and collaboration across disciplines. Iconic projects like the Bauhaus building in Dessau embodied Gropius's philosophy of merging aesthetics with practicality, creating designs that were innovative, sustainable, and accessible. His influence extended beyond architecture to urban planning, advocating for human-centered design that balanced form with purpose. Gropius's ideas laid the foundation for modernism, shaping global design principles and inspiring sustainable approaches to urban development that prioritize human needs and environmental stewardship. His legacy remains a cornerstone of contemporary architecture and planning.

How can the founding principles of the Bauhaus inspire contemporary urban design to balance functionality and creativity?

PASSING OF
T.E. LAWRENCE

"All men dream, but not equally. Night dreamers wake to find it was vanity; daydreamers may act with open eyes to make dreams real." – T.E. Lawrence. Archaeologist, military officer, and diplomat.

T E Lawrence and the Arab Revolt 1916 - 1918. Mecca - general view of the Haram from above. 1908. Photograph by Halladjian J H. Source: Imperial War Museums. Via Wikimedia Commons. Public Domain.

On this day in 1935, T.E. Lawrence, famously known as "Lawrence of Arabia," passed away from injuries sustained in a motorcycle accident. A British archaeologist, diplomat, and military officer, Lawrence became legendary for his role in the Arab Revolt during World War I, where he helped unite Arab tribes against the Ottoman Empire. His campaigns had a lasting impact on the cities and regions of the Middle East, with urban centers like Damascus, Aqaba, and Medina serving as pivotal sites in the struggle. These cities became symbols of Arab aspirations for independence and reflected the broader geopolitical shifts of the era. Lawrence's advocacy for Arab autonomy underscored the significance of cultural and political self-determination in shaping urban identities and regional dynamics. His complex legacy continues to provoke discussions on colonialism, nation-building, and the enduring influence of urban centers in the global historical landscape.

How do figures like T.E. Lawrence influence the cultural and political landscapes of cities, and what lessons can we learn from their legacy for modern urban development?

ADOPTION OF THE LAND ORDINANCE OF 1785 AND JEFFERSON'S GRID SYSTEM

"Cultivators of the earth are the most valuable citizens." – Thomas Jefferson. 3rd President of the United States and principal author of the Declaration of Independence.

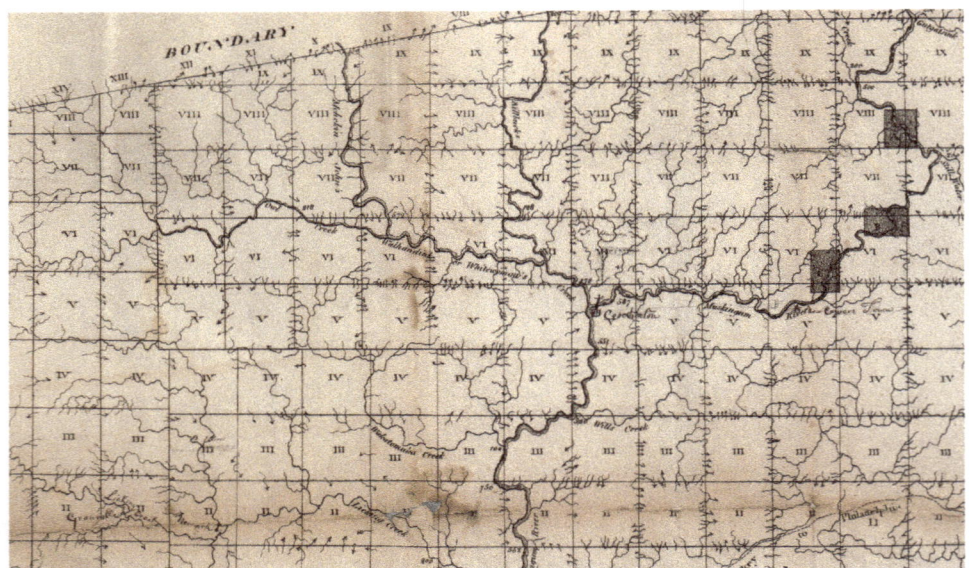

Plat of that tract of country in the territory northwest of the Ohio appropriated for military services and described in the Act of Congress intitled "An act regulating the grants of land appropriated for military services and for the Society of United Brethren for propagating the gospel among the heathen". Source: Library of Congress, Geography and Map Division. Public Domain.

On this day in 1785, the Land Ordinance of 1785 was adopted by the U.S. Congress of the Confederation, introducing Thomas Jefferson's visionary grid system for dividing and selling public land. This ordinance established the Public Land Survey System (PLSS), which divided land into 6-by-6-mile townships, further subdivided into 36 one-mile-square sections. One section in each township was reserved for public schools, reflecting Jefferson's commitment to education. The grid system aimed to standardize land division, facilitate westward expansion, and generate revenue for the government. It shaped the settlement patterns of the growing United States and influenced the planning of towns and cities, many of which adopted rectilinear street grids based on Jefferson's design. The grid became a defining feature of the American landscape, symbolizing rationality, efficiency, and order while laying the groundwork for urban and regional planning in the nation's early development.

How has Jefferson's grid system influenced modern land-use planning, and what challenges does it pose for contemporary urban development?

FIRST NATIONAL CONFERENCE ON CITY PLANNING HELD IN WASHINGTON, D.C.

"City planning is not merely the design of places but the design of the life within them."
– Frederick Law Olmsted Jr. American landscape architect and urban planner.

Aerial of Washington DC. Mall, 1901. By Graham, C., Detroit Publishing Co. Source: Library of Congress. Public Domain.

On this day in 1909, the First National Conference on City Planning convened in Washington, D.C., marking a transformative moment in the development of urban planning as a profession in the United States. The conference, organized by Frederick Law Olmsted Jr. and Flavel Shurtleff, brought together architects, engineers, public health officials, and policymakers to address the urgent challenges of industrialization and rapid urban growth. Discussions covered critical issues such as housing reform, street layout, public health, and the creation of parks, emphasizing the need for comprehensive and organized urban development. This historic gathering laid the groundwork for the modern planning profession, fostering a shared understanding of planning's role in improving urban life. It also inspired the creation of professional organizations like the American City Planning Institute (now the American Planning Association), cementing the conference's nationwide legacy in urban planning practices.

How did the First National Conference on City Planning shape the priorities and practices of modern urban planning?

MAY 22
1978

HAWAII BECOMES
THE FIRST STATE WITH STATEWIDE ZONING

"We must protect our land, our environment, and our way of life through thoughtful and unified land-use planning." — Hawaii Land Use Commission

Overlooking the taro farms in Hanalei Valley, Kauai, Hawaii. The image captures the agricultural landscape and traditional wetland farming system integral to Hawaiian cultural heritage and food sustainability. By Don Landwehrle. Licensed.

On this day in 1978, Hawaii became the first U.S. state to implement a statewide zoning system, revolutionizing land use planning. Unlike most states where local governments manage zoning, Hawaii established zoning laws at the state level to protect its limited land resources and balance competing needs, such as agriculture, conservation, and urban development. The system categorized land into three main districts—urban, rural, and conservation—placing land use decisions under the oversight of the state's Land Use Commission. This pioneering framework enabled Hawaii to address rapid growth while safeguarding its unique environment, cultural heritage, and agricultural lands.

The statewide zoning approach has since been recognized as a model for geographically constrained regions seeking to balance development with natural resource preservation. Hawaii's innovative land use system remains a testament to the power of proactive, centralized planning in achieving sustainable growth.

What can other regions learn from Hawaii's statewide zoning system in balancing development with environmental and cultural preservation?

GLOBAL URBAN POPULATION SURPASSES RURAL POPULATION

"The future of humanity lies in cities; their success will define our collective destiny."
– Ban Ki-moon. Former Secretary-General of the United Nations.

Abandoned Houtouwan Village, China's ghost fishing village on Shengshan Island, overtaken by nature. The image shows buildings and infrastructure reclaimed by vegetation, highlighting rural depopulation and nature's resilience. By Tada Images. Licensed.

On this day in 2007, the global urban population surpassed the rural population for the first time in history, a milestone often called the "Urban Millennium." This marked a pivotal shift driven by industrialization, economic opportunities, and improved living standards in cities, underscoring the rapid rapid urbanization worldwide. The transition highlighted the urgent need for sustainable urban planning to address challenges such as urban sprawl, environmental degradation, and the demand for adequate housing, transportation, and public services. It also emphasized the growing importance of resilient and inclusive urban environments to support the well-being of a majority-urban global population. For policymakers and planners, this moment reinforced the necessity of integrating sustainability, equity, and innovation into urban design to accommodate population growth while mitigating social and environmental impacts. The Urban Millennium remains a defining moment in shaping the future of cities and global development.

How can cities adapt their infrastructure and services to sustainably support the increasing urban population in the 21st century?

MAY 24
1921

BEGINNING OF
THE TULSA RACE MASSACRE

"The tragedy of Greenwood was not just in its destruction, but in the silence that followed."
– John Hope Franklin. American historian and scholar of African American history.

Aftermath of the Tulsa Race Riots, 1921. Author unknown. Source: Southern Methodist University. Via Wikimedia Commons. Public Domain.

On this day in 1921, events began to unfold that would culminate in the Tulsa Race Massacre, one of the deadliest acts of racial violence in U.S. history. In the days following May 24, tensions escalated in Tulsa, Oklahoma, after a young Black man was falsely accused of assaulting a white woman. By the night of May 31, a white mob launched a violent assault on Greenwood, a prosperous Black community known as 'Black Wall Street.' Over the next two days, an estimated 300 Black residents were killed, and more than 1,000 homes and businesses were destroyed. Greenwood, once a thriving center of Black entrepreneurship and cultural life, was reduced to rubble, displacing thousands and decimating generations of accumulated wealth. The massacre was largely omitted from official histories for decades, silencing the pain of survivors and their descendants. Today, the Tulsa Race Massacre stands as a powerful reminder of the enduring impacts of racial injustice and the importance of truth, equity, and reparative urban policy in addressing historical violence and rebuilding communities with justice at the core.

How can cities address historical injustices while fostering equitable growth and reconciliation in their communities?

PUBLICATION OF
THE FIRST ISSUE OF ARCHIGRAM MAGAZINE

"Architecture must become a 'plug-in' experience—alive, adaptable, and always in motion."
– Archigram Manifesto

Archigram Architects member Ron Herron at his drawing board in the Archigram Endell St architect office 1972 London. By Kathy deWitt Source: Alamy.

On this day in 1961, the first issue of Archigram magazine was published in the United Kingdom by Peter Cook and a group of visionary architects, marking the beginning of a movement that redefined urban and architectural theory. Emerging as a bold critique of postwar modernism, Archigram embraced futuristic ideas influenced by technology, pop culture, and science fiction. The group's speculative projects, including the Plug-In City, Walking City, and Instant City, envisioned adaptable and modular urban environments capable of evolving with society's changing needs. Their visually striking designs, featuring comic book-style graphics and bold colors, rejected the rigidity of traditional urban planning, favoring provocative and flexible solutions. Although their projects were never built, Archigram profoundly influenced high-tech architecture and experimental urbanism, inspiring architects to explore innovation and adaptability. Their legacy continues to shape contemporary discussions about integrating technology and creativity in urban design.

How can the experimental, adaptive visions of Archigram inspire solutions for today's urban challenges like climate adaptation, overpopulation, and mobility?

MAY 26
1927

THE LAST FORD MODEL T
ROLLS OFF THE ASSEMBLY LINE

"Any customer can have a car painted any color that he wants so long as it is black."
– Henry Ford. American industrialist and founder of the Ford Motor Company.

Model T's coming off the assembly line at the Highland Park plant, 1900. Source: Library of Congress, Geography and Map Division. Via Wikimedia Commons. Public Domain.

On this day in 1927, the final Ford Model T rolled off the assembly line at Ford's Highland Park plant in Michigan, marking the end of a revolutionary era in automotive history. With over 15 million units produced since its introduction in 1908, the Model T made automobiles affordable for the middle class and fundamentally changed transportation and urban development. Henry Ford's innovative assembly line production methods transformed manufacturing and reshaped how cities grew. Automobiles enabled suburban expansion, with cities sprawling outward and infrastructure evolving to accommodate car travel. However, this shift also introduced challenges, including traffic congestion, environmental degradation, and the decline of walkable neighborhoods. The Model T's legacy continues to shape modern transportation planning as cities seek to balance mobility with sustainability. Its profound impact remains a focal point in debates over the future of car-dependent urbanization and the design of equitable, livable cities.

How can urban planners today address the long-term impact of car-centric development while designing cities for sustainable, multimodal transportation?

OPENING OF
THE GOLDEN GATE BRIDGE

"A bridge is more than steel and concrete; it is a pathway to possibility and progress."
– Joseph Strauss. American civil engineer and chief engineer of the Golden Gate Bridge.

Golden Gate Bridge under construction from Fort Scott. 1930s. Source: US National Park Service. Via Wikimedia Commons. Public Domain.

On this day in 1937, the Golden Gate Bridge in San Francisco opened to pedestrian traffic, with vehicles allowed the following day. Spanning 4,200 feet, it was the longest suspension bridge in the world at the time, connecting San Francisco to Marin County and dramatically improving regional accessibility. The bridge supported economic growth, enhanced urban development, and became an iconic symbol of American ingenuity. Its Art Deco design and distinctive International Orange color captured global attention, cementing its status as an engineering marvel and an architectural masterpiece. Completed during the Great Depression, the project demonstrated the power of bold infrastructure to reshape urban areas, boost mobility, and inspire civic pride. The Golden Gate Bridge remains a landmark of innovation and ambition, continuing to influence infrastructure design and serving as a global symbol of connectivity and resilience in urban planning.

How can modern urban infrastructure projects balance aesthetic appeal with functionality to create structures that become enduring symbols of their cities?

MAY 28
1932

COMPLETION OF THE AFSLUITDIJK, PIONEERING LAND RECLAMATION

"While others live on land, we live in a struggle with water."
— Dutch Proverb

Construction of the Afsluitdijk, circa 1930. This monumental 32-kilometer dam transformed the Zuiderzee into the freshwater IJsselmeer, exemplifying Dutch engineering prowess in water management. Published in La Repubblica de Roma. Source: Wikimedia Commons. Via Wikimedia Commons. Public Domain.

On this day in 1932, the Afsluitdijk, a 32-kilometer-long dike, was completed, marking a transformative achievement in Dutch water management and land reclamation. The dike sealed off the Zuiderzee, a saltwater inlet of the North Sea, converting it into the freshwater IJsselmeer. This monumental project enabled the Netherlands to reclaim vast tracts of land for agriculture and settlement while protecting urban areas from devastating floods. As part of the Zuiderzee Works, the Afsluitdijk demonstrated innovative dike construction and water control techniques, showcasing Dutch leadership in sustainable infrastructure. Beyond flood prevention, it supported regional development and long-term urban growth. Today, the Afsluitdijk remains a symbol of resilience and ingenuity, continuing to be upgraded to address rising sea levels and climate change. Its legacy inspires global efforts to develop sustainable solutions for water management and urban planning in the face of environmental challenges.

How can the Dutch model of water management inspire global solutions to urban planning challenges posed by climate change and rising sea levels?

FALL OF CONSTANTINOPLE AND THE RISE OF ISTANBUL

"If the earth were a single state, Constantinople would be its capital."
– Napoleon Bonaparte. French military leader and emperor.

View of the Golden Horn bay with the Suleymaniye Mosque and the Sultanahmet district from the Galata Bridge. The image captures the colorful culture of the city and showcases the city's unique position between Europe and Asia. By Aquarius. Licensed.

On this day in 1453, Constantinople fell to the Ottoman forces led by Sultan Mehmed II, marking the Byzantine Empire's end and the city's transformation into Istanbul, the capital of the Ottoman Empire. The fall of Constantinople was a significant turning point in world history, as it shifted the balance of power in the Eastern Mediterranean and paved the way for Ottoman dominance. Mehmed II, often called "The Conqueror," revitalized the city by welcoming diverse populations, expanding infrastructure, and turning it into an Islamic cultural and political center. Key Byzantine structures, like the Hagia Sophia, were converted into mosques, while new architectural marvels, such as the Topkapi Palace, were constructed. Constantinople's unique geographic location continued to make it a bridge between Europe and Asia, shaping its identity as a vibrant, multicultural urban hub.

How can cities like Istanbul embrace their layered histories while meeting the demands of modern urbanization and globalization?

MAY 30
1899

FOUNDING OF NAIROBI AS A RAILWAY TOWN

"Cities are not just places of growth; they are arenas for negotiating history and identity."
– Njuguna Ng'ethe. Kenyan urbanist and scholar.

Nairobi Railway Station, 1899. The image documents the early stages of Nairobi's development as a transport hub, with the railway playing a key role in shaping the city's urban form and economic growth. Source: Unknown. CC0.

On this day in 1899, Nairobi was founded as a supply depot during the construction of the Uganda Railway, exemplifying transit-oriented development in colonial city planning. Strategically located between Mombasa and the interior, the railway established Nairobi as a crucial link for transporting goods and resources. The town grew rapidly around the rail infrastructure, with workshops, housing, and administrative offices catering to railway operations. Colonial planners organized Nairobi's layout to prioritize the railway, but this development also enforced racial segregation, with distinct zones for Europeans, Asians, and Africans. While the railway spurred Nairobi's growth into a key economic and administrative center, its transit-oriented origins created patterns of inequality that persisted after independence in 1963. Today, Nairobi's status as a regional hub reflects its foundation as a rail town. At the same time, efforts to modernize transportation infrastructure aim to address the colonial legacies embedded in its urban fabric.

How has Nairobi's colonial legacy shaped its modern urban form and development challenges?

THE JOHNSTOWN FLOOD CATASTROPHY

"The safety of our communities rests on the strength of our foresight and the care we give to what we build." – Clara Barton. American nurse, founder of the American Red Cross.

The Great Conemaugh Valley Disaster -- Flood & Fire at Johnstown, PA, 1890. Source: Reproduced from a lithograph print published by Kurz & Allison Art Publishers, 76 & 78 Wabash Avenue, Chicago, Illinois. Via Wikimedia Commons. Public Domain.

On this day in 1889, the South Fork Dam near Johnstown, Pennsylvania, catastrophically failed after days of heavy rain, unleashing 18.1 million cubic meters (4.8 billion gallons) of water in a devastating flood. The disaster claimed over 2,200 lives, destroyed thousands of homes, and left the town in ruins. Negligence and inadequate maintenance of the dam, combined with insufficient oversight, were identified as key factors in the tragedy, sparking outrage and calls for reform. The flood highlighted the dire consequences of ignoring infrastructure resilience and the importance of integrating disaster preparedness into urban planning. In its aftermath, engineering standards for dam safety were significantly improved, laying the groundwork for modern infrastructure oversight. The Johnstown Flood remains a reminder of the responsibility to maintain critical infrastructure, especially in disaster-prone areas, to protect urban populations from preventable catastrophes.

How can modern urban planners ensure that infrastructure is adequately maintained to prevent similar disasters in today's cities?

JUNE 1
1925

INTERNATIONAL CHILDREN'S DAY

"The true measure of any society can be found in how it treats its most vulnerable members." – Mahatma Gandhi. Indian independence leader and advocate for non-violence.

Children at play on a Georgetown sidewalk, Washington, D.C., September 1935—capturing an urban during the Great Depression. Photo by Carl Mydans for the U.S. Resettlement Administration, Source: Farm Security Administration - Office of War Information Photograph Collection. Library of Congress. Public Domain.

On this day in 1925, International Children's Day was first established during the World Conference on Child Welfare in Geneva, later gaining broader recognition following a 1954 United Nations proclamation. The day honors children's rights and well-being, emphasizing the importance of nurturing environments for their growth and development. Urban planning plays a vital role in this mission, as cities designed with children in mind promote safety, inclusivity, and opportunity. Child-friendly urban design includes safe routes to schools, accessible parks, green spaces, and playful public areas that encourage exploration and learning. Involving children in planning processes also offers

fresh, imaginative perspectives that can inspire more innovative and inclusive urban solutions. Such engagement not only fosters creativity and early civic involvement but ensures that the built environment supports all age groups. International Children's Day serves as a reminder that designing cities for children is an investment in a more just, vibrant, and sustainable urban future.

How can urban planners and policymakers ensure that cities are designed to meet the needs of children, fostering safe and inclusive environments for all?

CHARTER OF
THE COLONY OF VIRGINIA EXPANDED

"From sea to sea, west and northwest, the bounds of Virginia expand, charting a course for settlement and enterprise in the New World." – Second Charter of Virginia (1609)

A scene of a busy street in Jamestown, circa 1650. By Keith Rocco. Source: Publisher: Colonial National Historical Park, U.S. National Park Service. Public Domain.

On this day in 1608, the Colony of Virginia received an expanded charter from King James I of England, extending its territorial claims from "sea to sea." This transformative document authorized the establishment of towns, ports, and infrastructure, laying the groundwork for organized urban planning in the New World. Jamestown, the colony's capital, became North America's first permanent English settlement, serving as a blueprint for colonial governance and trade. The charter emphasized the strategic development of fortifications and public spaces to support economic growth and administrative control. However, it also set in motion the displacement and marginalization of Indigenous populations, highlighting the enduring tensions of colonial urbanism. This expansion of the Virginia Colony paved the way for the development of cities that would shape the trajectory of American urbanization, combining economic ambition with structured town planning.

How did early colonial charters influence the development of American urban centers and their relationship with Indigenous populations?

JUNE 3
1999

MIGUEL ANXO FERNÁNDEZ LORES BECOMES MAYOR OF PONTEVEDRA

"If you design cities for cars, you get cars. If you design cities for people, you get people."
– Miguel Anxo Fernández Lores. Spanish physician and mayor of Pontevedra.

Aerial view of the city of Pontevedra, Spain. The image showcases the compact urban fabric, historical core, and integration of pedestrian-friendly spaces within the city's design. By JackF. Licensed.

On this day in 1999, Miguel Anxo Fernández Lores was elected mayor of Pontevedra, Spain, initiating a transformative urban renewal that would earn global recognition. Under his leadership, Pontevedra prioritized pedestrians over cars, reclaiming public spaces and radically reducing vehicle traffic in the historic city center. Key policies included pedestrianization, traffic calming measures, and infrastructure improvements that enhanced walkability and accessibility. These changes led to remarkable outcomes: road fatalities dropped to nearly zero, air quality improved significantly, and public spaces became vibrant economic and social activity hubs. The "Pontevedra Model" has since become an international benchmark for sustainable and inclusive urban planning, demonstrating how bold, people-centered policies can revitalize cities. Today, Pontevedra is one of the world's most walkable and livable cities, inspiring urban planners to reimagine urban environments that prioritize community well-being and environmental sustainability.

How can cities replicate Pontevedra's success in creating pedestrian-friendly environments while addressing the unique challenges of larger urban centers?

TIANANMEN SQUARE PROTESTS AND CRACKDOWN

"A small spark can start a prairie fire."
– Chinese Proverb (used by activists and reformers)

Tiananmen Gate in front of the Forbidden City, Beijing, China. The image captures the historic gateway, symbolizing imperial architecture and its central role in Chinese political history. By Coward_lion. Licensed.

On this day in 1989, the Tiananmen Square Protests in Beijing culminated in a violent crackdown by the Chinese government, marking one of the most pivotal and tragic events in modern urban history. Beginning in April, students, workers, and citizens gathered in Tiananmen Square—a symbolic center of state power—to demand democratic reforms, freedom of expression, and anti-corruption measures. The square became a focal point for political discourse, dissent, and hopes for change. On June 3–4, the government declared martial law, deploying military forces armed with tanks and live ammunition to disperse protesters. The resulting violence claimed the lives of hundreds, possibly thousands, though the exact death toll remains disputed. The events of Tiananmen Square highlight the dual role of urban public spaces as arenas for collective action and as sites of state control, underscoring the fragile balance between civic expression and authority in cities worldwide.

How can urban planners and governments balance the need for public spaces as platforms for expression with concerns about order and state authority?

JUNE 5
1973

WORLD ENVIRONMENT DAY

"The environment is where we all meet; where we all have a mutual interest; it is the one thing all of us share." – Adapted from Lady Bird Johnson's speeches. American First Lady and environmental advocate.

Children adrift on a raft of discarded Christmas trees in Amsterdam's Hobbemakade canal, a haunting tableau of playful defiance amid urban waste. Set against a backdrop of aging cars and somber buildings, reflects the fragility of innocence in a world of environmental neglect. By Mieremet, Rob. Source: National Archives of the Netherlands, Anefo photo collection. CC0.

On this day in 1973, the first World Environment Day was celebrated, following its establishment by the United Nations General Assembly in 1972 during the Stockholm Conference on the Human Environment. This annual event became a cornerstone for raising global awareness and fostering action to address environmental challenges. Each year, World Environment Day focuses on critical issues such as climate change, biodiversity loss, pollution, and the sustainable use of resources. The event also underscores the vital role of cities and urban planning in preserving natural ecosystems and promoting sustainability. Activities like tree-planting campaigns, clean-up drives, and policy discussions demonstrate how urban areas can lead the way in achieving environmental resilience. World Environment Day has catalyzed change by encouraging collaboration and innovation, inspiring individuals, communities, and governments to envision and build a greener, more sustainable future.

What steps can cities take to ensure their growth is aligned with the principles of environmental sustainability and equity?

FOUNDING OF THE YMCA IN LONDON

"In all things, let charity guide your actions."
– George Williams. British philanthropist and founder of the YMCA.

Old YMCA building on South Tryon Street, Charlotte, NC, 1960s. The image highlights mid-20th-century civic architecture and the role of social institutions in American urban centers. By Clsdesign. Licensed.

On this day in 1844, George Williams founded the Young Men's Christian Association (YMCA) in London to support young men navigating the challenges of urban life during the Industrial Revolution. As cities expanded and industrialization drew people into urban centers, many young workers faced poor living conditions, isolation, and limited opportunities. The YMCA addressed these needs by providing affordable housing, social support, and a sense of community. Over time, its mission expanded to include recreation, education, and health programs, promoting urban populations' physical, mental, and spiritual well-being. The YMCA pioneered a community-centered approach to urban welfare, influencing the design of modern community centers and urban planning practices that prioritize inclusivity and accessibility. Today, the YMCA remains a global force for social cohesion and well-being, inspiring efforts to build resilient and compassionate urban communities in the face of ongoing challenges.

How can the legacy of organizations like the YMCA inform the creation of inclusive, multi-functional community spaces in modern cities to address today's urban challenges?

JUNE 7
1906

LEGISLATION & GOVERNANCE

THE ANTIQUITIES ACT OF 1906 PASSED BY THE SENATE

"A nation's history is written in its landscapes as well as its books."
– Theodore Roosevelt. 26th President of the United States and conservationist. (Adapted).

Statue of Liberty with New York Harbor in the background. One of the first designated urban monuments under the Act of 1906. By Grafficx. Licensed

On this day in 1906, the U.S. Senate passed the Antiquities Act, a groundbreaking piece of legislation establishing the legal foundation for protecting cultural and natural heritage in the United States. Signed into law later that month, the act authorized the President to designate national monuments on federal land to preserve historic landmarks, structures, and objects of scientific interest. This marked the first federal effort to conserve archaeological and cultural sites, reflecting a growing recognition of heritage preservation amid rapid urban and industrial expansion. The act led to the protection of iconic sites like the Grand Canyon and Mesa Verde, shaping land-use policies by prioritizing conservation alongside development. Its influence extended into urban planning, encouraging the integration of historical preservation in city design. The Antiquities Act remains a cornerstone of the preservation movement, ensuring that natural and cultural treasures are safeguarded for future generations.

How can legislative frameworks like the Antiquities Act be applied to protect urban cultural and natural heritage in rapidly growing cities?

INAUGURATION OF
THE HIGH LINE IN NEW YORK CITY

"The High Line is proof that when cities nurture innovation, they create something extraordinary."
– Amanda Burden. American urban planner and former director of the New York Planning Department.

Top view of the High Line, New York City—An elevated urban park transformed from a historic freight rail line, showcasing the creative reuse of industrial infrastructure in modern urban design. Photo by Wil Fyfordy, via Wikimedia Commons, licensed under CC BY-SA 4.0.

On this day in 2009, the High Line, a repurposed elevated railway, officially opened as a linear park in Manhattan. This transformative project turned an abandoned industrial structure into a 1.45-mile public space, blending nature, art, and community into the urban landscape. Designed with adaptive reuse and innovative architecture, the High Line redefined urban green spaces, demonstrating how neglected infrastructure can serve as a platform for public benefit and sustainable development. The park has become a cultural and economic catalyst, revitalizing surrounding neighborhoods and attracting millions of visitors annually. Its success has inspired similar projects worldwide, including Paris' Promenade Plantée and Toronto's Bentway. More than just a park, the High Line is a testament to the potential of adaptive reuse in urban revitalization, showcasing how creativity and community engagement can breathe new life into cities while setting a global standard for innovative urban redevelopment.

How can adaptive reuse of industrial spaces contribute to urban sustainability and community building?

JUNE 9
1859

APPROVAL OF
THE CERDÁ PLAN FOR BARCELONA

"Urban planning must serve society, ensuring health, equality, and freedom of movement."
— Ildefons Cerdà. Spanish urban planner and engineer.

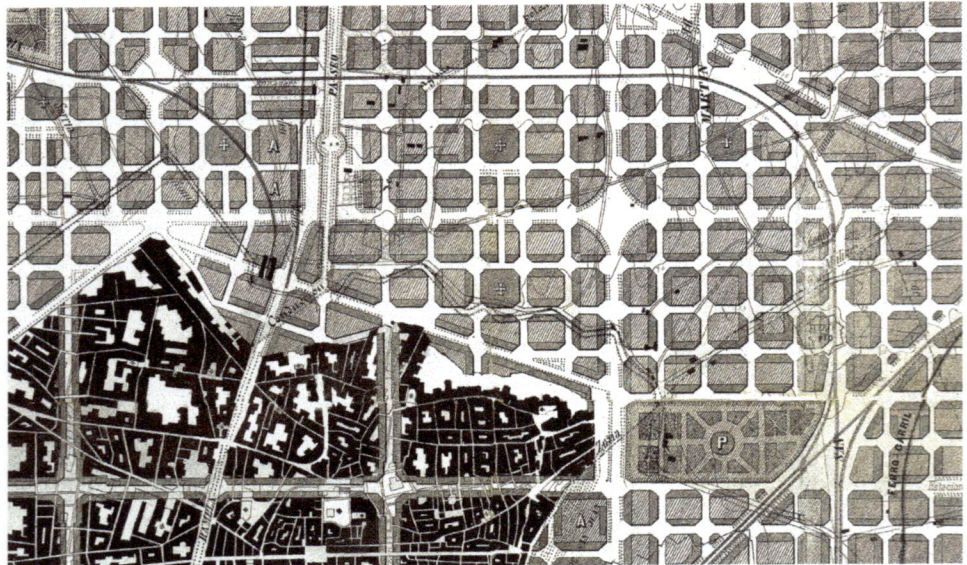

Detail of Cerdà's plan of Barcelona outlining the city's proposed expansion, featuring a regular grid, wide streets, and chamfered corners to improve health, mobility, and control uprisings, 1859. By Ildefons Cerdà i Sunyer. Source: Museu d'Història de la Ciutat, Barcelona. Public Domain.

On this day in 1859, the Spanish Ministry approved the Cerdà Plan, designed by Ildefons Cerdà, for Barcelona's expansion. Addressing overcrowding, poor sanitation, and public health crises, Cerdà proposed a rational grid layout that prioritized ventilation, mobility, and equality. The plan introduced wide streets to improve airflow and reduce disease, chamfered corners for better visibility and traffic flow, and generous green spaces to support health and recreation. One reason the Spanish government favored the plan was strategic—broad avenues made it harder for residents to erect barricades, helping to deter uprisings. Cerdà's vision also included mixed-use blocks that integrated residential and commercial functions and promoted community life through interconnected public spaces. Though initially controversial, the plan reshaped Barcelona, with the Eixample district standing as a lasting example of modern urban planning. Cerdà's innovative approach has influenced city design globally, showing how well-planned urban expansions can improve living conditions, foster inclusivity, and address both civic and political challenges in growing cities.

How can cities today adapt Cerdà's principles to balance urban growth with sustainability and livability?

DEATH OF ANTONI GAUDÍ

"To do things right, first you need love, then technique."
– Antoni Gaudí. Spanish architect and visionary of Catalan Modernism.

Proposal to open the Gaudí Avenue in Barcelona (1927) based on the Plan de Enlaces of 1917 and the layouts proposed by Léon Jaussely in 1904. By Comisión Especial del Ensanche. Source: Any Cerdà. Via Wikimedia Commons. Public Domain.

On this day in 1926, Antoni Gaudí, the renowned architect who shaped Barcelona's urban identity, died tragically after being struck by a tram. At the time, Barcelona's trams had recently transitioned from horse-drawn to quieter electric-powered vehicles, a technological shift that Gaudí, lost in thought and hard of hearing, may not have noticed. His death underscores the challenges cities face in adapting to new technologies while ensuring pedestrian safety. Gaudí's legacy endures through architectural masterpieces like the Sagrada Família and Park Güell, which embody his vision of blending creativity, nature, and functionality. His works have profoundly influenced urban design, emphasizing integrating artistic expression with practical urban needs. The circumstances of his death serve as a reminder of the need for thoughtful urban planning that prioritizes safety and accessibility as cities evolve with technological advancements—a lesson as relevant now as it was nearly a century ago.

How can cities design safer public spaces and systems to help pedestrians adapt to the introduction of quieter, faster, or less familiar transportation technologies?

JUNE 11
1580

RE-FOUNDING OF BUENOS AIRES FOLLOWING THE LAWS OF THE INDIES

"Let the city be laid out with a plaza at its heart, from which order and prosperity will flow."
– Laws of the Indies (1573)

The Cabildo. Former Town Council during the colonial era and now used for public service, Buenos Aires, Argentina. By Jobi_pro (edited). Licensed

On this day in 1580, Buenos Aires was re-established by Spanish conquistador Juan de Garay, following the urban planning principles outlined in the 1573 Laws of the Indies. As the first city intentionally founded under these regulations, Buenos Aires was designed with a rectilinear grid layout, organized around a central plaza that served as the focal point of civic life. Surrounding the plaza, space was allocated for government buildings, religious institutions, and commercial activities, reflecting the Spanish Crown's emphasis on order, functionality, and governance through carefully codified urban form. This intentional design laid the foundation for Buenos Aires' growth, economic integration, and social hierarchy, and served as a model for the planning of other colonial cities across the Americas. Today, the legacy of this early urban code and spatial logic can still be seen in the city's historic core, where the original grid and central plaza remain central to its identity and civic memory, influencing everything from public celebrations to modern zoning and infrastructure decisions.

How can principles of urban order and functionality, like those in Buenos Aires' founding, inform modern city design while incorporating contemporary values of equity and sustainability?

FOUNDING OF HELSINKI, FINLAND

"A city is a place where there is no need to wait for next week to get something done."
– Jan Gehl. Danish architect and urban design consultant.

Aerial view of Helsinki, Finland, showcasing the city's coastal relationship, architecture, and integration of green spaces and waterfront areas. By Artem. Licensed.

On this day in 1550, King Gustav I of Sweden founded Helsinki to challenge Tallinn's dominance in the Baltic Sea trade. The city's harsh climate and remote location from major trade routes initially limited its growth and influence. However, its relocation in the 1640s to a more strategic coastal site allowed Helsinki to expand and strengthen its position gradually. The city's transformation accelerated in 1812 when it was designated the capital of Finland under Russian rule, becoming the nation's political, cultural, and economic center. Over the centuries, Helsinki embraced innovative urban planning, prioritizing sustainability and livability, with initiatives in eco-friendly infrastructure, green spaces, and public transportation. Today, it is celebrated as one of the world's most livable cities, exemplifying how thoughtful urban planning can drive long-term resilience and prosperity. Helsinki's evolution from a modest trading post to a global model highlights the power of adaptability and visionary design.

How can the evolution of Helsinki from a small trade outpost to a global hub of sustainability inspire modern urban planners to adapt cities to changing needs and environments?

JUNE 13
313 CE

DECISIONS OF
THE EDICT OF MILAN IMPLEMENTED

"With this edict, let all religions flourish together in peace."
– Edict of Milan

Founding of a new world (1898). By George Dryer. Source: Publisher: New York, Eaton & Mains Cincinnati, Curts & Jennings. New York Public Library. Via Wikimedia Commons. Public Domain.

On this day in 313 CE, Emperor Constantine I and Emperor Licinius issued the Edict of Milan, legalizing Christianity across the Roman Empire and granting religious tolerance to all faiths. This pivotal decision ended centuries of persecution and profoundly shaped urban life and planning. Cities like Rome, Constantinople, and Antioch saw the rise of churches and Christian spaces, transforming their architectural and cultural landscapes. Integrating religious structures into the urban fabric set a precedent for the role of sacred spaces in city design, blending spiritual and civic priorities. The Edict also encouraged cultural and social diversity, influencing governance and fostering community cohesion within cities. This milestone marked the beginning of a shift in urban priorities, intertwining imperial power with religious expression and leaving a lasting legacy on the identity and development of cities throughout the Roman Empire and beyond. It paved the way for pilgrimage networks, charitable institutions, and public spaces oriented around shared spiritual life, embedding new layers of meaning into the streets and gathering places of ancient urban centers.

How did the legalization of Christianity through the Edict of Milan reshape the cultural and architectural identity of cities in the Roman Empire?

FOUNDING OF MUNICH BY HENRY THE LION

"A city is not an accident but the result of coherent visions and aims."
– Leon Krier. Luxembourgish architect and urban theorist.

Munich Marienplatz and the New Town Hall, a key landmark of the city's urban core and a prominent example of neo-Gothic architecture in Germany. By F11photo. Licensed.

On this day in 1158, the city of Munich was founded by Henry the Lion, Duke of Bavaria, on the banks of the River Isar. Originally established as a market and trading settlement, Munich's location capitalized on its proximity to important trade routes and the river, fostering its early growth and economic significance. The city's founding was closely tied to constructing a bridge over the Isar, which allowed Henry to control trade and levy tolls, solidifying Munich's position as a key commercial hub in medieval Bavaria. Over the centuries, Munich became a cultural and economic center renowned for its architecture, art, and vibrant traditions. Today, the city reflects its historic roots while embodying modern urban planning and innovation. Munich's founding highlights the importance of strategic location and infrastructure in shaping cities' development and enduring legacy.

How can modern cities balance their historical foundations with contemporary urban needs to preserve identity while fostering innovation?

JUNE 15
1902

INAUGURATION OF
THE 20TH CENTURY LIMITED TRAIN

"A great train is more than a means of travel; it is a bridge between cities and aspirations."
– George W. Kittredge. Railroad executive and advocate for passenger rail. (Paraphrased).

Observation Car on a deluxe overland limited train, 1910. Source: Detroit Publishing Co., publisher. Library of Congress Prints and Photographs Division. Public Domain.

On this day in 1902, the New York Central Railroad inaugurated the "20th Century Limited," a luxurious passenger train connecting New York City and Chicago. Renowned for its elegance, speed, and efficiency, the train epitomized the golden age of rail travel in the early 20th century. With amenities like fine dining, Pullman cars, and impeccable service, it set new standards for passenger comfort and technological sophistication. The 20th Century Limited fostered urban connectivity, efficiently linking two of the nation's largest economic and cultural hubs, and became a symbol of progress and modernity. Its success influenced rail infrastructure development, inspiring innovations in design and operations that enhanced the rail travel experience. Beyond its iconic status, the train played a critical role in shaping urbanization and economic growth, showcasing how advancements in transportation could drive the development and modernization of American cities.

How can lessons from the golden age of rail travel inspire sustainable and efficient urban transportation systems today?

CREATION OF THE PUBLIC WORKS ADMINISTRATION

"Public works mean work for the people."
– Harold L. Ickes. U.S. Secretary of the Interior during the New Deal.

Federal Public Works Administration building. Rapid City, South Dakota, 1938. Source: National Archives and Records Administration. Via Wikimedia Commons. Public Domain.

On this day in 1933, the Public Works Administration (PWA) was established under President Franklin D. Roosevelt's New Deal as part of the National Industrial Recovery Act (NIRA). Led by Harold L. Ickes, the PWA aimed to combat the Great Depression by creating jobs and stimulating economic recovery through large-scale infrastructure projects. Over its existence, the agency funded the construction of thousands of public works, including schools, hospitals, roads, bridges, and public housing developments, transforming urban America. Landmark projects such as the Triborough Bridge in New York City and the Hoover Dam showcased the PWA's commitment to modernizing infrastructure and supporting urban growth. By prioritizing long-term investments, the PWA improved public facilities and set new urban planning and development standards. Its legacy endures in the modernized infrastructure and public works that continue to serve communities across the United States.

How did the Public Works Administration's investments in infrastructure influence urban planning and development during and after the Great Depression?

JUNE 17
2011

GREEN, SUSTAINABLE, RESILIENT

GLOBAL SANITATION WORKERS DAY

"The health of a city depends on those who keep it clean and livable." – Nelson Mandela. South African anti-apartheid revolutionary and former president. (Paraphrased).

Garbage removal. By Visoot. Licensed

On this day in 2011, Global Garbage Man Day was established, honoring the vital contributions of sanitation workers in maintaining clean and healthy urban environments. These workers play a critical role in waste collection, recycling, and disposal, ensuring cities remain livable and sustainable. Sanitation services prevent the spread of disease, support environmental conservation, and underpin the functionality of urban areas. This day raises awareness about waste management challenges while promoting practices like reducing, reusing, and recycling. By celebrating the dedication of sanitation workers, Global Garbage Man Day highlights the importance of often-overlooked public services essential to urban health and sustainability. It also encourages communities to advocate for improved working conditions, better technologies, and efficient waste management systems that benefit cities worldwide. The day serves as a reminder of the collective responsibility to create cleaner, greener, and more resilient urban environments.

How can cities innovate waste management systems to create cleaner, healthier, and more sustainable urban environments?

FOUNDING OF THE TANG DYNASTY

"A well-ordered state begins with well-planned cities."
– Traditional Chinese Proverb

Aerial view of Dayan Pagoda (Giant Wild Goose Pagoda) in Xi'an, China. The pagoda is a prominent example of Tang Dynasty architecture and a key feature of the city's historical and cultural landscape. By Guang. Licensed.

On this day in 618 CE, Li Yuan proclaimed himself Emperor Gaozu of Tang. He founded the Tang Dynasty, which ruled China for nearly 300 years and ushered in a golden age of urban, cultural, and economic development. The Tang era's capital, Chang'an (modern Xi'an), became a model of urban planning, with its grid-based layout, bustling markets, and organized neighborhoods reflecting meticulous governance. As one of the largest cities in the world at the time, Chang'an served as a hub of trade, administration, and culture, attracting diverse populations and facilitating exchanges along the Silk Road. The dynasty's investments in infrastructure, such as the Grand Canal and an expansive road network, enhanced connectivity and economic integration across China and beyond. The Tang Dynasty's urban innovations profoundly influenced city planning in East Asia, inspiring capitals in Japan, Korea, and Vietnam and underscoring the transformative power of infrastructure and visionary governance in shaping civilizations.

How can the Tang Dynasty's legacy of urban innovation inspire modern cities to balance cultural heritage with contemporary urban needs?

JUNE 19
2021

JUNETEENTH
BECOMES A FEDERAL HOLIDAY

"Great nations don't ignore their most painful moments; they face them."
– President Joe Biden. 46th President of the United States.

The U.S. Capitol at night, illuminated on Juneteenth, 2021, marking the federal recognition of the holiday celebrating the end of slavery in the United States. By TSZ Enterprises. Licensed.

On this day in 2021, Juneteenth became a federal holiday in the United States when President Joe Biden signed the Juneteenth National Independence Day Act into law. Commemorating the emancipation of enslaved African Americans, Juneteenth specifically marks explicitly the announcement of freedom in Galveston, Texas, on June 19, 1865, over two years after the Emancipation Proclamation. Establishing Juneteenth as a federal holiday highlights the importance of confronting and understanding the legacy of slavery in the U.S. It also provides communities an opportunity to celebrate freedom, reflect on equality, and advocate for justice. Cities nationwide now host parades, festivals, and educational events that center African American history and culture, fostering inclusivity and public dialogue. This recognition embeds cultural significance into the urban fabric, making Juneteenth a pivotal reminder of the nation's progress while underscoring the work needed to create equitable and inclusive societies.

How can cities use public holidays like Juneteenth to promote community engagement and education on shared history and social justice?

OPENING OF THE KIEL CANAL

"A canal is more than a passage for ships; it is a corridor for commerce and progress."
– Otto von Bismarck. Statesman and first Chancellor of the German Empire. (Paraphrased)

Kiel Canal, Schleuse Holtenau (Holtenau Lock), Germany. The image shows key infrastructure connecting the North Sea and the Baltic Sea, crucial for maritime trade and engineering heritage. By Peter Hansen. Licensed.

On this day in 1895, the Kiel Canal (Nord-Ostsee-Kanal) officially opened, connecting the North Sea to the Baltic Sea across Germany's Jutland peninsula. Stretching 98 kilometers, the canal significantly reduced maritime travel distances by eliminating the need for ships to navigate around Denmark, quickly becoming the world's busiest artificial waterway. This engineering feat showcased the transformative power of infrastructure, enhancing trade, mobility, and economic efficiency. The canal bolstered Germany's strategic position and stimulated urban port development in cities like Kiel and Brunsbüttel, fostering regional growth. Its construction also demonstrated the integration of technological innovation with economic strategy, reshaping Europe's shipping networks. Over a century later, the Kiel Canal remains a crucial artery for global commerce, serving as a testament to the enduring influence of visionary engineering in shaping urban and economic landscapes while supporting international trade.

How can cities and regions today leverage similar infrastructure projects to enhance connectivity, boost trade, and create sustainable economic opportunities?

JUNE 21
1919

PAOLO SOLERI: ARCOLOGY: THE CITY IN THE IMAGE OF MAN

"A city is not an accident but the result of coherent visions and strategies."
– Paolo Soleri. Italian architect, urban theorist, and founder of Arcosanti.

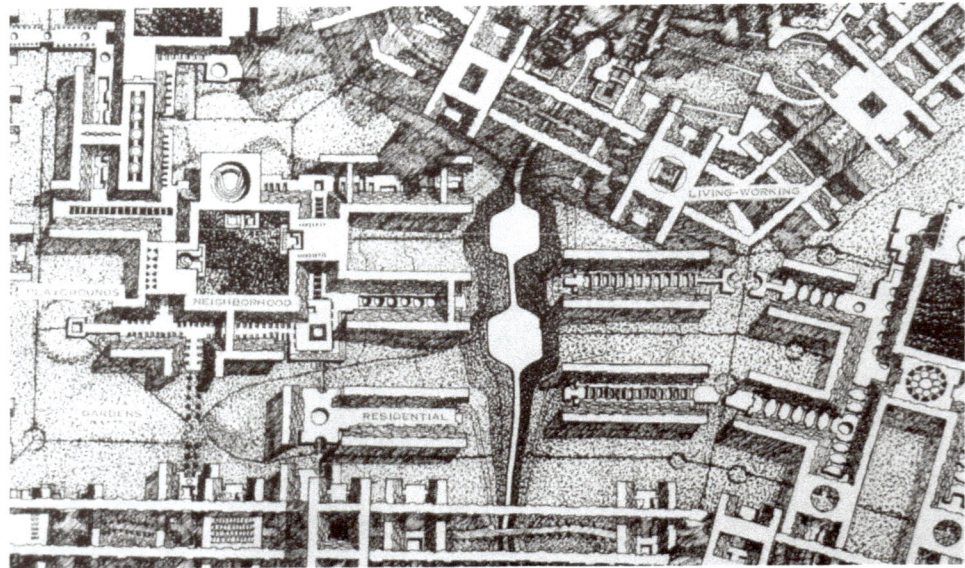

Arcology, City in the Image of Man 7. By Paolo Soleri. Initially published in 1973 by the MIT Press. Via Flickr. CC BY-SA 2.0

On this day in 1919, Paolo Soleri, a visionary architect and urban theorist, was born. Soleri is best known for pioneering the concept of arcology—a fusion of architecture and ecology—introduced in his 1969 book, Arcology: The City in the Image of Man. Arcologies envisioned compact, self-contained megastructures integrating living, working, and recreational spaces in vertical urban forms designed to minimize land use, resource consumption, and car dependency. Soleri's ideas directly addressed the challenges of urban sprawl, environmental degradation, and unsustainable development. His experimental community, Arcosanti, in Arizona, served as a living laboratory for his principles, demonstrating how innovative design could promote sustainability and reduce environmental impact. Although most of his arcologies remained conceptual, Soleri's work profoundly influenced urban planners and environmentalists, inspiring discussions on resource-efficient and climate-conscious cities. His legacy continues to shape sustainable urban development, offering solutions for the complexities of rapid urbanization.

How might the principles of arcology address the challenges of climate change and urban overpopulation today?

PASSAGE OF THE G.I. BILL

"An investment in the returning soldier is an investment in the future of America."
— Franklin D. Roosevelt. 32nd President of the United States.

Aerial view of Park Forest, Illinois, 1961 — one of America's first planned postwar suburbs, developed in 1946 to house returning WWII veterans. Enabled by GI Bill home loans, Park Forest became a model for suburban growth, embodying both the promise and contradictions of the American Dream. Courtesy Park Forest Historical Society. With Permission.

On this day in 1944, President Franklin D. Roosevelt signed the Servicemen's Readjustment Act, or the G.I. Bill, into law, transforming the postwar American landscape. This landmark legislation offered World War II veterans access to affordable mortgages, low-interest business loans, and funding for higher education, enabling millions to buy homes, pursue careers, and enter the middle class. The G.I. Bill fueled the rapid expansion of suburban America, reshaping urban and regional development as new neighborhoods flourished to accommodate returning soldiers and their families. However, its benefits were not distributed equitably: Black veterans and other minorities often faced systemic barriers, such as redlining and racial covenants, which restricted their access to housing and economic opportunities. Despite these shortcomings, the G.I. Bill profoundly impacted the U.S. economy and housing landscape, setting the stage for modern suburbanization and redefining the American Dream for a generation.

How can the lessons of the G.I. Bill inform current efforts to address housing inequities and support economic mobility for underserved populations?

JUNE 23
2005

U.S. SUPREME COURT RULES ON TAKINGS IN KELO V. CITY OF NEW LONDON

"Promoting economic development is a traditional and long-accepted function of government." – Justice John Paul Stevens, Majority Opinion

Generic image representing the authority of governments to acquire private property for public use. By Andrii. Licensed.

On this day in 2005, the U.S. Supreme Court issued its controversial decision in Kelo v. City of New London, expanding the scope of eminent domain under the Fifth Amendment. The court ruled in a 5-4 decision that the City of New London, Connecticut, could use eminent domain to seize private property for economic development projects as long as the taking served a "public purpose." The case involved seizing private homes for a waterfront redevelopment project, sparking a national debate about property rights versus community development. Critics argued the decision disproportionately benefited private developers and harmed low-income and marginalized communities, while supporters claimed it allowed cities to pursue vital economic revitalization efforts. The ruling led to widespread legislative backlash, with many states enacting laws to limit the use of eminent domain for private development.

What balance should cities and governments strike between using eminent domain for public good and protecting private property rights?

CHAMPLAIN TOWERS SOUTH PARTIAL COLLAPSE

"A structure is only as strong as the foundation upon which it is built."
— Marcus Vitruvius Pollio. Roman architect and engineer.

Aerial photo showing the empty parcel where the Champlain Towers once stood, Surfside, Miami, Florida. The site, now cleared of rubble, highlights the impact of the collapse on the urban fabric and serves as a reminder of the tragedy. By Felix Miznoznikov. Licensed.

On this day in 2021, the Champlain Towers South condominium in Surfside, Florida, partially collapsed, claiming the lives of 98 people in a devastating tragedy. The disaster exposed critical vulnerabilities in urban building safety, particularly the dangers of aging infrastructure, deferred maintenance, and inadequate oversight. Structural issues, including water infiltration and corroded reinforced concrete, had been identified but remained unaddressed, underscoring the consequences of neglect. The collapse prompted widespread reexamination of building inspection protocols and safety standards, with municipalities across the U.S. updating high-rise inspection requirements and revising building codes to mitigate future risks. This tragic event emphasized the need for proactive maintenance, rigorous oversight, and robust urban governance to safeguard residents in densely populated areas. It remains a sobering reminder of prioritizing infrastructure resilience, public safety, and accountability in urban planning and policy-making.

How can cities balance the costs of maintaining and inspecting aging infrastructure with the need to ensure safety and protect lives in urban environments?

JUNE 25
2012

NEOLITHIC SITE OF ÇATALHÖYÜK DESIGNATED A UNESCO WORLD HERITAGE SITE

"To uncover the earliest forms of urban life is to reveal the seeds of modern civilization itself." – James Mellaart. British archaeologist known for excavating Çatalhöyük.

Image of a reimagined Çatalhöyük based on existing descriptions of the city. By Plusurbia Design. Created using MidJourney.

On this day in 2012, during the UNESCO World Heritage Committee meeting held in St. Petersburg between June 25 and July 6, the Neolithic settlement of Çatalhöyük in present-day Turkey was inscribed as a UNESCO World Heritage Site, recognizing its profound contributions to the understanding of early urban life. First excavated in the 1960s by British archaeologist James Mellaart, Çatalhöyük dates back to approximately 7100 BCE and features a tightly clustered arrangement of mud-brick houses with shared walls and rooftop entryways—an early model of communal urban living. The site revealed rich archaeological findings, including wall paintings, symbolic objects, and evidence of early farming practices, shedding light on the social, spiritual, and architectural innovations of its inhabitants. UNESCO's designation highlights Çatalhöyük's significance as a precursor to urbanization, illustrating how early societies organized domestic, agricultural, and ritual spaces. It remains a critical site for examining the origins of settled life and the cultural foundations of human civilization.

How do the principles of shared spaces and sustainability at Çatalhöyük resonate with contemporary urban design challenges?

JUNE 26
1978

SUPREME COURT RULES ON PENN CENTRAL

"Land-use regulations do not constitute a taking simply because they restrict the use of private property." — Justice William J. Brennan, Jr., Majority Opinion

Interior of Grand Central Station in New York City, showcasing Beaux-Arts architecture, vaulted ceilings, and the iconic celestial dome. The terminal is a key example of early 20th-century urban infrastructure and transportation design. By Diegograndi. Licensed.

On this day in 1978, the U.S. Supreme Court issued its decision in Penn Central Transportation Co. v. New York City. This landmark ruling upheld the power of local governments to enact historic preservation laws under the Takings Clause of the Fifth Amendment. The case arose after New York City's Landmarks Preservation Commission denied Penn Central's request to construct a 55-story office tower above Grand Central Terminal, a designated historic landmark. Penn Central argued that the denial constituted a "taking" of its property without just compensation. The Supreme Court, in a 6-3 decision, disagreed, ruling that reasonable restrictions on land use to promote public welfare—such as preserving historic buildings—did not constitute a regulatory taking. This decision affirmed the legality of historic preservation ordinances across the United States, protecting significant cultural and architectural resources from unchecked development.

How does the Penn Central decision continue to shape the intersection of historic preservation, property rights, and urban development today?

JUNE 27
1934

HOUSING ACT OF 1934:
PRECURSOR TO SUBURBAN GROWTH

"Homeownership is the foundation of a sound economy and a stable community."
— Franklin D. Roosevelt. 32nd President of the United States.

Aerial view of houses in a typical suburban community, showcasing standardized layouts, low-density residential development, and separation of land uses characteristic of post-war suburbanization. By Condor 36. Licensed.

On this day in 1934, President Franklin D. Roosevelt signed the Housing Act of 1934, a landmark law that reshaped the U.S. housing market and spurred suburban expansion. The act established the Federal Housing Administration (FHA), which insured long-term, low-interest mortgages, making homeownership attainable for millions during the Great Depression. By standardizing lending practices, the legislation stabilized the construction industry and boosted housing development across the nation. However, FHA policies institutionalized racial discrimination through redlining, which excluded minority communities from accessing loans and opportunities for homeownership. While the act catalyzed suburban growth and created generational wealth for many Americans, it also entrenched racial segregation and economic inequality that persists today. The Housing Act of 1934 remains a pivotal moment in urban policy, demonstrating both the potential and pitfalls of government intervention in shaping housing markets and urban landscapes.

How can modern housing policies address the inequities created by the Housing Act of 1934 while promoting sustainable and inclusive growth?

NATIONAL
FOOD TRUCK DAY

"Street food is the soul of a city, served fresh from the heart."
– Roy Choi. Korean-American chef and food truck pioneer.

Imagined food truck festival on an urban street, visualizing vibrant public spaces activated by community gatherings and local food vendors, illustrating principles of placemaking and temporary urbanism. By Plusurbia Design. Created using MidJourney.

On this day in 2024, food lovers across the United States celebrated National Food Truck Day, a tribute to mobile culinary businesses' entrepreneurial spirit and cultural vibrancy. Rooted in the traditions of 17th-century street vendors and chuckwagons, food trucks have become an integral part of urban life, offering diverse cuisines and fostering community connections. The day highlighted their economic significance, with many food trucks run by small business owners contributing to local economies and enriching urban culture. Communities gathered to enjoy innovative dishes and share experiences online using the hashtag #NationalFoodTruckDay. Beyond celebrating creative street food, the event emphasized food trucks' role in redefining urban dining, providing accessible and inclusive culinary experiences, and strengthening community bonds. National Food Truck Day showcased how these mobile eateries bring people together and add a dynamic layer to the urban fabric.

How can cities better support food trucks as a dynamic part of the urban economy and cultural scene?

JUNE 29
1956

FEDERAL AID
HIGHWAY ACT SIGNED INTO LAW

"The interstate highways will provide a safe, efficient road system for defense and commerce." – President Dwight D. Eisenhower. 34th President of the United States.

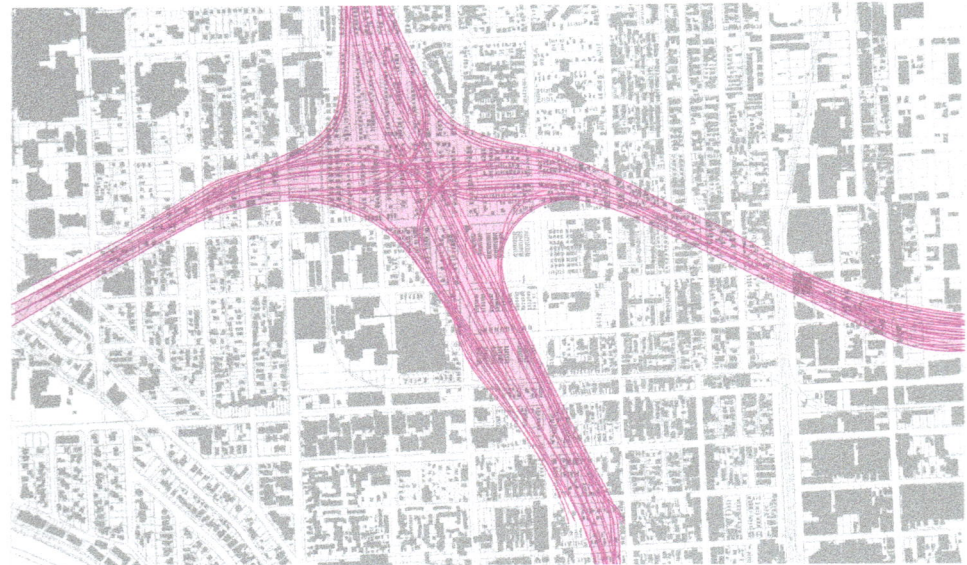

Map analysis of Overtown, FL, with highway overlap. Courtesy of University of Miami, Office of Community & Civic Engagement. By Professor Rafael Fornes and Professor Ricardo López. Source: University of Miami. With Permission

On this day in 1956, President Dwight D. Eisenhower signed the Federal Aid Highway Act, authorizing the creation of the Interstate Highway System. Allocating $25 billion for 41,000 miles of highways over 10 years, it became the largest public works project in U.S. history at the time. Inspired by Germany's autobahn, Eisenhower viewed the highways as essential for national defense, economic growth, and enhanced mobility. The Interstate Highway System revolutionized transportation, facilitating suburbanization, boosting commerce, and connecting cities nationwide. However, its construction also brought significant social and urban challenges, including the displacement of communities, particularly in minority neighborhoods, and the decline of many city centers. Despite these consequences, the act fundamentally reshaped the American landscape, laying the foundation for modern transportation and economic networks while sparking ongoing discussions about equity and sustainability in infrastructure planning.

How can modern infrastructure projects balance economic growth and mobility with social equity and environmental sustainability?

ABRAHAM LINCOLN
SIGNS THE YOSEMITE GRANT

"The battle we have fought, and are still fighting, for the forests is a part of the eternal conflict between right and wrong." – John Muir. Naturalist and environmental advocate.

Yosemite National Park, California, USA. Reflection in the Merced River of Yosemite Falls and the surrounding mountain landscape, highlighting the integration of natural beauty and protected areas in national park design. By Simon Dannhauer. Licensed.

On this day in 1864, President Abraham Lincoln signed a bill granting Yosemite Valley and Mariposa Grove to the State of California for preservation and public use. This landmark act, an early milestone in the conservation movement, set a precedent for protecting natural landscapes while influencing the development of urban green spaces. The Yosemite Grant highlighted the importance of nature in enhancing public health and well-being, inspiring the creation of urban parks like Central Park in New York City. The grant laid the foundation for integrating green spaces into urban planning by linking conservation to public recreation, emphasizing the balance between built and natural environments. It demonstrated the value of preserving natural landscapes for rural areas and as vital resources for urban populations. The Yosemite Grant remains pivotal in sustainable urbanism, underscoring the connection between conservation and urban quality of life.

How can cities today integrate natural spaces into urban environments to promote sustainability and improve the well-being of their residents?

JULY 1
1948

TOWN AND COUNTRY PLANNING ACT 1947

"The aim is to bring order to our towns and countryside, to ensure that development serves the people and preserves the beauty of the land." – Lewis Silkin, UK Minister of Town and Country Planning

Aerial view of Albury, Surrey Hills, UK, located within the Green Belt surrounding London. The image highlights the role of the Green Belt in preserving rural character, preventing urban sprawl, and maintaining open landscapes around major cities. By Victor Keech. Licensed.

On this day in 1948, the Town and Country Planning Act came into effect in the United Kingdom, following its passage by Parliament in 1947. This landmark legislation marked a transformative moment in urban planning history, empowering local authorities to comprehensively regulate land use and requiring the preparation of local development plans. One of its most enduring innovations was the creation of Green Belts to prevent urban sprawl, safeguard open countryside, and ensure public access to natural landscapes. Introduced amid the urgency of post-World War II reconstruction, the Act aimed to reconcile rapid housing and infrastructure needs with long-term environmental stewardship. By prioritizing the public good in land-use decisions, it redefined the planning system in the UK and established a model for integrating development control with sustainability. Its influence remains evident in planning practices worldwide, making it a foundational text in modern land-use policy.

How can the principles of the Town and Country Planning Act, such as Green Belts and comprehensive land use, be adapted to meet today's urban and environmental challenges?

SIGNING OF
THE TREATY OF TORDESILLAS

"The world is not divided by oceans but by the lines we draw upon it."
– Luís de Camões. Portuguese poet and author of The Lusiads. (Paraphrased).

Herrera and Tordesillas. Division of the Indies, 1601. Source: University of Texas at Arlington Libraries. Public Domain.

On this day in 1494, Spain signed the Treaty of Tordesillas, a pivotal agreement with Portugal that divided newly discovered lands outside Europe between the two powers. Portugal would sign the treaty later, on September 5 of the same year. Negotiated under papal guidance, the treaty drew a demarcation line west of the Cape Verde Islands: lands to the west were assigned to Spain, and those to the east to Portugal. This territorial division profoundly influenced the urban development of colonial cities. Spanish colonies in the Americas adopted grid-based city planning with central plazas, reflecting ideals of centralized governance and communal life, as seen in cities like Mexico City and Lima.

In contrast, Portuguese colonial urbanism prioritized fortified coastal enclaves oriented toward maritime trade, exemplified by cities such as Goa and Luanda. The treaty's legacy is still visible in the linguistic, cultural, and architectural distinctions across former colonial regions, illustrating how geopolitical decisions can shape urban forms and cultural identities for centuries.

How did the territorial divisions established by the Treaty of Tordesillas influence the urban forms, governance, and cultural evolution of cities in the Spanish and Portuguese empires?

JULY 3
1756

DEATH OF
GIOVANNI BATTISTA NOLLI

"To understand a city, one must first map its soul."
– Inspired by Giovanni Battista Nolli's work. Italian cartographer and architect.

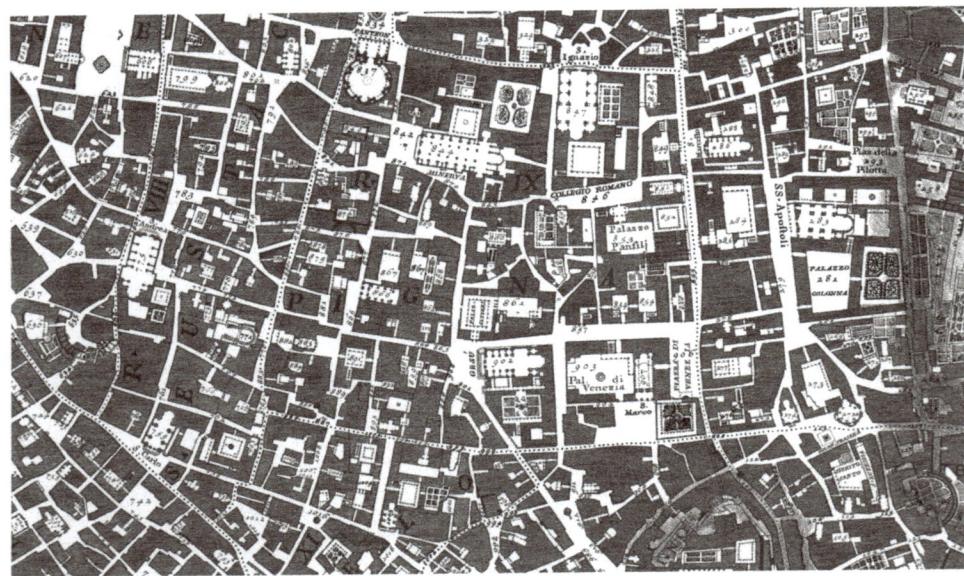

The New Plan of Rome, part 5/12, 1748. By Giambattista Nolli. Via Wikimedia Commons. Public Domain.

On this day in 1756, Giovanni Battista Nolli, the celebrated Italian architect and cartographer, passed away. Nolli is best remembered for his Pianta Grande di Roma (Large Plan of Rome), published in 1748, a groundbreaking map that set new standards for urban cartography. Using innovative figure-ground techniques, Nolli precisely illustrated the spatial relationship between open spaces, streets, and built environments, offering an unprecedented analytical tool for understanding urban form. His map went beyond mere representation; it highlighted Rome's intricate spatial dynamics and the interplay of public and private realms, making it invaluable for architects, planners, and historians. The Pianta Grande di Roma remains a timeless reference in urban planning, emphasizing the importance of clarity and detail in understanding and designing cities. Nolli's legacy is a foundational influence on modern urban analysis and the art of city mapping.

How can modern mapping technologies continue to build on Nolli's legacy to create more equitable and well-designed urban environments?

PUBLICATION OF
DANIEL BURNHAM'S PLAN OF CHICAGO

"Cities are built with the future in mind, shaped by the dreams of their creators."
– Daniel Burnham. American architect and urban planner. (Paraphrased).

Elevation showing the proposed Civic Center. Plate 131 from the Plan of Chicago, 1909. Source: Art Institute of Chicago. Via Wikimedia Commons. CC0

On this day in 1909, Daniel Burnham and Edward H. Bennett published the Plan of Chicago, a landmark document that laid the foundation for modern urban planning. Commissioned by the Commercial Club of Chicago, the plan addressed the city's rapid growth by creating a more orderly, efficient, and aesthetically pleasing urban environment. It proposed transformative improvements, including a coordinated street system, expanded lakefront parks, green spaces, civic centers, and regional transportation networks. Inspired by the City Beautiful Movement, the plan emphasized grandeur in design to foster civic pride and social harmony. While not all its ambitious elements were implemented, the Plan of Chicago profoundly influenced the city's development, shaping its infrastructure and public spaces. Its legacy extended far beyond Chicago, setting a global standard for comprehensive urban planning and demonstrating the transformative potential of visionary design in shaping cities.

How can Burnham's vision for civic beauty and functionality inspire modern urban planning in addressing today's challenges?

JULY 5
1994

JEFF BEZOS FOUNDS AMAZON

"Your margin is my opportunity."
– Jeff Bezos. American entrepreneur.

Package deliveries in a residential neighborhood. By Plusurbia Design. Created using MidJourney.

On this day in 1994, Jeff Bezos founded Amazon in Seattle as an online bookstore, sparking a revolution in global commerce that reshaped cities and economies. By offering unparalleled convenience, pricing, and variety through e-commerce, Amazon transformed how people shop, but its rapid rise also disrupted urban landscapes. Traditional "Main Street" shopping districts faced challenges like vacant storefronts and diminished foot traffic while small businesses struggled to compete. In response, cities adapted to the growth of fulfillment centers, last-mile delivery networks, and revamped logistics infrastructure. While Amazon's innovations improved access to goods and services, they also raised concerns about the homogenization of commerce and the sustainability of local economies. This evolution highlights the complex balance between technological progress and the vitality of community-centered urban spaces, pushing planners and policymakers to address the impacts of global retail on cities.

How can cities address the challenges posed by e-commerce while revitalizing local shopping areas to create vibrant urban communities?

LONDON AWARDED
THE 2012 SUMMER OLYMPICS

"The London Olympics were about much more than sport—they were about the regeneration of a city and the power of legacy." – Sebastian Coe. British politician and former Olympic runner.

Westminster Bridge, London, UK. The bridge connects the historic and political heart of London, offering views of key landmarks such as the Houses of Parliament and Big Ben. By Stuart Monk. Licensed.

On this day in 2005, the International Olympic Committee awarded London the 2012 Summer Olympics, making it the first city to host the Games three times. This milestone sparked one of modern history's most ambitious urban regeneration projects, transforming East London's Stratford area, characterized by industrial decline, into a vibrant urban hub. Central to this transformation was the creation of the Queen Elizabeth Olympic Park, alongside new residential neighborhoods and major infrastructure improvements, including the Stratford International Station. London's Olympic planning set a benchmark for sustainability, featuring energy-efficient venues, innovative water management systems, and a focus on long-term community benefits. Since the Games, the area has evolved into a thriving innovation, housing, and culture district with lasting economic and social impacts. The 2012 Olympics demonstrated how global events can drive sustainable urban development, leaving a legacy that continues to shape the city.

How can cities ensure that hosting global events leads to long-term benefits for local communities and sustainable urban growth?

JULY 7
1930

CONSTRUCTION BEGINS ON BOULDER DAM

"The Hoover Dam is more than concrete; it is the unyielding will of a nation to overcome challenges." – Franklin D. Roosevelt. 32nd President of the United States.

Looking upstram at the Boulder Dam's construction site, Boulder City, Nevada. By Ben D. Glaha. Source: Library of Congress Prints and Photographs Division. Public Domain.

On this day in 1930, industrialist Henry J. Kaiser began construction on the Boulder Dam, later renamed the Hoover Dam, on the Colorado River between Arizona and Nevada. This monumental project was designed to control floods, provide irrigation water, and generate hydroelectric power, addressing critical needs in the rapidly developing American Southwest. Built during the Great Depression, the dam provided thousands of jobs, symbolizing resilience and progress in a challenging era. Its completion enabled the urban growth of cities like Las Vegas, Los Angeles, and Phoenix, supplying the water and electricity essential for their expansion. Beyond its immediate functional impact,

the Hoover Dam became a global icon of engineering innovation and ambition, inspiring similar multi-purpose dam projects worldwide. It remains a testament to the transformative power of infrastructure in shaping urban and regional development, highlighting the role of visionary engineering in creating sustainable futures.

How can modern infrastructure projects replicate the success of Hoover Dam in addressing today's challenges of urban growth, climate change, and resource sustainability?

BIRTH OF
PHILIP JOHNSON

"Architecture is the art of how to waste space."
– Philip Johnson. American architect.

David H. Koch Theater at Lincoln Center, designed by Philip Johnson (completed in 1964), exemplifies modernist civic architecture integrated into mid-20th-century urban renewal. The theater helped transform the Upper West Side into a cultural district, showcasing the impact of high-profile design and cultural investment on reshaping urban identity and land use. By Ajay Suresh from New York, NY, USA. CC BY 2.0

On this day in 1906, Philip Johnson, one of the most influential architects of the 20th century, was born in Cleveland, Ohio. Johnson, A key figure in modernist and postmodernist architecture, shaped urban development through his iconic skyscrapers and cultural institutions. His landmark works, including the Glass House (1949), the Seagram Building (1958, with Mies van der Rohe), and the AT&T Building (1984), redefined the relationship between architecture and urban space. Johnson's impact extended beyond individual structures—his advocacy for architectural experimentation helped cities embrace evolving styles, from the sleek minimalism of modernism to the expressive forms of postmodernism. His work transformed urban skylines, integrating bold design with functional city planning. By challenging conventions and fostering innovation, Johnson played a crucial role in shaping how cities adapt to changing architectural movements, leaving a lasting imprint on the built environment and the ongoing dialogue between architecture and urbanism.

How have Johnson's architectural innovations shaped the way cities balance aesthetic expression with functional urban spaces?

JULY 9
1970

CREATION OF THE
ENVIRONMENTAL PROTECTION AGENCY

"Restoring nature to its natural state is a cause beyond party and beyond factions."
— Richard Nixon. 37th President of the United States.

United States Environmental Protection Agency building in Washington, DC. By Leonid Andronov. Licensed

On this day in 1970, President Richard Nixon submitted a reorganization plan to Congress to create the Environmental Protection Agency (EPA), consolidating various federal functions into a single agency dedicated to protecting human health and the environment. This proposal came amid growing public concern over environmental degradation, spurred by events such as oil spills, smog crises, and polluted waterways. Officially launched on December 2, 1970, the EPA was tasked with implementing landmark environmental legislation, including the Clean Air Act, Clean Water Act, and Endangered Species Act. Its establishment represented a transformative shift toward federal environmental regulation, emphasizing the need to balance industrial development with ecological preservation. The EPA's work has since been pivotal in addressing pollution, conserving natural resources, and fostering sustainable urban planning practices. Its creation set a global precedent for prioritizing environmental stewardship in policy-making, shaping the trajectory of modern environmental governance.

How can agencies like the EPA balance environmental protection with economic and urban development in today's world?

MARTIN LUTHER KING JR. AGAINST HOUSING DISCRIMINATION

"We are here today because we are tired of being segregated and humiliated... we are tired of being denied what is ours by right." – Martin Luther King Jr. Civil rights leader and activist.

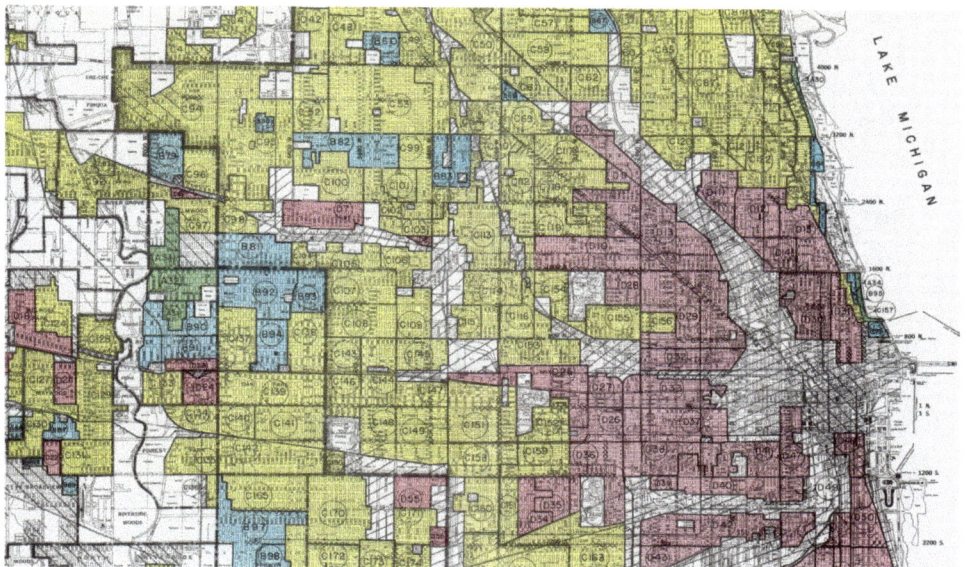

Redlining map for Richmond, Virginia, created by the Home Owners' Loan Corporation. The map illustrates discriminatory housing practices that shaped racial and economic segregation in American cities. Source: National Archives Catalog. Public Domain.

On this day in 1966, Dr. Martin Luther King Jr. launched the Chicago Freedom Movement, a pivotal campaign to combat housing discrimination and systemic inequities in northern urban areas. This marked a significant expansion of the civil rights movement to address entrenched issues like redlining, restrictive covenants, and unequal housing opportunities, which confined Black residents to substandard living conditions. King's campaign included a massive rally at Soldier Field on July 10, demanding fair housing and economic justice, followed by marches through segregated neighborhoods that met with intense resistance. Though progress was slow, the movement laid the groundwork for the Fair Housing Act of 1968, which sought to outlaw housing discrimination nationwide. King's efforts in Chicago underscored the deep connections between civil rights, urban development, and housing access, influencing policy discussions and advocacy for equitable urban environments that continue to resonate today.

How did Martin Luther King Jr.'s efforts in Chicago influence the broader fight for housing equity, and what progress still needs to be made?

JULY 11
1917

BIRTH OF
WILLIAM H. WHYTE

"What attracts people most, it would appear, is other people."
— William H. Whyte. American urbanist, sociologist, and author.

Bryant Park, one of White's favorites and a focus of his documentary "Social Life of Small Urban Spaces" (1980). By Charles. Licensed

On this day in 1917, William H. Whyte, a pioneering American urbanist, sociologist, and author, was born in West Chester, Pennsylvania. Whyte's influential work reshaped urban planning by emphasizing the critical role of human behavior and social interaction in the design of public spaces. His seminal book The Social Life of Small Urban Spaces (1980) showcased the importance of plazas, parks, and sidewalks in fostering vibrant, connected communities. Through meticulous observation, Whyte developed practical principles for creating public spaces that encourage engagement, accessibility, and social vitality, focusing on features like seating, sunlight, and the natural flow of pedestrian movement. Earlier in his career, Whyte's groundbreaking book The Organization Man (1956) offered a critical examination of corporate culture and its impact on individuality and community life, sparking broader discussions about work-life balance and societal values. Today, his human-centered approach remains a cornerstone of urban planning, inspiring architects and planners to prioritize livability, inclusivity, and the well-being of city inhabitants.

How can modern urban spaces be designed to foster stronger community connections and social engagement?

BIRTH OF HUGH FERRISS

"The buildings, relieved of all except their essential form, stand in majestic isolation."
– Hugh Ferriss. American architect and delineator.

Drawing, Study for Maximum Mass Permitted by the 1916 New York Zoning Law, Stage 1 and 4, 1922. Source: Gift of Mrs. Hugh Ferriss to the Cooper Hewitt Collection, Smithsonian Design Museum. Public Domain.

On this day in 1889, Hugh Ferriss, a pioneering American architect, illustrator, and urban theorist, was born. Renowned for his dramatic and futuristic depictions of skyscrapers and cityscapes, Ferriss profoundly shaped 20th-century urban design and architecture. His seminal book, The Metropolis of Tomorrow (1929), presented visionary concepts for dense urban centers, addressing issues like zoning laws, mass transit, and the human experience within towering cityscapes. Ferriss's work explored the balance between monumental urban forms and livability, emphasizing architecture's psychological and social dimensions. His striking renderings influenced the evolution of zoning ordinances, including New York City's 1916 Zoning Resolution, which introduced setback requirements to allow light and air into urban environments. Ferriss's artistic and theoretical contributions inspire architects and urban planners, offering enduring insights into how cities can harmonize ambition with functionality and human-centered design.

How can the balance of monumental urban architecture and human-scale environments shape sustainable cities in the future?

JULY 13
1573

ISSUANCE OF THE URBAN PLANNING ORDINANCES IN THE LAWS OF THE INDIES

"Let the town be set on a plain, at the foot of a mountain, near a river, with fertile soil and sufficient water." — Ordinances Concerning the Laying Out of New Towns

Mexcaltitán de Uribe, Nayarit, Mexico. The image shows the island's gridded urban layout, reflecting the influence of the Laws of the Indies, a Spanish colonial planning code that mandated orderly, orthogonal street patterns in new settlements. By Luis Méndez Covarrubias. Via Wikimedia Commons. CC BY-SA 4.0

On this day in 1573, King Philip II of Spain issued the "Ordinances Concerning the Laying Out of New Towns" as part of the Laws of the Indies (Leyes de Indias), creating one of the earliest codified frameworks for urban planning. These ordinances outlined detailed requirements for designing settlements in Spanish territories in the Americas, focusing on orderly town layouts that balanced functionality and aesthetics. Key elements included a central plaza, a rectilinear street grid, and strategically placed public buildings like churches and administrative offices around the plaza. The ordinances emphasized access to resources like water and farmland while incorporating defenses against natural disasters and enemy attacks. This planning model profoundly influenced the design of colonial cities throughout Latin America and the Philippines, and many retain these features today, highlighting their enduring impact on urban form and planning history.

How can the principles of the Laws of the Indies guide contemporary planning in fostering sustainable and human-centered urban development?

PASSAGE OF
THE HOUSING ACT OF 1949

"A decent home is not just a housing goal; it is a moral imperative."
— Harry S. Truman. 33rd President of the United States.

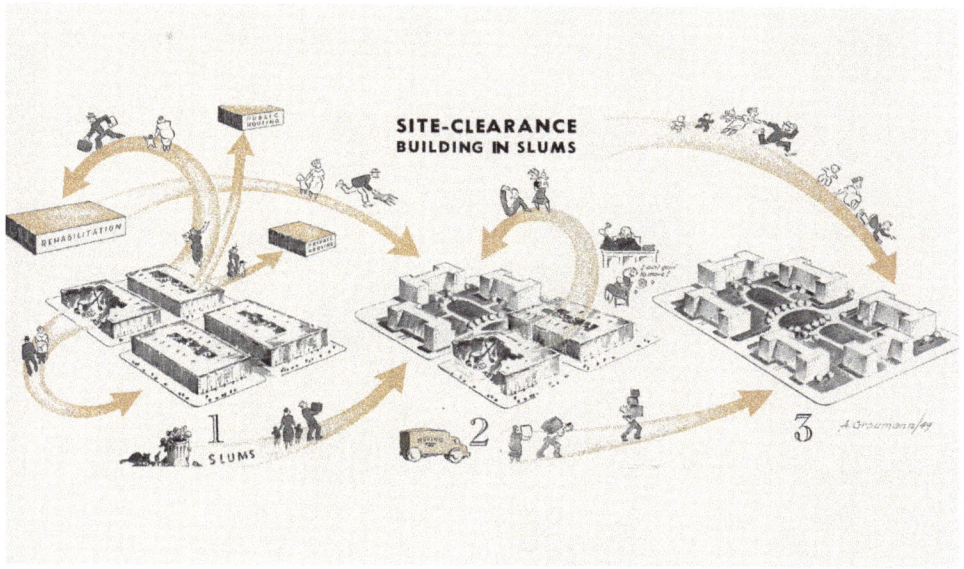

Site Clearance Drawing. 1949. By New York City Housing Authority (reconstructed image). Source: New York Public Library. Public Domain.

On this day in 1949, President Harry S. Truman received the final draft of the Housing Act of 1949, which he would sign into law on July 15 as a key component of his Fair Deal agenda. The act represented a transformative moment in U.S. housing policy, setting the ambitious federal goal of providing "a decent home and suitable living environment for every American family." It authorized substantial funding for slum clearance, public housing construction, and urban renewal projects, catalyzing widespread redevelopment in American cities. While the legislation aimed to improve living conditions and address postwar housing shortages, its implementation often led to the displacement of low-income and minority communities, with entire neighborhoods razed and inadequate relocation support provided. Despite its complex legacy, the Housing Act of 1949 marked a pivotal expansion of federal involvement in urban development and laid the groundwork for future housing initiatives such as Section 8. Its influence remains visible in contemporary housing debates and urban policy frameworks.

How did the Housing Act of 1949 shape urban renewal policies, and what lessons can be learned to ensure equitable housing solutions today?

JULY 15
1799

DECREE OF MEMPHIS: THE ROSETTA STONE

"The ability to govern well depends on communicating clearly with all who dwell within the city." – Ptolemy V Epiphanes. Pharaoh of Egypt. (Paraphrased).

Detail of the Rosetta Stone. By Jens Teichmann. Licensed

On this day in 1799, the Rosetta Stone was discovered near the Egyptian town of Rosetta (modern-day Rashid) by French soldiers during Napoleon Bonaparte's Egyptian campaign. While the exact date is not definitively recorded, experts generally agree that July 15 is the most likely. Inscribed in 196 BCE in Memphis, Egypt, the stone bears a decree issued by Ptolemy V Epiphanes, written in hieroglyphic, Demotic, and Greek to communicate royal policies across different social strata. The text addresses land use, tax reforms, and the maintenance of essential infrastructure such as temples and irrigation systems—key components of urban management in ancient Egypt. It also granted tax exemptions to religious institutions and mandated the restoration of public works, highlighting the central role of governance in sustaining urban life and social stability. The Rosetta Stone's discovery was instrumental in the decipherment of Egyptian hieroglyphs, unlocking a deeper understanding of ancient urban systems, administrative practices, and cultural history.

How can modern cities use lessons from ancient governance systems to balance authority and infrastructure needs?

FOUNDING OF WASHINGTON, D.C.

"We plan for posterity, but they must also provide for themselves."
– Pierre Charles L'Enfant. Architect and planner (attributed).

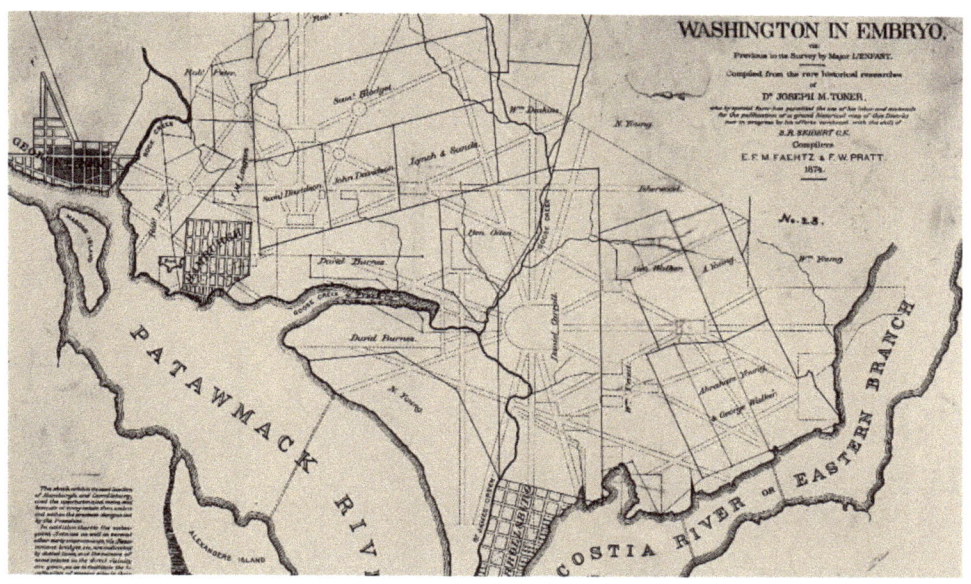

Sketch of Washington in embryo - previous to its survey by Major L'Enfant, 1792. Source: Published by authority of the Capitol Centennial Committee, 1893. Library of Congress Geography and Map Division. Public Domain.

On this day in 1790, the Residence Act was signed into law, designating the Potomac River as the location of the U.S. federal capital. This decision was a pivotal compromise between Northern and Southern states during the republic's early years. In 1791, Washington, D.C., was officially founded and named after President George Washington, with its design entrusted to French-American engineer Pierre Charles L'Enfant. L'Enfant envisioned a grand city with a geometric layout featuring wide avenues radiating from significant landmarks, emphasizing functionality and symbolism. His plan incorporated public squares and open spaces, culminating in the monumental core that includes the National Mall. Washington, D.C., became a model for capital city planning, influencing urban design principles worldwide. Today, it remains a living embodiment of L'Enfant's vision, serving as both the political center and a cultural symbol of the United States, blending history with modern governance.

How does Washington, D.C.'s founding reflect the relationship between politics, geography, and urban design in creating capital cities?

JULY 17
1744

BIRTH OF ELBRIDGE GERRY

"The evils we experience flow from the excess of democracy."
– Elbridge Gerry. American statesman, diplomat, and fifth US Vice President.

Gerrymander, a definition. Image by Casimiro. Licensed

On this day in 1744, Elbridge Gerry was born in Marblehead, Massachusetts, a key figure in early American governance and the 5th Vice President of the United States. A prominent statesman and signer of the Declaration of Independence, Gerry is most famously associated with the term "gerrymandering," which originated from his approval of a controversial redistricting plan in Massachusetts designed to favor his political party. This act shaped electoral practices and highlighted the complex relationship between urban representation and political power. As cities grew, gerrymandering underscored the tension between fair representation and partisan strategy, affecting urban governance and the equitable distribution of resources. Gerry's legacy remains a pivotal lesson in how political boundaries and urban planning intersect, emphasizing the need for fair representation in cities as they expand and evolve. His contributions continue to influence debates on democracy and governance in urban contexts.

How does urban planning intersect with political boundaries to ensure equitable representation today?

THE FOUNDATION OF GIOTTO'S BELL TOWER

"Architecture is frozen music, and in its harmony, a city finds its soul."
– Johann Wolfgang von Goethe. German poet, playwright, and philosopher.

Cityscape of Florence, Italy, with a view of Giotto's Bell Tower (Campanile di Giotto), a landmark of Italian Gothic architecture that forms part of the Florence Cathedral complex, symbolizing the city's cultural and urban identity. By Sergey Novikov. Licensed

On this day in 1334, the Bishop of Florence blessed the first foundation stone of the Campanile (bell tower) of the Florence Cathedral, a masterpiece designed by Giotto di Bondone. Standing beside the Cattedrale di Santa Maria del Fiore, this striking example of Gothic architecture is celebrated for its elegant proportions and intricate marble detailing in white, green, and pink hues. Giotto, one of the most influential artists of the Renaissance, designed the tower to harmonize with the cathedral while incorporating sculptural reliefs and geometric patterns that reflect the era's artistic advancements. Though Giotto passed away in 1337, construction continued under Andrea Pisano and later Francesco Talenti, culminating in the tower's completion in 1359. Today, the Campanile di Giotto remains one of the most recognizable landmarks of Florence, embodying the city's rich architectural heritage and pioneering role in shaping urban aesthetics during the Renaissance.

How can historical landmarks be preserved while adapting to the needs of modern urban environments?

JULY 19
1900

OPENING OF
THE PARIS MÉTRO

"May this new means of communication serve as a symbol of progress and a source of pride for the French people." – Émile Loubet, President of the French Republic.

The Opéra Paris Metro crossing. Source: Illustreret Norsk Konverastionsleksikon 1913. Via Wikimedia Commons. CC0

On this day in 1900, Paris's Line 1 of the Métro opened, connecting Porte de Maillot to Porte de Vincennes and providing vital transportation for the Summer Olympic Games in the Bois de Vincennes. Planned by engineer Fulgence Bienvenüe, the Métro aimed to ensure that no point in Paris was more than 500 meters from a station, revolutionizing urban mobility. Construction on additional lines quickly followed, establishing the Métro as a key part of the city's infrastructure. Renowned for its art nouveau entrances designed by Hector Guimard, many of which remain iconic landmarks, the Métro embodied functionality and aesthetic innovation. Its compact, efficient design connected key parts of the city, reducing congestion and transforming Paris into one of the most accessible cities in the world. The Métro's integration into the urban fabric set a global standard for public transit, exemplifying Paris's leadership in urban planning and design.

How has the Paris Métro influenced the development of urban transit systems in other cities worldwide?

CREATION OF
THE NATIONAL PLANNING BOARD

"Planning must be seen as the foundation of a productive and equitable nation."
— Adapted from Frederick Law Olmsted Jr.'s essays on national planning.

Public Works Administration (PWA), through the NPB oversaw the construction of the Overseas Highway, connecting Key West to mainland Florida via a 113-mile roadway across the Florida Keys. By Aiisha. Licensed

On this day in 1933, the National Planning Board (NPB) was established as part of the Public Works Administration (PWA) under President Franklin D. Roosevelt's New Deal. Created to respond to the economic and social crises of the Great Depression, the NPB coordinated infrastructure projects and promoted regional planning to combat unemployment and urban decline. Led by prominent urban thinkers like Frederick Law Olmsted Jr., the board emphasized sustainable development, efficient resource use, and long-term strategies for urban growth. Though short-lived—it evolved into the National Resources Planning Board in 1934—the NPB laid crucial groundwork for federal involvement in urban and regional planning. Its efforts helped shape future large-scale public works by linking infrastructure investment with thoughtful, innovative planning. The board's legacy endures in how federal agencies address urban challenges today, underscoring the importance of aligning economic recovery with environmental sustainability and social equity.

How did the creation of the National Planning Board shape the role of the federal government in urban and regional planning?

JULY 21
1970

INAUGURATION OF THE ASWAN HIGH DAM

"The Aswan High Dam is a symbol of the new era of development and progress."
– Gamal Abdel Nasser. Egyptian president and revolutionary leader.

Aswan High Dam, Egypt, a major infrastructure project completed in 1970, regulating the Nile River's flow, enabling hydroelectric power generation, and reshaping the surrounding urban and agricultural landscape. By Oksana. Licensed

On this day in 1970, the Aswan High Dam in Egypt was officially inaugurated, marking a pivotal achievement in the country's post-independence modernization under President Gamal Abdel Nasser. Built across the Nile River near Aswan, the dam was designed to control annual flooding, provide irrigation water, and generate hydroelectric power, fueling Egypt's agricultural productivity and urban expansion. The project created Lake Nasser, one of the world's largest artificial lakes, transforming the region's economy and landscape. However, the dam also had significant social and environmental consequences, displacing tens of thousands of Nubian people, submerging ancient cultural heritage sites, and disrupting the Nile's ecosystem. Despite its challenges, the Aswan High Dam remains a landmark of 20th-century engineering and urban planning, symbolizing the complexities of balancing development, environmental preservation, and social equity in large-scale infrastructure projects. It continues to shape Egypt's growth and identity.

How can contemporary planners learn from the successes and challenges of large-scale projects like the Aswan High Dam to ensure equitable and sustainable urban development?

U.S. GOVERNMENT IMPLEMENTS GASOLINE RATIONING

"The car has become an article of dress without which we feel uncertain, unclad, and incomplete." – Marshall McLuhan. Canadian philosopher and media theorist.

Traffic Los Angeles Downtown. By OutdoorPhoto. Licensed

On this day in 1942, the United States government implemented mandatory gasoline rationing, prioritizing fuel for military operations during World War II. This measure drastically curtailed civilian automobile use, reshaping mobility across the nation. Americans adapted by carpooling, relying more heavily on public transit, and rediscovering walking and cycling as practical alternatives. The rationing exposed the vulnerabilities of car-dependent systems during global crises and highlighted the importance of diversified mobility options. This pivotal moment in U.S. transportation history serves as a reminder of how resource scarcity can drive societal shifts in urban mobility. Today, as cities face challenges like rising gas prices and climate change, urban planners draw lessons from this period to advocate for walkable cities, enhanced public transit networks, and expanded cycling infrastructure. These strategies aim to reduce fossil fuel dependence and create more sustainable, resilient urban environments for future generations.

How can the lessons from gasoline rationing during World War II inspire modern cities to prioritize alternative transportation systems and pedestrian-friendly design?

JULY 23
1927

THE DEBUT OF
LE CORBUSIER'S FIVE POINTS OF ARCHITECTURE

"A house is a machine for living in."
– Le Corbusier. Swiss-French architect and urban planner.

Weissenhof Estate – A pioneering showcase of modernist housing, reflecting Le Corbusier's Five Points of Architecture, including pilotis, open plans, and horizontal windows, which redefined urban residential design.By Lukas Schill/ Wirestock Creators. Licensed.

On this day in 1927, at the opening of the Weissenhof Estate Exhibition in Stuttgart, Germany, Le Corbusier introduced his groundbreaking Five Points of Architecture: pilotis (supporting columns), flat roofs, open floor plans, horizontal windows, and free façades. These principles represented a dramatic shift from traditional architectural norms, emphasizing simplicity, functionality, and modernity while redefining housing design for a new era. The Weissenhof Estate served as a showcase for innovative housing prototypes, propelling Le Corbusier's ideas to the forefront of the modernist movement. These concepts reached their pinnacle in the Villa Savoye (1931), a masterpiece embodying the Five Points and a manifesto for modern design. Le Corbusier's vision also influenced urban planning, promoting efficiency, light, and space in residential development. Today, the Five Points remain integral to sustainable and functional design, illustrating their enduring relevance in shaping contemporary architecture and urban landscapes across the globe.

How can Le Corbusier's Five Points be adapted to address the needs of sustainable and socially inclusive housing today?

RE-DISCOVERY OF
MACHU PICCHU BY HIRAM BINGHAM III

"The city above the clouds reveals the genius of a civilization attuned to its environment."
– Hiram Bingham III. American explorer and historian. (Paraphrased).

View of Machupichu. By Carlos. Licensed

On this day in 1911, American historian and explorer Hiram Bingham III re-discovered Machu Picchu, a breathtaking Inca citadel high in the Andes Mountains of Peru. Constructed in the 15th century during Emperor Pachacuti's reign, Machu Picchu represents a pinnacle of Inca urban planning, featuring terraced agricultural fields, religious temples, and advanced water management systems. The site's rediscovery brought global attention to the engineering and architectural ingenuity of the Inca civilization, showcasing their ability to harmonize human settlement with challenging mountainous terrain. Designated as a UNESCO World Heritage Site in 1983, Machu Picchu has become a symbol of cultural heritage and resilience, attracting millions of visitors annually. Its preservation raises essential discussions about balancing tourism with conservation, ensuring that ancient urban centers like Machu Picchu remain intact for future generations while continuing to inspire awe and appreciation for the ingenuity of past civilizations.

How can the preservation of ancient urban sites like Machu Picchu inspire sustainable practices in modern city planning and development?

JULY 25
1916

NEW YORK CITY ADOPTS
THE FIRST COMPREHENSIVE ZONING RESOLUTION

"Zoning is the most powerful tool for creating orderly, sustainable cities."
— Edward M. Bassett. American lawyer and pioneering city planner.

New York illustrated Publication, 1916. Source: Publisher New York : Success Postal Card Co., Seymor B. Durst Old York Library. Columbia University Libraries. CC0

On this day in 1916, New York City adopted the nation's first Comprehensive Zoning Resolution, a pioneering policy that established the framework for modern land-use regulation in the United States. Motivated by concerns over overcrowding, industrial encroachment into residential neighborhoods, and the massive shadows cast by skyscrapers, the resolution introduced innovative controls on building heights, setbacks, and the separation of land uses (residential, commercial, and industrial). Spearheaded by reformers like Edward M. Bassett, the policy aimed to enhance public health, safety, and urban quality of life. The 1916 Zoning Resolution addressed immediate urban challenges and became a model for cities across the country, shaping zoning as a key tool for urban planning. However, it also laid the foundation for exclusionary zoning practices, which contributed to socioeconomic divides and spatial inequalities in American cities, leaving a complex legacy that continues to influence urban development.

How can zoning policies balance the goals of regulating urban growth with promoting equitable access to housing and resources?

PASSAGE OF
THE AMERICANS WITH DISABILITIES ACT

"Let the shameful wall of exclusion finally come tumbling down."
— George H. W. Bush. 41st President of the United States.

Book with title The Americans with Disabilities Act (ADA). By Vitalii Vodolazskyi. Licensed

On this day in 1990, President George H. W. Bush signed the Americans with Disabilities Act (ADA) into law, marking a historic milestone in civil rights. The ADA prohibits discrimination against individuals with disabilities and mandates accessibility across employment, transportation, public accommodations, and government services. Title II requires local governments to ensure accessibility in public transportation, housing, and facilities, while Title III sets standards for businesses and public spaces, including historic properties. The ADA popularized universal design principles, leading to widespread urban improvements such as ramps, elevators, and curb cuts, transforming cities into more inclusive environments. This legislation reshaped urban planning, encouraging architects and policymakers to prioritize accessibility in the built environment. Over three decades later, the ADA remains a cornerstone of equity, fostering greater independence and participation for individuals with disabilities and setting global benchmarks for inclusive urban design.

How can urban planners build on the principles of the ADA to create cities that are accessible and inclusive for all?

GOOGLE EXTENDS
REMOTE WORK POLICY AMID PANDEMIC

"Work is not a place; it is what we do."
— Sundar Pichai. CEO of Google and Alphabet.

Video call, online conference. By Kateryna. Licensed

On this day in 2020, Google announced that its employees could continue working from home until July 2021, making it the largest tech company to commit to long-term remote work during the COVID-19 pandemic fully. This decision signaled a significant shift in work culture, urban economies, and city infrastructure as businesses reevaluated the necessity of physical office spaces. The widespread adoption of remote and hybrid work models led to declining office occupancy, shifting real estate demand, and changing public transit usage in major urban centers. Cities were forced to rethink zoning laws, transit funding, and commercial space utilization to accommodate a more dispersed workforce. Meanwhile, suburban and smaller cities saw an influx of remote workers seeking improved quality of life. Google's move underscored the evolving relationship between work and urban design, highlighting the need for adaptable, resilient cities that balance economic vitality with the realities of a more flexible workforce.

How do you think remote work has reshaped your city? Should urban planners prioritize office space revitalization or invest in infrastructure for decentralized work communities?

FORMATION OF THE KERNER COMMISSION TO ADDRESS URBAN RIOTS

"Segregation and poverty have created in the racial ghetto a destructive environment totally unknown to most white Americans." – Kerner Commission Report

President Lyndon Baines Johnson with some members of the National Advisory Commission on Civil Disorders (Kerner Commission) in the Cabinet Room of the White House, Washington, D.C. 1967. By: Trikosko, Marion S. Source: Library of Congress Prints and Photographs Division. U.S. News & World Report Magazine Collection. Public Domain.

On this day in 1967, President Lyndon B. Johnson established the National Advisory Commission on Civil Disorders, known as the Kerner Commission, to investigate the causes of widespread urban unrest and riots in U.S. cities. The Commission's 1968 report delivered a stark warning, stating that the nation was "moving toward two societies, one Black, one white—separate and unequal." It identified systemic racism, poverty, and urban inequality as underlying causes of the unrest and recommended bold investments in housing, education, and employment to address disparities in urban areas. The report also emphasized fostering integration and equitable urban development to prevent future conflict. Although many of its recommendations went unheeded, the Kerner Commission's findings remain a seminal work in urban policy and social justice, highlighting the critical relationship between equity, urban stability, and the well-being of diverse communities in American cities.

How can modern cities address systemic inequality and segregation to ensure that urban environments promote equity and opportunity for all residents?

JULY 29
1836

INAUGURATION OF
THE ARC DE TRIOMPHE, PARIS

"Monuments are the anchors of a city's memory, binding past triumphs to future aspirations."
– Inspired by French architect Jean Chalgrin's legacy.

Aerial view of the Arc de Triomphe, Paris—Twelve grand avenues radiate from this iconic monument, a symbol of French national pride. Photo by Eric Isselée, licensed via Adobe Stock.

On this day in 1836, the Arc de Triomphe in Paris was inaugurated to honor those who fought and died for France during the French Revolutionary and Napoleonic Wars. Commissioned by Napoleon Bonaparte in 1806 and designed by Jean Chalgrin, the monument stands at the western end of the Champs-Élysées. It forms the centerpiece of a star-shaped configuration of radiating avenues, exemplifying 19th-century urban design principles emphasizing grandeur, symmetry, and centrality. The Arc's monumental scale and strategic placement reflect the period's fascination with blending architecture and urban planning to create powerful national pride and historical remembrance symbols. Over time, the Arc de Triomphe has become an enduring icon of Paris, inspiring the design of triumphal arches and ceremonial spaces worldwide. It remains a gathering place for significant events, continuing to connect its historical legacy with the city's modern identity.

How can the preservation and integration of historical monuments shape the identity and cultural continuity of modern cities?

FOUNDING OF BAGHDAD, IRAQ

"I have never seen a city of greater height, perfect circularity, and superior merits than Al Zawra (Baghdad)." – Al-Jahiz, Arab prose writer and scholar.

View of Bagdad on the Persian side of the Tigris. Image extracted from page 008 of Travels in Asia and Africa, etc. [Edited by J. P. Berjew.]", by Abraham Parsons. Source: British Library. Via Wikimedia Commons. Public Domain.

On this day in 762 CE, Caliph Al-Mansur founded Baghdad near the Tigris River, designing it as a perfect circle known as the "Round City." As the capital of the Abbasid Caliphate, Baghdad quickly became a center of learning, culture, and commerce, symbolizing the Islamic Golden Age. Its innovative circular layout reflected advanced urban planning, with the caliph's palace and grand mosque at the center, surrounded by administrative, residential, and commercial zones. The design emphasized centralized governance, efficient administration, and strong defenses. Baghdad's prosperity attracted scholars, traders, and artisans worldwide, fostering a thriving intellectual and economic environment where science, philosophy, and the arts flourished. The city's pioneering urban form and cultural achievements influenced the development of cities throughout the Islamic world, leaving a legacy of architectural, intellectual, and urban innovation that continues to inspire city planning.

How did the unique design and planning of Baghdad influence the development of urban centers in the Islamic world and beyond?

JULY 31
1919

CREATION OF
THE UK'S COUNCIL HOUSING PROGRAM

"The quality of housing determines the quality of the nation."
– Christopher Addison, British politician and social reformer.

English Rowhouses. 1920s efforts to provide affordable, government-supported homes were shaped by the ideals of the "Homes Fit for Heroes" movement after World War I. Photo by Mubus. Licensed

On this day in 1919, the UK's Housing Act, known as the Addison Act, was enacted, marking the country's first major council housing initiative. Named after Dr. Christopher Addison, the Minister of Health, the Act addressed severe post-World War I housing shortages by empowering local authorities to build affordable, high-quality homes for working-class families. It marked a historic shift in government responsibility for public welfare, redefining housing as a social right rather than a market commodity. By setting minimum standards for space and amenities, the Act aimed to eliminate the cramped, unsanitary conditions of industrial-era housing. While financial challenges limited its full implementation, the Addison Act laid the foundation for modern social housing policies, influencing similar initiatives worldwide. It remains a milestone in urban planning, symbolizing a commitment to addressing inequality and improving living conditions through thoughtful government-supported housing solutions.

How did early council housing programs shape the perception of government responsibility in addressing housing needs?

HOLC ISSUES FIRST REDLINING MAPS

"The geography of inequality was drawn in red ink, and its consequences still stain our cities." – Richard Rothstein, American academic and author, The Color of Law.

sections.   The beneficial influences from a negro standpoint are the good negro schools, playgrounds, and proximity to downtown Miami, while the detrimental influences are poor sanitation and critical condition of the majority of the buildings.   Present sales prices are about 30 % of the 1925 peak and at the low in 1933 were about 20 % of the peak prices. Present volume is about 10 to 15 % of the 1925 peak levels and at the low in 1933 was about 5 % of the peak volume.   Present occupancy is about 90 %, was 100 % in 1925, and 70 % in 1933.   Present rental prices are about 35 % of the 1925 peak prices and at the low in 1933 were about 30 %.   There is no surplus of housing in these sections and new housing is needed on a slum-clearance basis.   There is no new residential construction in these sections other than the $1,000,000. P. W. A. low cost negro project at Sixty-third Street and N. W. Seventeenth Avenue, which is about 30 % completed.   About 50 % of the loans made in these sections were foreclosed or re-financed.

Redlining document for Liberty City, Miami, FL, A majority Black neighborhood needing new housing "on a slum - clearance basis." Reference: NARA85713724 (p22). Source: U.S. National Archives and Records Administration at College Park - Archives II (College Park, MD). Via Wikimedia Commons. Public Domain.

In August 1935, the Home Owners' Loan Corporation (HOLC) completed its redlining maps, known as the Security Maps for Analysis of Mortgage Lending Areas, a federal initiative to stabilize the housing market during the Great Depression. These maps categorized neighborhoods into four risk levels for investment, with minority and immigrant communities frequently labeled as "hazardous" and outlined in red. This discriminatory practice excluded these areas from federal mortgage programs and private lending, entrenching racial and economic segregation in American cities. Redlining steered investment away from marginalized neighborhoods, reinforcing cycles of poverty, underdevelopment, and infrastructure decay. Its impact is still evident today in homeownership rates, wealth accumulation, and neighborhood quality disparities. Although outlawed by the Fair Housing Act of 1968, redlining's legacy underscores the profound influence of policy and planning on systemic inequality, highlighting the enduring need for equitable urban development practices.

What strategies can urban planners and policymakers use to repair the long-term impacts of redlining and promote equitable access to housing and resources?

AUGUST 2
1790

THE FIRST
UNITED STATES CENSUS

"The census is intended to enable them to adapt the public measures to the particular circumstances of the community." – James Madison, American statesman and Founding Father.

Distribution of the population east of the 100th meridian: 1820. (Prepared under the supervision of Henry Gannett, Geographer of the Twelfth Census. United States Census Office, 1903). Julius Bien & Co., N.Y. Source: David Rumsey Map Collection, David Rumsey Map Center, Stanford Libraries. Public Domain.

On this day in 1790, the Bureau of the Census was inaugurated. The first United States Census was conducted, overseen by Secretary of State Thomas Jefferson. This landmark effort recorded a population of nearly 4 million and was the foundation for apportioning seats in the House of Representatives and allocating federal resources. Beyond its political function, the census offered critical insights into urban and rural populations' demographic makeup and geographic distribution. As cities like Philadelphia and New York began to expand, the data provided a framework for understanding societal changes and planning for the needs of a growing nation. The 1790 Census reflected the priorities of a young republic, establishing a precedent for using population data to inform governance, urban development, and resource distribution. This tradition has since become a cornerstone of American policy, shaping the evolution of cities and communities nationwide.

How has the role of census data evolved in shaping urban policy and planning over time?

FORMAL ADOPTION OF THE GREEN BELT POLICY

"A breathing space for the metropolis—a Green Belt that preserves nature for both recreation and necessity." – Patrick Abercrombie. British urban planner.

Aerial view of the North Downs in Surrey, part of London's Green Belt, established to limit urban sprawl and preserve open countryside. By Beataaldridge. Licensed.

On this day in 1955, the Green Belt Policy was formally adopted as national planning guidance in the United Kingdom through Circular 42/55, issued by the Ministry of Housing and Local Government. The policy encouraged local councils to establish Green Belts around urban areas to restrict sprawl, preserve the countryside, and provide open recreational spaces. Building on ideas from Patrick Abercrombie's Greater London Plan of 1944, the policy extended Green Belt principles nationwide, ensuring a consistent approach to managing urban growth. By protecting rural land from development, the Green Belt policy has played a pivotal role in balancing the needs of expanding cities with environmental conservation. Its enduring influence shapes the spatial development of urban areas in the UK, serving as a global model for sustainable land-use planning that prioritizes ecological preservation and urban livability.

How has the Green Belt Policy influenced urban sustainability, and what challenges does it face in modern urban development?

AUGUST 4
1463

BIRTH OF
LORENZO DI PIERFRANCESCO DE' MEDICI

"The beauty of a city lies in its ability to inspire its people through art and design."
– Inspired by Lorenzo di Pierfrancesco de' Medici's patronage of arts and urban design.

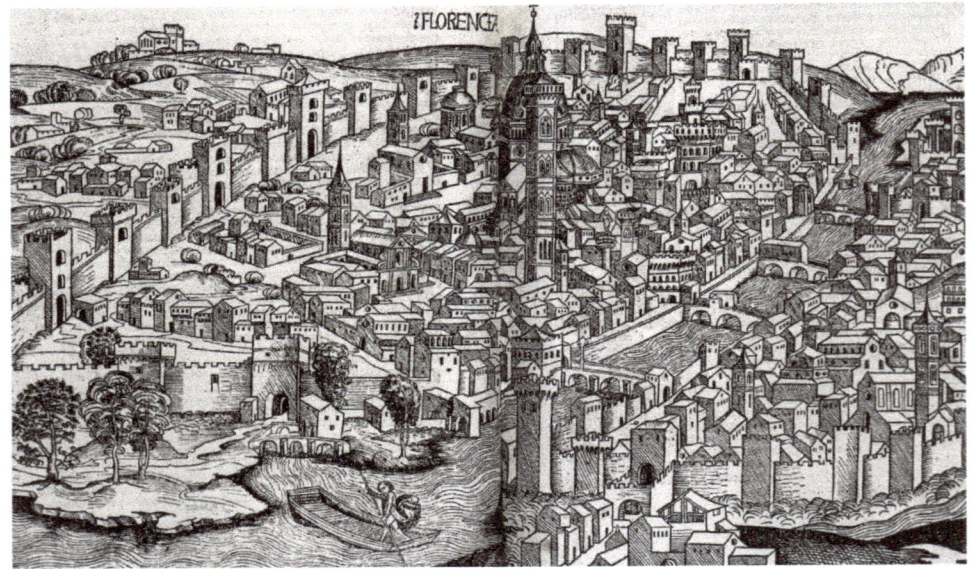

Mappa di Firenze, 1493. By Hartmann Schedel. Source: Hartmann Schedel. Liber chronicarum LXXXVII, Nuremberg. Via Wikimedia Commons. Public Domain.

On this day in 1463, Lorenzo di Pierfrancesco de' Medici was born in Florence, Italy. A prominent member of the Medici family, Lorenzo played a pivotal role in the cultural and architectural flourishing of Renaissance Florence. As a patron of the arts, he supported luminaries such as Sandro Botticelli, commissioning works that have become timeless symbols of artistic excellence. Beyond individual commissions, Lorenzo contributed to urban beautification projects that transformed Florence into a cultural and architectural innovation hub. His investment in public art and civic spaces enhanced the city's aesthetic appeal and social cohesion, making Florence a model of how art and architecture can elevate urban life. The Medici family's holistic approach to integrating art, culture, and urban design continues to influence city planning, demonstrating the enduring power of cultural investments to shape vibrant, community-centered urban environments.

How can the integration of art and architecture into urban spaces enhance the cultural identity and community cohesion of modern cities?

DEATH OF FRIEDRICH ENGELS

"An industrial city can only be understood as a machine for creating wealth for the few and misery for the many." – Paraphrased from Friedrich Engels' writings.

A glimpse into the harsh realities of life in the London slums – a stark reminder of the social challenges of the industrial age, 1872. By Gustave Doré. Source: Wellcome Collection gallery. Via Wikimedia Commons. CC BY 4.0

On this day in 1895, Friedrich Engels, co-founder of Marxist theory and a leading critic of urban inequality, passed away in London, England. Engels dedicated much of his life to studying the social impacts of industrialization on urban life. His groundbreaking work, The Condition of the Working Class in England (1845), vividly detailed the overcrowded slums, worker exploitation, and public health crises in cities like Manchester during the Industrial Revolution. These observations exposed the stark inequalities created by industrial capitalism, inspiring labor movements and influencing urban reform efforts to improve living conditions in industrial cities. After

Karl Marx died in 1883, Engels edited and published additional volumes of Das Kapital, ensuring their lasting influence on global economic and social thought. Engels' critiques remain foundational to the study of urbanization, offering enduring insights into the relationship between industrial development, social justice, and the structure of cities.

How do Engels' critiques of urban inequality during the Industrial Revolution resonate with modern debates about wealth inequality and urban development today?

AUGUST 6
1945

ATOMIC BOMBING
OF HIROSHIMA

"The human spirit, like a city, can rise again from the ashes, stronger and more determined."
– Inspired by Sadako Kurihara's writings. Japanese poet and peace activist.

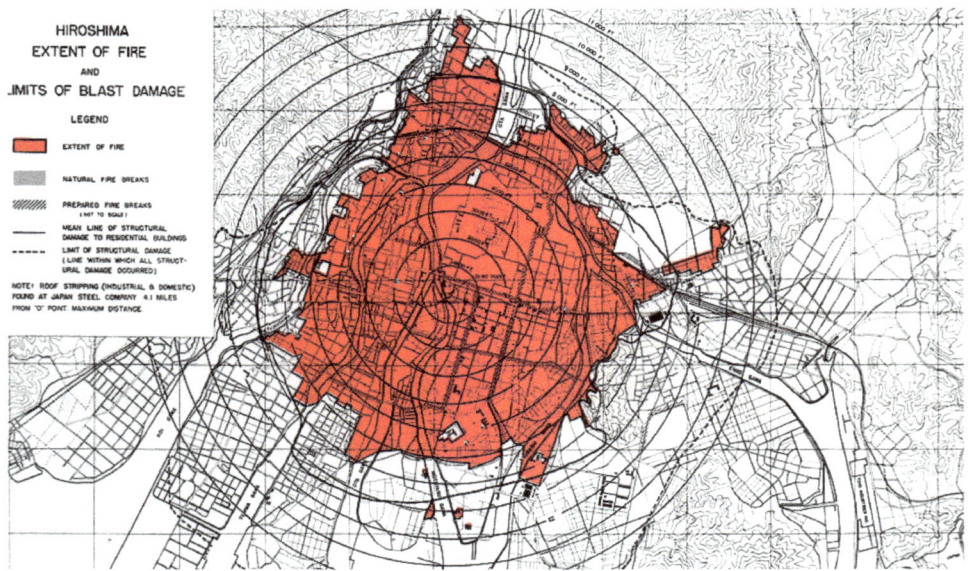

Map of Blast and Fire Damage to Hiroshima. Source: U.S. Strategic Bombing Survey. Via Wikimedia Commons. Public Domain.

On this day in 1945, Hiroshima, Japan, became the first city to endure an atomic bombing, leading to catastrophic loss of life and the near-total destruction of its infrastructure. The explosion devastated the urban landscape, creating unprecedented challenges for recovery and resilience. In the aftermath, Hiroshima's reconstruction efforts became a testament to human perseverance, with the city rebuilding as a global symbol of peace and sustainability. Urban planners emphasized memorialization, creating spaces such as the Hiroshima Peace Memorial Park to honor the victims while advocating for nuclear disarmament. The city's transformation highlights the role of urban planning in disaster recovery, focusing on resilience, sustainability, and community well-being. Hiroshima's experience underscores the vital need for cities worldwide to develop comprehensive disaster preparedness and recovery strategies to build more resilient, adaptive, and peaceful urban environments in the face of future challenges.

How can urban planning integrate lessons from past disasters to enhance resilience and promote peace in contemporary cities?

BIRTH OF
ROBERT DUDLEY

"Maps are the mirrors of our exploration and the blueprints of our urban aspirations."
– Adapted from Robert Dudley's philosophy.

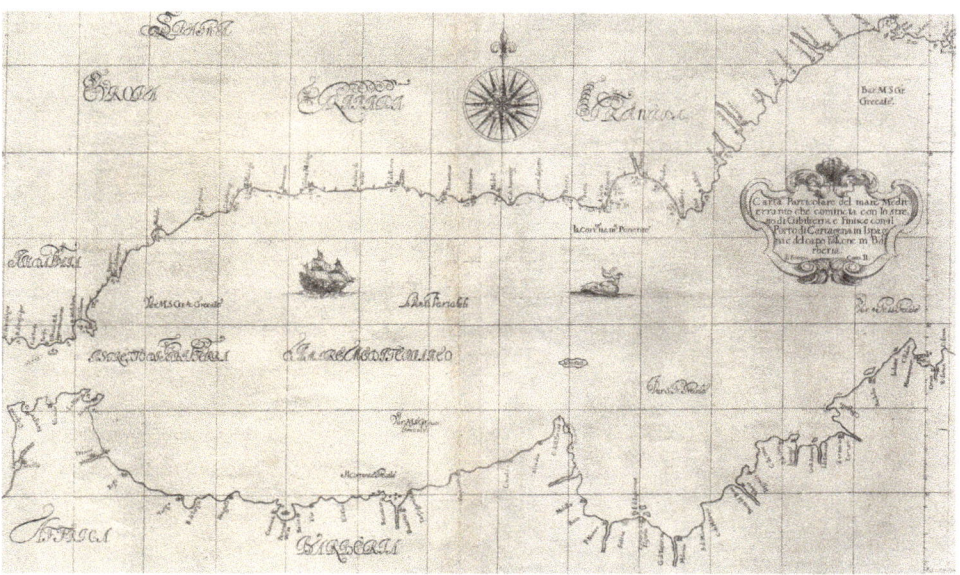

Map of the Western Mediterranean and Gibraltar, 1646. By Robert Dudley. Source: Lawrence Ruderman Antique Maps, Inc. CC0

On this day in 1574, Robert Dudley, an English explorer, naval engineer, and cartographer, was born. Dudley is celebrated for his pioneering work, Dell'Arcano del Mare (The Mystery of the Sea), a six-volume atlas published in 1646–1647. This groundbreaking atlas featured some of the earliest detailed charts of global coastlines and harbors, revolutionizing maritime cartography and influencing coastal urban planning. Dudley's meticulous studies of navigation and harbor design emphasized safety, efficiency, and resilience, shaping the development of port cities during the early modern period. His work reflected the era's growing interconnectedness between exploration, mapping, and urbanization, providing tools that expanded global trade networks and facilitated the growth of coastal urban centers. Dudley's legacy endures as a testament to cartography's essential role in advancing maritime exploration and the strategic planning of urban infrastructure in coastal regions.

How can historical advancements in cartography and navigation inform modern urban coastal planning and resilience strategies?

AUGUST 8
2019

CELEBRATION OF
DIGITAL NOMAD DAY

"Work is no longer where you go; it's what you do, wherever you are."
– Pieter Levels. Dutch entrepreneur and digital nomad advocate.

Remote working. By Shellygraphy. Licensed

On this day in 2019, Digital Nomad Day was first celebrated to recognize the growing movement of remote workers who use technology to work from anywhere in the world. The observance reflects the shift toward location-independent careers, a trend accelerated by the COVID-19 pandemic. The rise of digital nomads is reshaping urban environments as cities adapt to accommodate a more mobile workforce. Many have responded by developing co-working hubs, expanding high-speed internet access, and repurposing office spaces for flexible work arrangements. Some destinations even offer digital nomad visas to attract remote professionals, fostering economic growth and innovation. This evolving work culture challenges traditional urban planning, influencing housing markets, transportation patterns, and local economies. Digital Nomad Day highlights how cities must balance infrastructure, sustainability, and community engagement to support a workforce redefining where and how we live and work.

How can urban planners and policymakers design cities that accommodate the growing population of digital nomads and remote workers?

BIRTH OF
GORDON CULLEN

"The purpose of the environment we build is to create conditions in which the eye and mind can be engaged, rather than simply confronted with monotony." – Gordon Cullen.

Cullen's principles of deflected and terminated vistas in Najac village in the south of France. By Stockbym. Licensed

On this day in 1914, Gordon Cullen, the influential urban designer and author of Townscape (1961), was born in Calverley, Yorkshire, England. Cullen was a trailblazer in highlighting the visual and experiential dimensions of urban environments, introducing the concept of "serial vision" to explain how pedestrians perceive a sequence of views as they move through a city. His landmark book Townscape championed the importance of designing for human scale, encouraging architects and planners to thoughtfully integrate buildings, streets, and open spaces to create visually engaging and emotionally resonant urban areas. Cullen's work combined artistic sensibility with practical urban design principles, inspiring a generation of planners to prioritize placemaking and aesthetic harmony. His legacy continues influencing efforts to create livable, walkable, and visually cohesive cities that celebrate the human experience.

How can Cullen's concept of "serial vision" inspire the design of contemporary urban spaces to engage residents and visitors alike

AUGUST 10
1933

ADOPTION OF PRINCIPLES FOR
THE ATHENS CHARTER FOR URBAN PLANNING

"The city is an immense social organ that should be shaped for efficiency and health."
– Le Corbusier. Swiss-French architect and urban planner.

Amsterdam Zuidoost – A modernist urban experiment shaped by the ideals of the 1933 CIAM Congress, featuring elevated roads, metro tracks, expansive green spaces, and honeycomb-patterned housing blocks that embody the Athens Charter's vision of a functionally zoned, efficient, and health-oriented city. By Milos. Licensed.

On this day in 1933, the 4th International Congress of Modern Architecture (CIAM) concluded aboard the SS Patris II en route to Athens, solidifying principles that would shape modern urban planning. Led by Le Corbusier, the Congress laid the groundwork for the Athens Charter, a manifesto addressing urban challenges in the industrial age. The Charter emphasized zoning, dividing cities into four functions—dwelling, work, recreation, and transportation—to tackle issues like overcrowding, poor housing, and inadequate infrastructure. It advocated for high-density housing, integrated green spaces, and transit-oriented development to create more efficient and livable cities. Published formally by Le Corbusier in 1943, these ideas profoundly influenced mid-20th-century urban design, inspiring planning approaches worldwide. However, critics later argued that its rigid, top-down principles often overlooked local cultural and social dynamics. The Athens Charter remains a landmark in urban planning history, embodying modernism's ambitions and limitations.

In what ways has the Athens Charter's focus on functional zoning shaped today's cities, positively or negatively?

HEDY LAMARR & GEORGE ANTHEIL PATENT FREQUENCY-HOPPING SYSTEM

"Hope and curiosity about the future seemed better than guarantees. The unknown was always so attractive to me... and still is." – Hedy Lamarr. Austrian-American inventor and actress.

Conceptual digital network connections. Hong Kong Downtown. Financial district Aerial. By Tampatra. Licensed

On this day in 1942, actress Hedy Lamarr and composer George Antheil were awarded a patent for a frequency-hopping spread spectrum communication system. Conceived initially to secure torpedo guidance during World War II, their invention laid the foundation for modern wireless technologies, including Wi-Fi, Bluetooth, and cellular networks. This innovation has profoundly transformed urban life, enabling seamless real-time communication, remote work, and the development of smart city technologies. Lamarr and Antheil's work revolutionized transportation systems, emergency response, and public infrastructure by enhancing urban connectivity and fostering greater efficiency and adaptability in city management. Their frequency-hopping system exemplifies how technological breakthroughs can drive urban transformation, creating more interconnected and resilient cities. Despite the monumental impact of their work, Lamarr and Antheil's contributions went largely unrecognized during their lifetimes, highlighting the often-overlooked role of unconventional innovators in shaping modern urban experiences.

How has the development of wireless communication technologies influenced urban planning and the connectivity of cities globally?

AUGUST 12
1848

DEATH OF
GEORGE STEPHENSON

"The rage for railroads is so great that many will be laid in parts where they will not pay."
– George Stephenson

Image of the Scotswood, Newburn and Wylam Railway and the cottage in which George Stephenson was born (crop without border or text), 1887. By E. Hodgson. Source: Tomlinson, William Weaver, 1858-1916 (1915) The North Eastern Railway; its rise and development, p. 720. Public Domain.

On this day in 1848, George Stephenson, celebrated as the "Father of Railways", passed away, leaving an enduring mark on the form and function of modern cities. As the chief engineer of the Liverpool and Manchester Railway, opened in 1830, Stephenson oversaw the world's first public inter-city railway to use steam locomotives for both passengers and freight. This innovation sparked the railway age, dramatically accelerating urban growth and reshaping regional connectivity. Cities began expanding outward along rail corridors, while new industrial zones and suburban communities emerged with direct access to rail. The mobility revolution introduced by Stephenson synchronized daily life with railway timetables, connected rural markets with urban centers, and reduced travel times in ways previously unimaginable. His work laid the infrastructural and spatial foundation for the modern metropolis, influencing not only transportation planning but also patterns of land use, economic development, and social mobility in urban settings worldwide.

How did the advent of intercity railways alter the scale, shape, and socioeconomic patterns of urban development in the 19th century?

TONY GARNIER'S INDUSTRIAL CITY

"The city of tomorrow must unite work, life, and nature in a harmonious balance."
– Tony Garnier, French architect and urban planner. (Paraphrased).

Plate 164 from the book "Une Cité industrielle", Volume 2. By Tony Garnier. Source: Bibliothèque municipale de Lyon. Via Wikimedia Commons. Public Domain.

On this day in 1869, French architect Tony Garnier, a pioneer in modern urban planning, was born. Garnier's groundbreaking work, Une Cité Industrielle (The Industrial City), conceptualized in 1904, envisioned a self-sufficient city designed to harmonize industry, education, health, and recreation. Dividing the city into functional residential, industrial, civic, and recreational zones, Garnier's vision incorporated innovative elements like prefabricated concrete buildings, green spaces, and efficient transportation systems. His design prioritized productivity and quality of life, emphasizing integrating environmental and social needs within an industrialized urban framework.

Although Une Cité Industrielle was never built, it became a cornerstone of modern urban planning, influencing movements like modernism and inspiring planners to consider sustainability and functionality in city design. Garnier's ideas remain relevant, guiding efforts to create urban environments that balance progress, human well-being, and environmental stewardship, cementing his legacy as a visionary in urban development.

How do visionary designs like Une Cité Industrielle shape contemporary approaches to sustainable urban planning?

AUGUST 14
1959

FIRST SATELLITE
IMAGES CAPTURED

"From space, we see the patterns of our cities—how they breathe, grow, and falter."
– Karen C. Seto, Urbanization Scientist.

Charlotte Harbor, Florida, satellite image map: NASA LANDSAT-1, 1:500,000, N2723W08143, 1970. By Geological Survey (U.S.); United States. National Aeronautics And Space Administration. Source: Library of Congress. Via Wikimedia Commons. Public Domain.

On this day in 1959, the Explorer 6 satellite transmitted the first images of Earth from space, capturing cloud cover over the Pacific Ocean. Though primitive by modern standards, these images marked the dawn of using aerial and satellite technology to study Earth's surface. This breakthrough paved the way for advanced satellite programs like Landsat in the 1960s and 1970s, transforming urban and environmental planning. Satellite imagery gave planners a new perspective on urban growth, land use, and natural resource management, enabling more precise analysis of sprawling cities, transportation networks, and the environmental impact of urbanization. These insights allowed for data-driven approaches to planning, improving resource management and designing sustainable cities. Today, satellite imagery plays a critical role in monitoring climate change, mapping informal settlements, and managing disaster response, offering planners up-to-date, high-resolution data that supports smarter, more resilient interventions. The legacy of Explorer 6 lives on in the widespread use of satellite data, which continues to shape how cities and regions adapt to global challenges in planning, infrastructure, and conservation.

How has satellite imagery transformed urban and regional planning, and what future innovations could further improve data-driven planning practices?

INAUGURATION OF
THE PANAMA CANAL

"The Panama Canal is a testament to human ingenuity and perseverance."
– David McCullough. American author and historian. The Path Between the Seas.

In the Panama Canal, approaching the Chagres River railroad crossing, 16 July 1915. View looks north, with USS Ohio (BB-12) and USS Wisconsin (BB-9) in the background. Source: Collection of Admiral Thomas C. Kinkaid, 1973. U.S. Naval History and Heritage Command Photograph. National Museum of the U.S. Navy. Public Domain.

On this day in 1914, the Panama Canal officially opened with the transit of the SS Ancon, marking a groundbreaking achievement in engineering and global trade. Spanning approximately 50 miles (80 km) across the Isthmus of Panama, the canal connects the Atlantic and Pacific Oceans, reducing maritime travel distances by about 8,000 miles and significantly enhancing international commerce. Initiated by the French in the late 19th century and completed by the United States, its construction overcame immense challenges, including tropical diseases like malaria and yellow fever and the complexities of the rugged terrain. The canal's opening revolutionized global shipping, providing a faster, more efficient route for goods and shaping economic and urban development in Panama and beyond. A century later, the Panama Canal remains a critical artery for global trade, handling a substantial portion of the world's maritime traffic and exemplifying the transformative power of infrastructure.

How did the construction and opening of the Panama Canal influence urban development and economic growth in Panama and globally?

AUGUST 16
1744

BIRTH OF
PIERRE MÉCHAIN

"Our task was to measure the world—so that all humanity might share in its standard." —Reflecting Méchain and Delambre's stated goal of creating a universal length based on the Earth's meridian

Official engraved marble standard meter, installed in Place Vendôme in Paris during the French Revolution to introduce the metric system in France. By HJBC. Licensed

On this day in 1744, Pierre Méchain was born, a French astronomer and geodetic surveyor whose work helped define the very measurements we use to shape cities and nations. In 1791, under the direction of the French Academy of Sciences and as part of the revolutionary government's vision to base all measurements on nature, Méchain, alongside fellow astronomer Jean-Baptiste Delambre, undertook the ambitious meridian arc survey between Dunkirk and Barcelona. Méchain was responsible for the southern portion, traversing the Pyrenees and parts of Spain. Their calculations formed the basis of the meter, conceived as one ten-millionth of the Earth's meridian quadrant. This immense geodetic task laid the groundwork for the metric system and modern cartographic precision, enabling cadastral mapping and standardized urban planning worldwide. Despite political upheaval, including Méchain's arrest and internment during the French Revolution, his commitment to scientific accuracy endured. His work continues to define how we measure, map, and plan the physical world.

How do standardized systems of measurement influence the way planners map, regulate, and organize urban space today?

WOODSTOCK PERFORMERS JAM THROUGH THE FINAL NIGHT

"Woodstock was not about sex, drugs, and rock 'n' roll. It was about unity and peace."
– Richie Havens. American singer-songwriter and activist.

Photo taken near the Woodstock music festival on August 18, 1969. By Ric Manning. Via Wikimedia Commons. CC BY 3.0

On this day in 1969, the Woodstock Music and Art Fair concluded with an iconic marathon of performances, including Jimi Hendrix's legendary rendition of "The Star-Spangled Banner." Held on a farm near Bethel, New York, Woodstock drew over 400,000 attendees, temporarily transforming the rural setting into a massive, makeshift "city" of music and culture. The festival became a defining moment of the counterculture movement, symbolizing ideals of peace, love, and community amidst the social upheavals of the 1960s. Performances by legendary artists such as Janis Joplin, Joe Cocker, and Santana electrified the crowd and left an enduring cultural legacy. Woodstock's spontaneous, ad-hoc nature highlighted the challenges and opportunities of large-scale event management in temporary urban environments. It influenced the design and planning of future music festivals, showcasing the importance of infrastructure, resource coordination, and community spirit in creating successful shared cultural experiences.

How can large-scale gatherings shape our understanding of community and shared urban experiences?

AUGUST 18
1917

THE GREAT FIRE
OF THESSALONIKI

"The fire cleared the way for a new Thessaloniki, designed to meet the needs of a modern city while respecting its past." – Ernest Hébrard. French architect and urban planner.

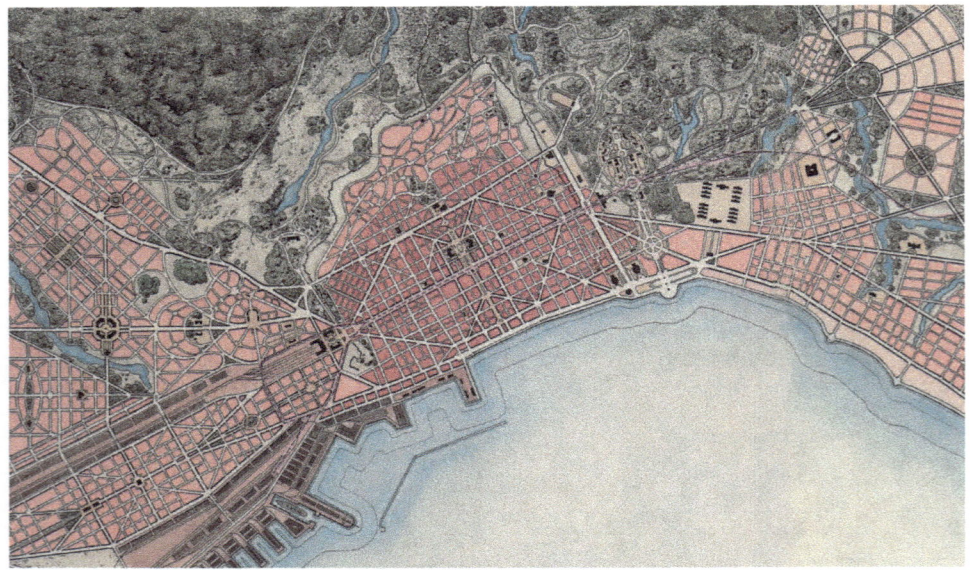

Map of Thessaloniki after the Great Fire of 1917. By Thomas Hayton Mawson, Architect, 1918. Via Wikimedia Commons. Public Domain.

On this day in 1917, a devastating fire swept through Thessaloniki, Greece, destroying 32% of the city and leaving 70,000 residents homeless. The blaze obliterated the historic city center, including markets, homes, and cultural landmarks, dramatically altering the urban landscape. In the wake of the tragedy, French architect Ernest Hébrard led a visionary urban redevelopment effort to transform Thessaloniki into a modern European city. His plan introduced wider streets, public squares, and zoning regulations while preserving key elements of the city's historical and cultural heritage. The reconstruction blended modern urban planning principles with respect for Thessaloniki's diverse identity, setting a new standard for post-disaster urban renewal. While the fire was a tragic event, it became a turning point in Thessaloniki's history, demonstrating resilience and the potential to rebuild cities in ways that embrace both progress and cultural preservation.

How can cities recovering from disaster integrate historical preservation with the demands of modern urban planning?

FIRST RACE AT
INDIANAPOLIS MOTOR SPEEDWAY

"The Speedway is more than a racetrack; it's part of our community's identity."
– Louis Schwitzer, American engineer and racer. (Paraphrased).

Indianapolis Race, 1913. By Meurisse Press Agency. Source: Bibliothèque nationale de France. Via Wikimedia Commons. Public Domain.

On this day in 1909, the Indianapolis Motor Speedway hosted its first motor race, marking the beginning of a legacy that shaped motorsports culture and the surrounding urban area. Initially built as a testing ground for the emerging automobile industry, the Speedway quickly gained prominence, attracting visitors nationwide. Its success spurred investments in local infrastructure, including better roads, public transit, and visitor amenities, transforming the area into a bustling hub of activity. This development fueled economic growth, reshaped land use, and solidified Indianapolis as the epicenter of motorsports. The Speedway's impact extends beyond racing, demonstrating how large-scale attractions can define city identity, stimulate innovation, and catalyze regional development. Over time, the Indianapolis Motor Speedway has become a lasting symbol of the connections between transportation, culture, and urban planning, illustrating the transformative potential of iconic landmarks in shaping urban landscapes.

How can cities leverage major sporting events and venues to promote sustainable urban development and community identity?

AUGUST 20
1964

CREATION OF THE
COMMUNITY ACTION PROGRAMS

"The War on Poverty is not a struggle simply to support people, but to help them support themselves." – Lyndon B. Johnson. 36th President of the United States.

President Lyndon B. Johnson on the telephone, 1968. Source: LBJ Presidential Library. Public Domain.

On this day in 1964, President Lyndon B. Johnson signed the Economic Opportunity Act into law, launching Community Action Programs (CAPs) as a centerpiece of the War on Poverty. CAPs aim to empower low-income communities by engaging residents directly in decision-making processes to address poverty and inequality. These programs, administered through local agencies, provided critical services such as education, job training, housing assistance, and healthcare, fostering self-sufficiency and community development. This marked a significant shift in federal policy, emphasizing grassroots participation and local control in combating poverty and promoting equity.

While CAPs faced challenges, including political resistance and funding constraints, they were pivotal in addressing systemic inequities and supporting marginalized populations. The legacy of CAPs endures in contemporary community development efforts, demonstrating the transformative power of localized, participatory approaches to creating more equitable and sustainable urban and regional environments.

What role do grassroots community action programs play in fostering equity and resilience in today's urban planning efforts?

BIRTH OF
VINCENT SCULLY

"We have to remember that what we build will shape the lives of those who come after us."
– Vincent Scully. American architectural historian.

Vincent Scully, Professor of Architecture, Yale. By Ben Holloway. Courtesy of Catherine Lynn. From her personal collection, with permission.

On this day in 1920, Vincent Scully was born in New Haven, Connecticut. A transformative voice in architecture and urban planning, Scully profoundly shaped the discourse through his teaching at Yale and his influential writings. Renowned for his inspiring lectures, he championed urban design rooted in human scale, historical continuity, and cultural meaning. At a time when modernist planning often prioritized abstraction and efficiency, Scully advocated for cities that foster community, memory, and connection. His works, including The Shingle Style and American Architecture and Urbanism, underscored the value of traditional urban forms and their capacity to reflect shared histories. Scully's emphasis on place-making helped spark the rise of New Urbanism and advanced the cause of historic preservation. He urged planners and architects to design not just for utility, but for the soul of the city. His legacy endures as a call to create urban environments that are thoughtful, rooted, and responsive to the human experience.

How can Scully's emphasis on human scale and historical context inform current urban planning practices to create more livable and sustainable cities?

AUGUST 22
1974

DEVELOPMENT OF
THE CDBG PROGRAM

"Community development is about empowering local governments to shape their future."
— Gerald Ford. 38th President of the United States.

The Atlanta Beltline, Atlanta, Georgia, USA, 2020. The image shows the multi-use trail and redevelopment project funded in part by CDBG grants, illustrating the transformation of former railway corridors into public space. By Aerial Stock Footage. Licensed.

On this day in 1974, President Gerald Ford signed the Housing and Community Development Act into law, establishing the Community Development Block Grant (CDBG) Program. Administered by the U.S. Department of Housing and Urban Development (HUD), the program consolidated numerous urban aid initiatives into a single, flexible funding source. CDBG grants empower local governments to address diverse community development needs, including affordable housing, infrastructure upgrades, public services, and economic development, focusing on supporting low- and moderate-income residents. By emphasizing local control, the program allows cities and counties to tailor funding to their unique priorities, fostering urban revitalization and long-term growth. Over nearly five decades, the CDBG program has remained one of HUD's most impactful tools for improving urban environments and addressing socioeconomic disparities, serving as a cornerstone of community-focused federal support in the United States.

How can the flexibility of the CDBG program be leveraged to address modern challenges like housing affordability and climate resilience?

JACQUES CARTIER LANDS NEAR QUEBEC CITY

"We came seeking a new land, but met an old world of its own."
– Attributed to Jacques Cartier. French explorer. (Paraphrased).

A perspective view of the City of Quebec, 16th C. Source: Print Collection, The New York Public Library. Public Domain.

On this day in 1541, French explorer Jacques Cartier landed near present-day Quebec City during his third voyage to Canada. Charged with establishing a permanent French colony, Cartier founded Charlesbourg-Royal, one of the earliest European settlements in North America. Despite its failure due to harsh winters, disease, and conflicts with Indigenous peoples, the settlement marked an important attempt at colonization. Cartier's expedition reflected European ambitions for expansion, wealth, and religious conversion, often at great cost to native communities. Though short-lived, the effort foreshadowed the eventual founding of Quebec City by Samuel de Champlain in 1608, which became a major center of French influence in the Americas. Cartier's voyages highlight the complex interactions between exploration, urban settlement, the displacement of Indigenous populations, and the challenges of creating sustainable urban communities in unfamiliar and hostile environments.

How can lessons from early colonial settlements inform modern approaches to urban development in regions with deep Indigenous histories?

AUGUST 24
79 CE

MOUNT VESUVIUS
ERUPTION AND THE PRESERVATION OF POMPEII

"What better way to read the life of the past than in the streets of Pompeii, frozen in its final moment?" – Adapted from historical reflections on Pompeii's significance.

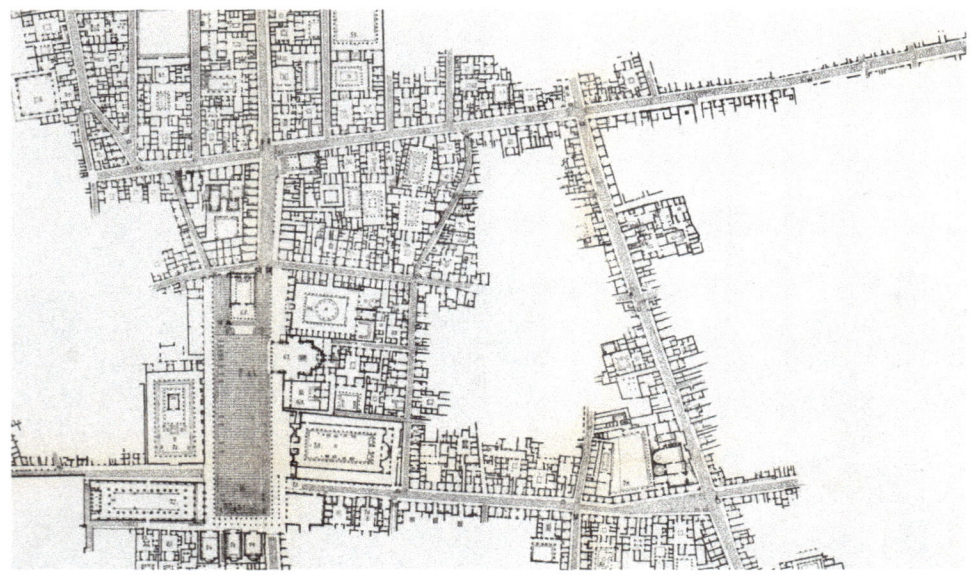

New Plan of the Pompei excavations, 1862. Source: Boston Public Library. Norman B. Leventhal Map & Education Center. Public Domain.

On this day in 79 CE, Mount Vesuvius erupted, burying the Roman cities of Pompeii and Herculaneum under volcanic ash and preserving a remarkably detailed snapshot of ancient urban life. Pompeii, with its planned grid layout, central forum, aqueducts, and mixed-use buildings, exemplifies the sophistication of Roman urban planning and engineering. Its streets, lined with shops, temples, and homes, reveal the vibrant commercial and social dynamics of the Roman Empire. Rediscovered in the 18th century, Pompeii's ruins uncovered vivid frescoes, inscriptions, and everyday objects, offering unparalleled insight into Roman society, architecture, and infrastructure. Though the eruption is traditionally dated to August 24 based on Pliny the Younger's eyewitness account, more recent archaeological evidence, such as an October 17 inscription, suggests a later date. Regardless, Pompeii endures as a powerful symbol of both the resilience and fragility of urban life—capturing the lasting legacy of Roman urbanism and the ever-present threats posed by natural disasters.

How do cities balance preservation of history with modern urban needs, especially when those sites are as fragile as Pompeii?

CREATION OF
THE NATIONAL PARK SERVICE

"National parks are the best idea we ever had. Absolutely American, absolutely democratic, they reflect us at our best." — Wallace Stegner. American historian and novelist.

Nine park rangers called the first rangers of Yosemite National Park, shown mounted on horses lined up in meadow in Yosemite Valley, 1915; with Yosemite Falls in distance. Courtesy of the U.S. National Park Service. Public Domain.

On this day in 1916, President Woodrow Wilson signed the Organic Act, establishing the National Park Service (NPS) within the Department of the Interior. Created to manage and protect the nation's growing number of parks and monuments, the NPS balanced conservation with public access, ensuring natural and cultural treasures could be enjoyed by future generations. Initially responsible for 35 sites, including Yellowstone, Yosemite, and the Grand Canyon, the agency has expanded to manage over 400 sites, ranging from iconic landscapes to historic landmarks. The creation of the NPS was a turning point in environmental stewardship, formalizing the movement to preserve America's natural beauty and cultural heritage. Its innovative park planning and sustainable management model has inspired similar conservation systems worldwide. By promoting education, recreation, and preservation, the NPS has remained a symbol of environmental responsibility, linking the past to the future in protected public spaces.

How can the principles of the National Park Service inspire modern urban park planning and environmental conservation efforts?

AUGUST 26
1542

FRANCISCO DE ORELLANA'S COMPLETION OF AMAZON RIVER NAVIGATION

"The Amazon has been occupied by Indigenous people for over 12,000 years."
– Science Panel for the Amazon

Amazon River. By Marco. Licensed

On this day in 1542, Francisco de Orellana reached the Atlantic Ocean, completing the first known navigation of the Amazon River. Initially part of Gonzalo Pizarro's expedition in search of El Dorado, Orellana's journey became a landmark exploration of the vast Amazon basin. His voyage introduced Europeans to the region's immense waterways and diverse indigenous populations, though European biases and exaggerations shaped his accounts. This expedition laid the groundwork for further colonization, urban development, and exploitation of the Amazon's resources, often at significant cost to native communities and ecosystems. Settlements along the Amazon, developed to capitalize on its resources, displaced indigenous populations and reshaped the region's landscape. Orellana's journey represents the dual legacy of exploration: advancing geographic knowledge while catalyzing colonization, ecological disruption, and long-term challenges for native societies and environmental sustainability in one of the world's most vital regions.

How can modern urban planning in historically indigenous regions balance development with the preservation of native cultures and rights?

DISCOVERY OF
THE TRANSMISSION OF YELLOW FEVER

"The health of the people is really the foundation upon which all their happiness and all their powers as a state depend." – Benjamin Disraeli. British Prime Minister and writer.

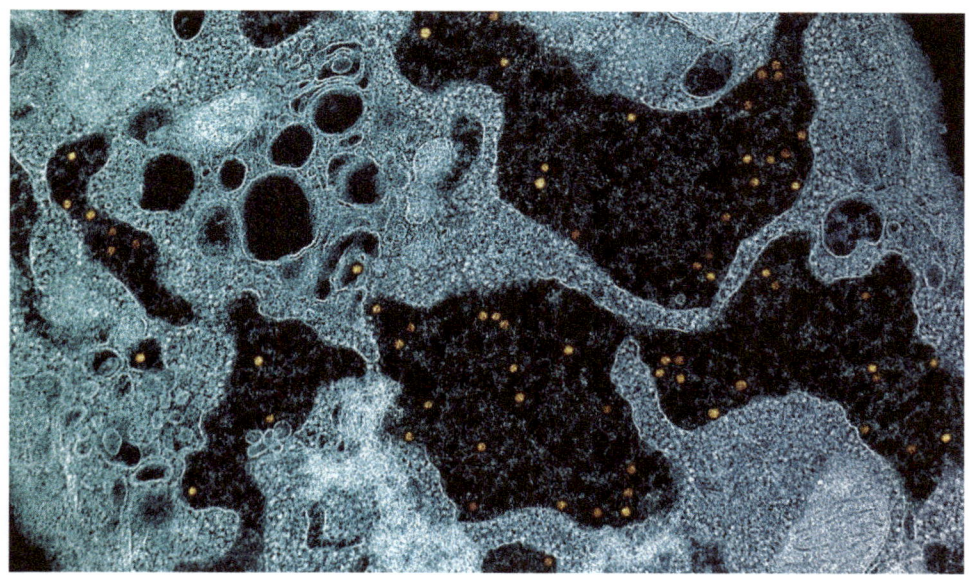

Yellow fever virus. By National Institute of Allergy and Infectious Diseases (NIAID). Via Wikimedia Commons. CC BY 2.0

On this day in 1900, U.S. Army physician James Carroll voluntarily allowed an infected mosquito to feed on him, contracting a severe yellow fever. His courageous self-experimentation, part of research led by Walter Reed, conclusively proved that mosquitoes transmit yellow fever. This groundbreaking discovery revolutionized public health and urban planning, prompting widespread mosquito control initiatives. Cities such as Havana and New Orleans launched aggressive sanitation and vector-control campaigns, including draining standing water, fumigating homes, and improving waste management. These efforts significantly reduced yellow fever outbreaks, saving countless lives and enhancing the livability of urban areas. The research underscored the vital role of pest control in safeguarding public health, particularly in densely populated cities vulnerable to disease outbreaks. Carroll's sacrifice and the resulting advancements continue to influence urban health practices, highlighting the importance of integrating disease prevention into city planning and management.

How can modern cities build on past successes in pest control to address contemporary public health challenges?

AUGUST 28
2008

OPENING OF
THE SHANGHAI WORLD FINANCIAL CENTER

"A skyline is a city's signature, written in steel and glass."
– Attributed to Kohn Pedersen Fox (KPF). (Paraphrased).

Shanghai city skyline. By Gui Yong Nian. Licensed

On this day in 2008, the Shanghai World Financial Center (SWFC) officially opened, symbolizing China's rapid economic transformation and urban ambition. Standing at 492 meters (1,614.2 feet), it was the second tallest building in the world, with the highest roof height globally. Designed by Kohn Pedersen Fox, the 100-story tower features a distinctive trapezoidal opening near the top, nicknamed "the bottle opener," which reduces wind resistance. Initially planned for 1997, construction was delayed by the Asian Financial Crisis and design changes. Located in Pudong's Lujiazui Financial District, the SWFC is a mixed-use skyscraper, housing offices, retail spaces, a luxury hotel, and observation decks with panoramic views of Shanghai's skyline. The building reflects Shanghai's emergence as a global financial hub and was named the Best Tall Building Overall for 2008 by the Council on Tall Buildings and Urban Habitat (CTBUH).

How do globalized financial hubs like Shanghai influence local culture and urban identity?

AUGUST 29
2005

HURRICANE KATRINA
REACHES THE GULF COAST

"We can rebuild homes, but we must also rebuild hope and equality in our cities."
– Barack Obama. 44th President of the United States.

Aftermath of Hurricane Katrina in New Orleans, showing a flooded residential street. The image highlights the impact of extreme weather on urban areas and the importance of disaster resilience in city planning. By Bernard. Licensed

On this day in 2005, Hurricane Katrina made landfall along the U.S. Gulf Coast, leaving a trail of destruction in cities like New Orleans, Gulfport, and Biloxi. The storm caused catastrophic flooding, with levee failures inundating 80% of New Orleans, highlighting critical vulnerabilities in urban infrastructure and emergency response systems. Over a million residents were displaced, and the disaster exposed deep racial and socioeconomic disparities in disaster preparedness and recovery efforts. Katrina's impact reshaped the urban fabric of affected areas, altering economies, demographics, and community structures. The disaster sparked national and global discussions about climate resilience, urban planning, and equitable disaster management, emphasizing the urgent need for infrastructure investments and policies prioritizing vulnerable populations. Hurricane Katrina remains a stark reminder of cities' profound challenges in adapting to climate change and ensuring sustainable, inclusive disaster preparedness and recovery strategies.

How can cities better prepare for and recover from climate-related disasters in the face of increasing risks?

FOUNDING OF HOUSTON, TEXAS

"Houston has always been a city of innovation and opportunity."
– Sylvester Turner. Mayor of Houston.

Bird's Eye View Of the City of Houston, Texas, 1873. By Augustus Koch. Source: Published by J. J. Stoner, Madison, Wis. Center for American History, The University of Texas at Austin. Via Wikimedia Commons. Public Domain.

On this day in 1836, the city of Houston was founded by brothers Augustus Chapman Allen and John Kirby Allen. Named after General Sam Houston, a hero of the Texas Revolution, the city was strategically located near Buffalo Bayou as a key transportation and trading hub in the Republic of Texas. Initially planned as a settlement, Houston's grid layout reflected early American city-building principles, prioritizing accessibility and economic development. The city's growth was fueled by its pivotal role in regional trade, agriculture, and, later, the booming oil and energy industries. Over the decades, Houston evolved into one of the largest and most diverse cities in the United States, showcasing adaptability in urban planning to accommodate rapid expansion and economic shifts. Today, it is a global metropolis, highlighting the importance of resilience, innovation, and strategic planning in urban development.

How can the lessons from Houston's early growth inform sustainable planning for rapidly expanding cities today?

ZEPPELIN PATENTS HIS NAVIGABLE BALLOON

"Man is not made for crawling. He has wings."
– Count Ferdinand von Zeppelin. German general and inventor of the rigid airship

Postcard: Zeppelin in St Gallen, pre-1934. Author unknown. Via Wikimedia Commons. Public Domain.

On this day in 1895, Count Ferdinand von Zeppelin patented his navigable balloon, sparking visions of a future where cities embraced airship travel as a core part of urban life. These massive airships, seen as marvels of innovation, inspired utopian ideas of skyscrapers crowned with zeppelin ports, transforming city skylines into bustling hubs of vertical transportation. Imagine urban centers where airships dock seamlessly atop towering structures, connecting cities across continents with gravity-defying ease. This vision celebrated the integration of technology and urban planning, emphasizing how advancements in transportation could reshape cities into dynamic, interconnected hubs. While airplanes eventually supplanted airships for practicality and speed, the dream of integrating aviation into urban infrastructure stands as a testament to humanity's boundless imagination. Zeppelin's invention remains a symbol of how technology can inspire ambitious urban designs that push the boundaries of possibility and redefine the future of cities.

How could reimagining airships and vertical transport systems influence the design of future sustainable cities?

SEPTEMBER 1
1903

CONSTRUCTION BEGINS ON LETCHWORTH GARDEN CITY

"Town and country must be married, and out of this joyous union will spring a new hope, a new life, a new civilization." — Ebenezer Howard. English urban planner.

Aerial photograph showing Broadway Gardens at the center of Letchworth Garden City, England. Conceived as the town's civic and social heart, the garden anchors the radial layout and embodies Ebenezer Howard's vision of integrating green space into everyday urban life. By Nasim. Licensed

On this day in 1903, First Garden City Limited was established to purchase land and begin construction on Letchworth Garden City in England, the world's first garden city. Conceived by urban planner Ebenezer Howard, Letchworth brought to life the vision outlined in his influential book To-Morrow: A Peaceful Path to Real Reform (1898). Howard's model aimed to combine the benefits of urban and rural living, creating a self-sufficient community with designated areas for housing, industry, and green spaces. Letchworth prioritized community well-being, environmental harmony, and sustainable development, serving as a prototype for the Garden City Movement.

This revolutionary approach influenced urban planning worldwide, inspiring developments like Radburn, New Jersey, and Greenbelt, Maryland, and shaping the principles of modern sustainable planning. Letchworth's legacy endures as a model for integrating nature, housing, and industry, offering innovative solutions to contemporary issues like urban sprawl and environmental challenges.

What lessons from Letchworth Garden City can be applied to creating sustainable and livable communities in today's urban planning efforts?

THE GREAT FIRE OF LONDON BEGINS

"London rises from its ashes with greater splendor than ever before."
– John Evelyn, diarist and observer of the fire.

Print of the Great fire of London, 1666. Image scanned from Robert Chambers' Book of Days, 1st edition. Via Wikimedia Commons. Public Domain.

On this day in 1666, the Great Fire of London began in Thomas Farriner's bakery on Pudding Lane, quickly spreading through the densely packed medieval city. Over four days, the fire consumed approximately 13,000 homes, 87 churches, including the iconic St. Paul's Cathedral, and numerous public buildings, leaving an estimated 70,000 people homeless. The disaster, while devastating, became a catalyst for significant urban transformation. Plans emerged for wider streets, the implementation of stricter fire codes, and the widespread use of fire-resistant materials like brick and stone. Architect Christopher Wren played a central role in the city's reconstruction, designing key landmarks that redefined London's skyline, including the new St. Paul's Cathedral and several churches. The Great Fire marked a turning point in London's history and demonstrated the potential of resilience and innovation in urban planning to rebuild and modernize cities after disasters.

How can cities recovering from disasters use reconstruction as an opportunity to innovate while preserving cultural and historical significance?

SEPTEMBER 3
1783

THE TREATY OF PARIS: REDEFINITION OF URBAN CENTERS

"Peace and independence are inseparable; only by standing united can our cities flourish."
– Inspired by John Adams' writings. U.S. negotiator of the Treaty of Paris.

American Commissioners - Preliminary Peace Agreement with Great Britain, 1783-1784 (British commissioners refused to pose; the painting was never finished). London, England. By Benjamin West. Source: Winterthur Museum Garden and Library. Via Wikimedia Commons. Public Domain.

On this day in 1783, the Treaty of Paris was signed, officially ending the American Revolutionary War and recognizing the independence of the United States. This monumental agreement marked a political milestone and reshaped the trajectory of urban centers across North America. Cities such as New York, Boston, and Philadelphia transitioned from colonial outposts to vital hubs of governance, commerce, and culture for the burgeoning nation. The treaty's resolution also highlighted contrasting developments in British-held cities like Montreal and Quebec City, which continued under colonial rule. Additionally, the recognition of U.S. sovereignty paved the way for westward expansion, fostering the establishment of new towns and urban centers that would shape the nation's growth and identity. The Treaty of Paris serves as a reminder of the interplay between political change and urban development, setting the stage for the United States' transformation into a network of thriving cities.

How can cities embrace moments of political transformation to reshape their roles as centers of governance, culture, and innovation in a changing world?

BIRTH OF
DANIEL BURNHAM

"Make no little plans; they have no magic to stir men's blood."
— Daniel Burnham. American architect and urban planner.

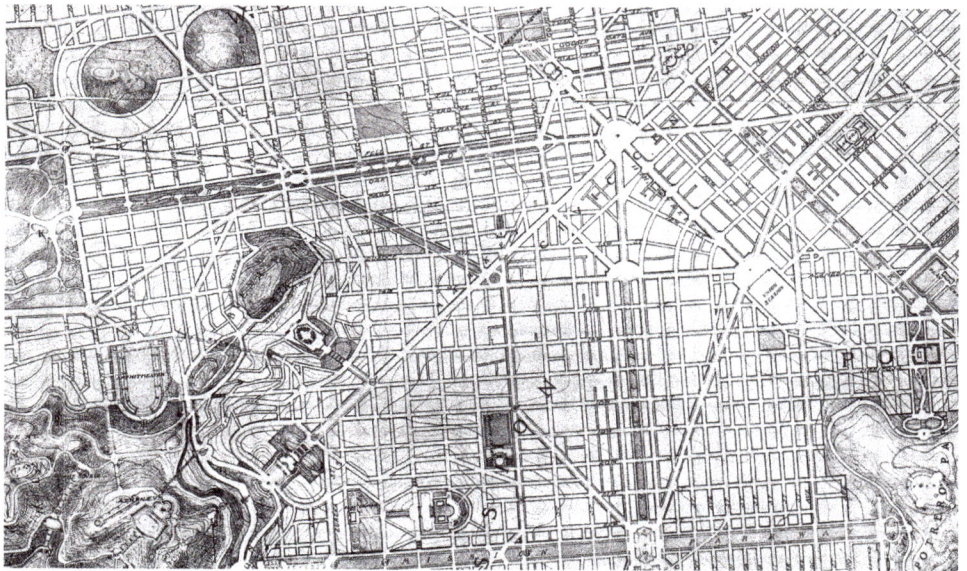

Plan of San Francisco. Recommended report to the Association for the Improvement and Adornment of San Francisco. By D.H. Burnham, 1905. Source: David Rumsey Historical Map Collection. Via Wikimedia Commons. Public Domain.

On this day in 1846, Daniel Burnham, a pioneering architect and urban planner, was born in Henderson, New York. Widely regarded as one of the founding figures of modern urban planning in the United States, Burnham championed the idea that cities should not only serve practical needs but also uplift the human spirit through beauty and order. As a key leader of the City Beautiful movement, he promoted the integration of monumental architecture, formal boulevards, and expansive public spaces to instill civic pride and social harmony. Burnham's most enduring legacy is the Plan of Chicago (1909), co-authored with Edward H. Bennett, which laid out a visionary blueprint for the city's development, including lakefront access, green park systems, civic centers, and efficient transportation networks. This plan became a model for future city planning efforts across the country. Burnham also served as chief architect of the 1893 World's Columbian Exposition in Chicago, whose Beaux-Arts design profoundly influenced American urban aesthetics. His belief that "Make no little plans" continues to inspire planners toward ambitious, human-centered urban visions.

How can Burnham's legacy inspire bold urban planning projects in contemporary cities?

SEPTEMBER 5
1882

FIRST U.S.
LABOR DAY PARADE HELD IN NEW YORK CITY

"The strength of a nation lies in the hands of its workers." – Samuel Gompers (Paraphrased). American labor union leader and founder of the American Federation of Labor (AFL).

Illustration of the first American Labor parade held in New York City on September 5, 1882 as it appeared in the September 16, 1882 issue of Frank Leslie's Illustrated Newspaper. By Staff Illustrator. Source: Frank Leslie's Illustrated Newspaper, 1882. Via Wikimedia Commons. Public Domain.

On this day in 1882, the first Labor Day parade took place in New York City, organized by the Central Labor Union to celebrate workers' contributions to the nation's economic and social progress. Thousands of workers, unions, and their families marched through the city, demanding fair labor practices, better wages, and improved working conditions. Held during a period of rapid industrialization and urban growth, the parade also underscored the need for cities to prioritize public health, green spaces, and humane environments amidst the challenges of overcrowding and poor working conditions. Labor Day became a national holiday in 1894, reflecting the critical role of workers in shaping modern cities and advancing urban progress. The day serves as a reminder of the enduring connection between labor rights and the development of livable, equitable urban environments where communities can thrive.

How can the legacy of Labor Day inspire cities to prioritize equitable living and working conditions for their residents?

DEATH OF CLARENCE PERRY

"The neighborhood unit is a plan for creating communities that foster strong relationships and support self-expression." – Clarence Perry, American urban planner. (Adapted).

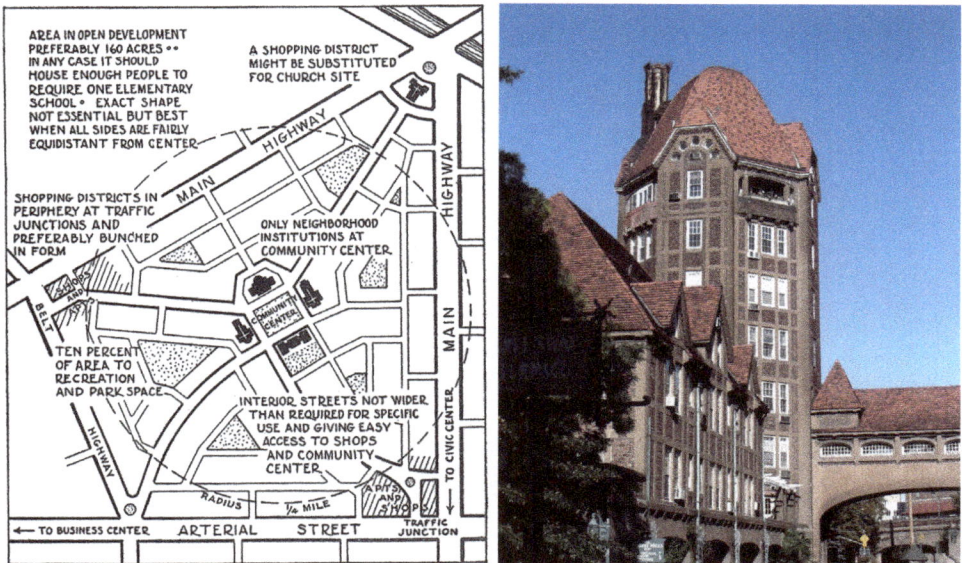

Left: Diagram of Clarence Perry's Neighbourhood unit, 1929. By Clarence Perry / Committee on Regional Plan of New York and Its Environs. Source: New York Regional Survey, Volume 7. PDM 1.0. Right: Forest Hills Gardens – An early example of Clarence Perry's neighborhood unit, By Юкатан CC BY-SA 3.0

On this day in 1944, Clarence Arthur Perry, a pioneering urban planner and sociologist, died in New Rochelle, New York. Perry is best remembered for his influential Neighborhood Unit Concept, first introduced in 1929 as part of the Regional Plan of New York and Its Environs. This model proposed organizing urban neighborhoods around elementary schools, with clearly defined boundaries, limited through-traffic, and essential services such as shops, parks, and community facilities within walking distance. Perry's vision aimed to foster community identity, safety, and social cohesion by emphasizing human-scaled design and walkability. The Neighborhood Unit became a foundational idea in 20th-century planning, shaping suburban development and inspiring planners worldwide. However, the model has also drawn criticism for inadvertently reinforcing socio-economic segregation and contributing to car-dependent urban sprawl. Despite its limitations, Perry's work remains a vital reference in contemporary planning discourse, reminding practitioners of the importance of community-centered design in creating inclusive, sustainable, and livable cities.

How can Perry's vision of walkable, community-centered neighborhoods be adapted to tackle modern challenges like sustainability and urban density?

SEPTEMBER 7
1630

FOUNDING OF
BOSTON, MASSACHUSETTS

"Boston is not just a city, it's an idea."
– Martin Luther King Jr. American civil rights leader and minister.

Bonner's map depicting Boston before centuries of landfill transformed its coastline., 1723-1733. Source: Boston Public Library. Norman B. Leventhal Map & Education Center; Bonner, John. Via Wikimedia Commons. Public Domain.

On this day in 1630 (Julian calendar), Boston, Massachusetts, was founded by Puritan settlers on the Shawmut Peninsula. The date reflects the Julian calendar, which was in use at the time. Named after Boston in Lincolnshire, England, the settlement quickly became a key center for commerce, governance, and religious life in the American colonies. Its early urban form followed English town planning traditions, featuring a central meetinghouse and Boston Common—a public green space still in use today. Boston's layout and civic institutions laid the groundwork for its emergence as a leading city during the American Revolution and a lasting symbol of democratic ideals. The city's historical architecture, including sites like Faneuil Hall and the Old North Church, preserves its colonial legacy while coexisting with contemporary development. As Boston has grown, it has become a national model for integrating historic preservation with modern infrastructure, transportation, and housing strategies. The city's founding marks the beginning of a remarkable trajectory as one of America's most influential and continuously evolving urban centers.

How can historical cities like Boston adapt to modern urban challenges while preserving their cultural legacy?

FOUNDING OF
ST. AUGUSTINE, FLORIDA

"This is the fairest land my eyes have ever beheld."
– Pedro Menéndez de Avilés. Spanish admiral and founder of St. Augustine, Florida.

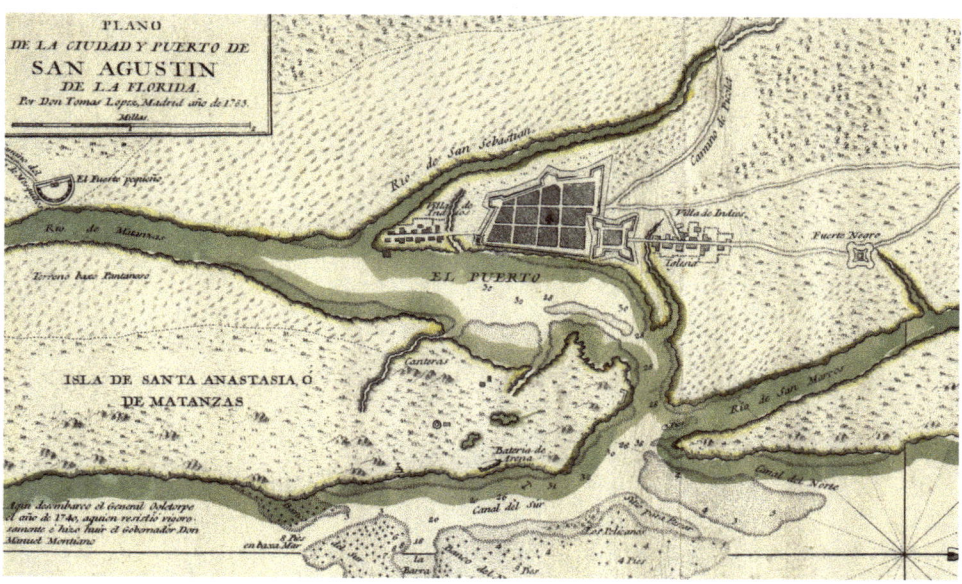

Plan of the City and Port of St. Augustin, FL. 1780. By Tomas Lopez de Vargas Machuca. Source: State Library and Archives of Florida. Via Wikimedia Commons. Public Domain.

On this day in 1565, Spanish explorer Pedro Menéndez de Avilés founded St. Augustine, Florida, making it the oldest continuously occupied European-established city in the United States. Established as a military outpost and trade hub, St. Augustine played a key role in Spain's colonial ambitions in North America. The city's design showcased Spanish colonial urban planning principles, including a central plaza, a grid street system, and robust defensive structures, later exemplified by the Castillo de San Marcos. These elements ensured both functionality and protection while fostering a sense of community. Over the centuries, St. Augustine has preserved much of its historic architecture and urban layout, offering a living example of early colonial urbanism. Today, the city remains a vibrant cultural destination, attracting visitors intrigued by its rich history and enduring heritage while highlighting the influence of Spanish colonial planning on American urban development.

How can cities like St. Augustine balance the preservation of historic urban forms with the demands of modern growth and tourism?

SEPTEMBER 9
1965

DEPARTMENT OF HOUSING AND URBAN DEVELOPMENT LAUNCHES

"We seek a decent home and a suitable living environment for every American family."
— Lyndon B. Johnson. 36th President of the United States.

Riverwalk affordable housing apartments, Roosevelt Island, Manhattan, 2019. The image showcases HUD-supported housing initiatives designed to promote equitable urban development, with a focus on mixed-income communities in high-cost cities. By Tdorante10. Via Wikimedia Commons. CC BY-SA 4.0

On this day in 1965, the Department of Housing and Urban Development (HUD) was officially established as a Cabinet-level agency under President Lyndon B. Johnson's Great Society agenda. HUD was tasked with addressing housing inequality, urban poverty, and the challenges of rapidly growing cities. Its core responsibilities included administering public housing programs, enforcing fair housing laws to combat racial discrimination, and supporting initiatives like the Community Development Block Grant (CDBG) to revitalize urban areas. HUD also promoted affordable housing and worked to improve living conditions in underserved communities. Despite facing budget constraints, policy controversies, and debates over urban renewal's social impact, HUD became a central force in shaping American housing and urban policy. It continues to influence urban development through programs promoting equitable access to housing and sustainable urban planning, remaining a key player in efforts to create inclusive and thriving communities nationwide.

How can HUD adapt its programs and policies to address today's housing crises and promote equitable urban development?

BIRTH OF THOMAS ADAMS

"Planning must be both local and regional, as cities are not isolated entities."
— Thomas Adams. British urban planner and regional planning pioneer.

Network map of the City of Ottawa. By Kostiantyn. Licensed.

On this day in 1871, Thomas Adams, a pioneering figure in regional planning in Canada and Britain, was born. A visionary advocate for integrating urban and rural development, Adams emphasized the need for cohesive policies addressing the interdependencies between cities and their surrounding regions. His work focused on balancing population growth, economic development, and environmental preservation, laying the foundation for modern regional planning practices. As the first President of the Town Planning Institute of Canada, Adams played a pivotal role in establishing infrastructure, housing, and agricultural land protection frameworks. His influence extended to significant projects like the National Capital Plan for Ottawa and planning guidelines in the UK. Adams' legacy continues to shape contemporary regional governance, promoting that urban centers and rural areas function as interconnected ecosystems, essential for sustainable development and harmonious growth.

How can regional planning balance urban expansion and the preservation of natural resources today?

SEPTEMBER 11
1921

NAHALAL, THE FIRST
JEWISH MOSHAV, IS ESTABLISHED

"The land is small, but every inch is imbued with meaning and care."
– Richard Kauffmann. German-Jewish architect and planner of early Zionist settlements.

Nahalal, Moshav in northern Israel. Layout devised by Richard Kauffmann. By ZeevStein. Via Wikimedia Commons. CC BY-SA 4.0

On this day in 1921, Nahalal, the first moshav, was founded in Palestine—now Israel—in the Jezreel Valley, also known as the Valley of Esdraelon. Designed by architect Richard Kauffmann, Nahalal featured a distinctive circular layout with communal facilities such as schools and meeting halls at the center, surrounded by individual agricultural plots radiating outward. This spatial arrangement symbolized equality, shared responsibility, and a deep connection to the land. Unlike kibbutzim, moshavim allowed for private farming alongside cooperative decision-making, balancing personal initiative with collective support. Nahalal became a model for Zionist rural and urban planning,

embodying the ideals of self-sufficiency, sustainability, and social cohesion. Its innovative design inspired the development of other moshavim and kibbutzim throughout the region, shaping the spatial and social fabric of modern Israel. Nahalal's legacy underscores the power of intentional planning in cultivating resilient, inclusive, and productive communities.

How can the principles of cooperative living and sustainable design seen in Nahalal inspire modern urban and rural planning?

VIENNA'S TRANSFORMATION OF DEFENSIVE SPACES

"The greatness of a city lies in its ability to reclaim and redefine its history."
– Camillo Sitte, urban theorist and advocate for Vienna's planning traditions

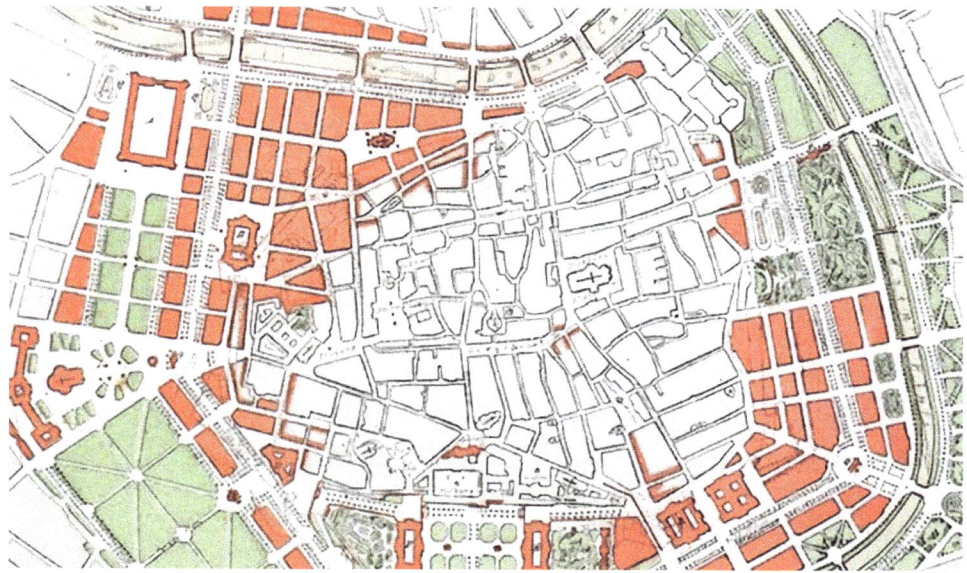

Approved plan for Vienna's expansion, 1860. By K. K. Hof - und Staatsdruckerei in Wien. Source: Wien Museum. Via Wikimedia Commons. Public Domain.

On this day in 1683, Vienna successfully repelled the Ottoman Empire during the Battle of Vienna, marking a major turning point in European history and halting Ottoman expansion into Central Europe. The prolonged siege led to the construction of extensive military defenses, including thick walls, bastions, and cleared zones—features typical of 17th-century military urbanism. These fortifications influenced the city's growth for more than a century. By the mid-19th century, with the military threat gone, Emperor Franz Joseph I ordered their demolition and commissioned the creation of the Ringstrasse, a grand circular boulevard encircling the old city. This bold urban transformation reimagined former military zones as spaces for civic pride and cultural life. Lined with monumental architecture such as the Vienna State Opera and the Parliament, the Ringstraße became a model of integrated urban design. Today, Vienna's historic center, including the Ringstraße, is a UNESCO World Heritage Site, symbolizing how cities can turn legacies of conflict into assets for modern urban identity and cohesion.

How can cities learn from Vienna's example to transform spaces of conflict or obsolete infrastructure into thriving areas for public and cultural life?

SEPTEMBER 13
1898

HANNIBAL GOODWIN PATENTS CELLULOID PHOTOGRAPHIC FILM

"The camera is an instrument that teaches people how to see without a camera."
– Dorothea Lange. American documentary photographer and photojournalist.

Celluloid film negative. By Cafera13. Licensed

On this day in 1898, Hannibal Goodwin was awarded a patent for celluloid photographic film, a groundbreaking invention that revolutionized the photography and film industries. The flexible and durable nature of celluloid enabled capturing moving images, laying the foundation for cinema and modern mass media. This innovation profoundly impacted urban life, enabling the documentation of cityscapes and the everyday experiences of urban dwellers, shaping how cities were represented and understood. The rise of cinema, made possible by celluloid film, transformed urban centers into cultural hubs, with theaters becoming spaces for entertainment and social interaction. Additionally, photography and advertising flourished, influencing how cities marketed themselves and creating a shared visual culture. Goodwin's invention not only reshaped industries but also contributed to the cultural and social dynamics of urban spaces, making cities central to the development and consumption of visual media.

How has the ability to document urban life through photography and film influenced the evolution of cities and their cultural identity?

PUBLICATION OF
KARL MARX'S DAS KAPITAL

"The conditions of the working class in the cities are the visible truth of capitalism."
– Karl Marx. German philosopher, economist, and revolutionary socialist.

Postage stamps from GERMANY, DDR, showing a portrait of the philosopher and political economist Karl Marx. With Manifestos of the Communist Party and Das Kapital. Circa 1968. By Zabanski. Licensed

On this day in 1867, the first volume of Karl Marx's Das Kapital was published in Hamburg, Germany, offering a foundational critique of industrial capitalism. While primarily an economic analysis, the work profoundly impacts urban planning and city-building by exposing the exploitative conditions prevalent in 19th-century urban centers. Marx detailed the severe inequality, overcrowded housing, and unsanitary living conditions workers face in rapidly industrializing cities, fueling labor movements and calls for urban reform. His insights into class struggle and economic disparity have shaped discussions about social justice and informed approaches to equitable urban development. Das Kapital continues to influence debates about the role of public policy in addressing inequality, particularly in housing, infrastructure, and access to resources in cities. Marx's critique underscores the importance of planning cities prioritizing fairness and sustainability, ensuring they serve all inhabitants rather than perpetuating economic divides.

How can Marx's critiques of inequality in industrial cities inform urban planners working to address modern issues like affordable housing and homelessness?

SEPTEMBER 15
1821

CENTRAL AMERICAN INDEPENDENCE AND THE TRANSFORMATION OF CITIES

"The city is a reflection of its people and their aspirations, evolving with each new era of independence." – Inspired by Manuel José Arce's advocacy, Central American leader.

Market place. Antigua, former capital of Guatemala, c. 1880. By Maudslay, Alfred Percival. Source: The New York Public Library. Public Domain.

On this day in 1821, the countries of Central America—Guatemala, Honduras, El Salvador, Nicaragua, and Costa Rica—declared independence from Spain, marking a transformative moment in the region's history. Urban centers like Guatemala City and San Salvador, once Spanish colonial administrative hubs, began evolving into capitals of newly independent nations. The colonial grid layouts, characterized by plazas, cathedrals, and governmental buildings, were adapted to reflect sovereignty's political and cultural aspirations. Independence spurred the construction of new government buildings, monuments, and public spaces, which reshaped these cities' identities and symbolized national pride. However, this transition also brought challenges as Central American cities grappled with defining their roles in the post-colonial era. Today, these capitals strive to balance the preservation of their colonial heritage with the pressures of rapid urbanization and social inequality, embodying the enduring complexities of independence in their urban landscapes.

How can post-colonial cities strike a balance between preserving their heritage and adapting to the demands of modern urban growth?

INAUGURATION OF INDEPENDENCE DAY CELEBRATIONS AT THE ZÓCALO

"The Zócalo is the heart of Mexico, where history, culture, and the people converge."
– Carlos Fuentes. Mexican writer and diplomat. (Paraphrased).

Constitution Square (Zócalo), Mexico City, Mexico. The image depicts the historic heart of Mexico City, a key civic space used for political gatherings, cultural events, and public life. By A Medvedkov. Licensed

On this day in 1825, Mexico held its first large-scale Independence Day celebration at the Zócalo in Mexico City, officially commemorating the nation's liberation from Spanish colonial rule. Organized under President Guadalupe Victoria, the event established a patriotic tradition that continues to this day. The Zócalo—Mexico's political and ceremonial heart—was chosen as the symbolic center of the festivities, reinforcing its role as a space for national identity and civic unity. The celebration introduced enduring rituals, most notably the reenactment of the Grito de Dolores, Miguel Hidalgo's 1810 call to arms. Each year on the night of September 15th, the President of Mexico delivers the "cry for independence" from the National Palace balcony, followed by fireworks, music, and jubilant gatherings. A military parade the next day further emphasizes national pride and sovereignty. This celebration highlights the enduring power of urban public space—especially the Zócalo—as a stage for historical memory, collective expression, and the ongoing shaping of civic culture.

How do large public spaces like the Zócalo help shape and preserve a nation's collective memory and identity through annual rituals?

SEPTEMBER 17
1787

SIGNING OF THE U.S. CONSTITUTION AND THE VISION FOR WASHINGTON, D.C.

"A city ought to be designed to inspire its citizens, to represent the ideals of its nation, and to be worthy of its name." – Pierre Charles L'Enfant. French-American architect and planner. (Adapted).

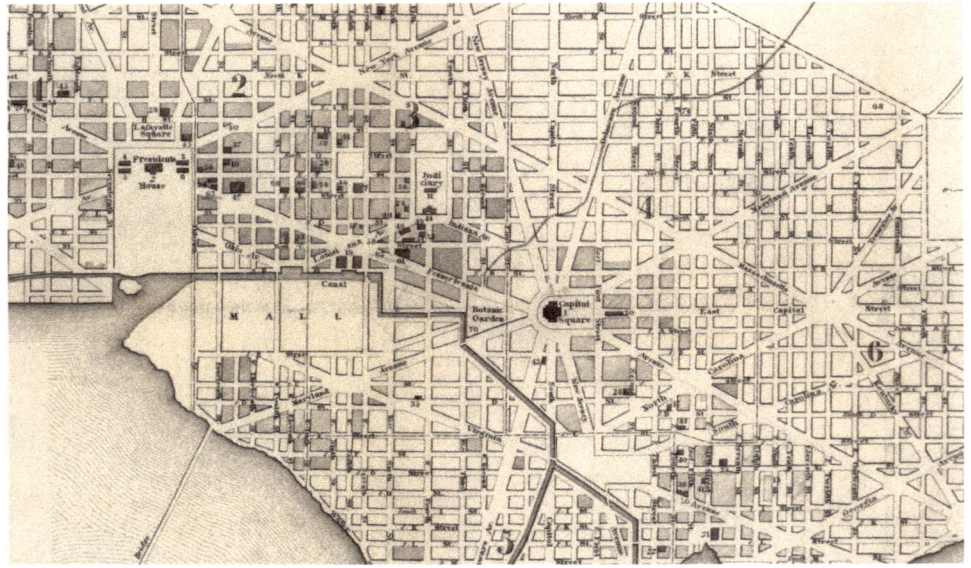

1845 Plan of Washington. Published in [Philadelphia? : s.n.], 1845. Retrieved from the Library of Congress. Public Domain.

On this day in 1787, the United States Constitution was signed in Philadelphia, establishing the framework for the nation's government and laying the groundwork for creating Washington, D.C., the nation's capital. Authorized by the Residence Act of 1790, Washington, D.C., was planned in 1791 by Pierre Charles L'Enfant, who envisioned a city that symbolized democracy and unity. Influenced by Enlightenment ideals, L'Enfant's design featured grand avenues radiating from key public spaces, monumental landmarks such as the Capitol and White House, and a grid layout punctuated by open spaces. These elements reflected the principles of governance and national identity enshrined in the Constitution. Over time, Washington, D.C., has evolved into a global symbol of democracy and civic ideals. Its design remains a powerful example of how urban planning can embody political values, uniting form and function to represent a nation's aspirations.

How can the design of national capitals reflect the values of their societies while adapting to the needs of modern urban life?

THE ATLANTA COMPROMISE SPEECH

"In all things that are purely social we can be as separate as the fingers, yet one as the hand in all things essential to mutual progress." – Booker T. Washington. American educator and leader.

Dr. Booker T. Washington at desk. Author unknown. Source: Washington, Booker T. (1903) The Successful Training of the Negro, New York City: Doubleday, Page & Company. Via Wikimedia Commons. Public Domain.

On this day in 1895, Booker T. Washington delivered his iconic "Atlanta Compromise" speech at the Cotton States and International Exposition in Atlanta, Georgia. Addressing a racially divided audience, Washington advocated for African Americans to prioritize economic progress and vocational education as practical paths to uplift rather than seeking immediate social and political equality. While controversial, the speech underscored the economic potential of Southern cities in creating opportunities for African Americans during the post-Reconstruction era. Washington's message sparked a national dialogue about race relations, labor, and urban growth, highlighting how cities could serve as hubs for economic and educational advancement despite systemic barriers. The speech remains significant for its nuanced take on racial equity challenges, offering insights into the historical intersections of urban policy, education, and social justice that continue to influence discussions on inclusive urban development.

How can cities address the historical legacies of inequality while fostering equitable access to education, housing, and economic opportunities?

SEPTEMBER 19
1985

MEXICO CITY EARTHQUAKE:
URBAN DESTRUCTION AND RESILIENCE

"The 1985 earthquake shook more than just buildings; it shook the soul of Mexico City, awakening a spirit of solidarity and resilience." – Carlos Monsiváis, Mexican writer.

Mexico City. Aftermath of the Earthquake. 1985. By Gobierno de la Ciudad de México. Source: Museo Archivo de la Fotografía Mexico. Via Wikimedia Commons. Public Domain.

On this day in 1985, a catastrophic earthquake struck Mexico City, registering 8.1 on the Richter scale and causing widespread devastation. Approximately 10,000 lives were lost, thousands were injured, and hundreds of buildings—including hospitals, schools, and housing complexes—collapsed. The disaster revealed significant vulnerabilities in urban infrastructure, particularly in older and poorly constructed buildings, highlighting the urgent need for improved seismic safety. However, the tragedy also showcased the strength of grassroots movements, as citizens organized rescue efforts and demanded accountability in urban planning and disaster preparedness. In response, Mexico City implemented stricter building codes, enhanced emergency response systems, and introduced policies to mitigate future risks. These reforms transformed the city into a global model of resilience, demonstrating how urban centers can adapt and improve after natural disasters. The 1985 earthquake remains a pivotal moment in urban history, underscoring the importance of proactive planning and community engagement.

How can cities ensure their infrastructure and urban design are resilient to natural disasters while fostering a culture of preparedness and solidarity among citizens?

ROME BECOMES
THE CAPITAL OF A UNIFIED ITALY

"Rome is the city of echoes, the city of illusions, and the city of yearning."
– Giotto di Bondone. Italian painter and architect.

The outer face facade of the Porta Pia, a city gate in the Aurelian Walls of Rome, designed by Virginio Vespignani. By Debbie Ann Powell. Licensed

On this day in 1870, Italian forces captured Rome during the Breaching of the Porta Pia, ending centuries of Papal rule and incorporating the city into the Kingdom of Italy. This event marked the final act of the Italian Unification (Risorgimento) and established Rome as the capital of a unified Italy. Urban planners faced the monumental task of transforming Rome into a modern capital while respecting its unparalleled historical and religious legacy. In the following decades, the city underwent significant changes, including the development of administrative buildings, public squares, and modern infrastructure to support its new role. Yet, planners also worked to preserve Rome's ancient monuments and religious landmarks, maintaining its unique character. Today, Rome is a remarkable synthesis of ancient and contemporary elements, exemplifying the challenges and opportunities of balancing historical preservation with the demands of modern urban life.

How can historic cities like Rome adapt to the demands of modern governance and infrastructure while preserving their cultural and architectural heritage?

LONDON CELEBRATES CAR-FREE DAY

"The car has become the carapace, the protective and aggressive shell, of urban and suburban man." – Marshall McLuhan. Canadian philosopher and media theorist.

London's financial district (City of London), UK, showing dense urban development, contemporary architecture, and the concentration of global financial institutions. By IRStone. Licensed

On this day in 2019, London marked Car-Free Day by closing over 16 miles of central roads to traffic, transforming the city into a pedestrian-friendly space. The initiative aimed to reduce air pollution, encourage walking and cycling, and showcase the potential of streets designed for people rather than cars. More than 20,000 residents and visitors participated, highlighting widespread interest in rethinking urban mobility. The event aligned with London's broader goals to combat climate change, improve air quality, and promote sustainable transportation options. The day fostered conversations about reducing automobile dependency and prioritizing greener urban infrastructure by offering a glimpse of a car-free future. Car-Free Day, celebrated in cities worldwide, continues to inspire innovative approaches to urban planning, emphasizing walkability, public transit, and cycling as key components of more sustainable and livable cities. London's participation underscored its commitment to addressing climate and mobility challenges through bold, community-centered initiatives.

How can events like Car-Free Day influence long-term shifts in transportation planning and public attitudes toward pedestrian-friendly cities?

OPENING OF
THE FOUR LEVEL INTERCHANGE

"The highways destroyed the hearts of many cities."
– Anthony Foxx, former U.S. Secretary of Transportation

Four Level Interchange of Arroyo Seco Parkway and Highway 101, looking north-east from Downtown Los Angeles - in 1999. Source: Historic American Engineering Record; Library of Congress HAER CAL,19-LOSAN,83-16. Via Wikimedia Commons. Public Domain.

On this day in 1953, the Four-Level Interchange in Los Angeles, the world's first stack interchange, opened to traffic, heralding a new era of freeway design and car-centric urban planning. While celebrated as an engineering marvel, such infrastructure development often came at a heavy cost to urban communities. In Los Angeles and across the United States, freeway construction frequently destroyed the fabric of thriving urban neighborhoods, disproportionately affecting African American communities. The construction of interchanges like this uprooted families, decimated local businesses, and perpetuated racial and economic segregation. The Four-Level Interchange symbolized mid-20th-century priorities that favored suburban expansion and automobile travel over preserving the vitality of urban centers. Today, its legacy is a reminder of the social and environmental consequences of infrastructure decisions, inspiring efforts to design transportation systems that prioritize equity and inclusivity in urban planning.

How can urban planning reconcile the legacy of past infrastructure projects with the need for equitable and sustainable cities?

SEPTEMBER 23
1932

UNIFICATION OF SAUDI ARABIA AND THE URBAN EVOLUTION OF RIYADH

"A nation without a past is a nation without a future."
– King Abdulaziz Ibn Saud

Aerial view of Riyadh, Saudi Arabia, showing the city's modern expansive layout, skyscrapers, and key arterial roads within the desert landscape. By Swisshippo. Licensed

On this day in 1932, Saudi Arabia was unified under King Abdulaziz Ibn Saud, marking the establishment of the modern Kingdom of Saudi Arabia. At unification, Riyadh was a modest desert settlement, but its designation as the national capital catalyzed its transformation into a thriving urban center. Fueled by the discovery of oil and strategic urban planning, Riyadh grew rapidly, blending traditional Islamic design with modern architectural innovations, exemplified by landmarks like the Kingdom Centre and Al Faisaliah Tower. Over the decades, Riyadh's urban evolution has reflected Saudi Arabia's broader modernization and economic diversification efforts. Today, initiatives like Vision 2030 aim to position Riyadh as a sustainable, globally competitive city, with plans for green spaces, smart city technologies, and cultural hubs. Riyadh's development underscores the dynamic interplay of tradition and innovation in shaping a city's identity on the global stage.

How can rapidly urbanizing cities like Riyadh balance cultural heritage preservation with the demands of global modernity and sustainable growth?

BIRTH OF
F. SCOTT FITZGERALD

"So we beat on, boats against the current, borne back ceaselessly into the past."
– F. Scott Fitzgerald. American novelist.

Broadway north from 38th St., New York City, showing the Casino and Knickerbocker Theatres, a sign pointing to Maxine Elliott's Theatre. By American Studio, N.Y. Source: Library of Congress's Prints and Photographs division. Via Wikimedia Commons. Public Domain.

On this day in 1896, F. Scott Fitzgerald was born in St. Paul, Minnesota. Celebrated as one of the defining literary voices of the 20th century, Fitzgerald is best known for The Great Gatsby (1925), a novel that captures the essence of the Roaring Twenties—a transformative period marked by rapid urbanization, shifting social norms, and unprecedented economic growth in American cities. Fitzgerald's portrayal of New York City and Long Island serves as both a glamorous backdrop and a symbolic landscape, reflecting the complexities of urban life during a time when cities were emerging as powerful cultural and economic epicenters. His exploration of themes like ambition, excess, disillusionment, and the American Dream provides a layered critique of the social stratification and moral ambiguity embedded in urban modernity. Through his sharp prose and vivid characterizations, Fitzgerald illuminated the allure and alienation of city life, offering timeless insights into the human condition. His work continues to resonate as a mirror of both the promise and pitfalls of metropolitan ambition and identity.

How do works like The Great Gatsby provide a lens into the cultural and social transformations of rapidly growing cities?

SEPTEMBER 25
1957

THE LITTLE ROCK NINE AND THE INTEGRATION OF CENTRAL HIGH SCHOOL

"Mob rule cannot be allowed to override the decisions of our courts."
– President Dwight D. Eisenhower. 34th President of the United States.

Arkansas National Guard at Little Rock Central High School, Little Rock Central High School National Historic Site, 1957. Author unknown. Source: U.S. National Park Service. Public Domain.

On this day in 1957, nine African American students, known as the Little Rock Nine, entered Central High School in Little Rock, Arkansas, under the protection of federal troops. This pivotal event in the Civil Rights Movement followed the Supreme Court's landmark Brown v. Board of Education (1954) decision, which declared racial segregation in public schools unconstitutional. Initially, under orders from Governor Orval Faubus, the Arkansas National Guard blocked the students' entry, sparking national outrage. President Dwight D. Eisenhower deployed the 101st Airborne Division to escort the students and enforce desegregation. The integration of Central High School revealed the deep resistance to desegregation in urban public institutions, highlighting the challenges of implementing civil rights laws. It also underscored the federal government's critical role in upholding constitutional protections, marking a significant step toward racial equity in education and public spaces.

How can cities continue to address systemic inequality in public education and ensure that schools foster inclusivity, equity, and opportunity for all?

THE RELEASE OF ABBEY ROAD
AND THE ICONIC ZEBRA CROSSING

"It's been a great honor, and it's amazing to think that the crossing on Abbey Road has become a landmark for the world." – Paul McCartney. British musician.

Abbey Road Zebra Crossing, 2007. By Misterweiss. Via Wikimedia Commons. Public Domain.

On this day in 1969, The Beatles released their iconic Abbey Road album in the United Kingdom, an event that forever transformed a simple zebra crossing into a globally recognized cultural landmark. The album's cover, featuring the band walking across the pedestrian crossing outside Abbey Road Studios in London's St. John's Wood neighborhood, captured an ordinary urban scene and elevated it into one of the most enduring images in music history. The crossing quickly became a pilgrimage site for Beatles fans, drawing visitors from around the world and embedding itself in London's cultural and visual identity. This moment highlighted how everyday urban infrastructure—normally seen as purely functional—can acquire profound symbolic meaning when tied to popular culture. In 2010, the British government granted the crossing Grade II listed status, recognizing its historic and artistic significance. The continued popularity of Abbey Road illustrates the powerful role cities play in shaping and preserving cultural memory, and how public space can become a canvas for collective identity and global recognition.

How can cities identify and preserve urban spaces that gain cultural importance through art, history, or global influence, while maintaining their functionality?

SEPTEMBER 27
1962

PUBLICATION OF
RACHEL CARSON'S SILENT SPRING

"In nature, nothing exists alone."
— Rachel Carson. American marine biologist, author, and conservationist.

Rachel Carson conducts Marine Biology Research with Bob Hines — in the Atlantic, 1952. By U.S. Fish and Wildlife Service. Via Wikimedia Commons. Public Domain.

On this day in 1962, Rachel Carson published Silent Spring, a landmark book that exposed pesticides' devastating environmental and public health effects, particularly DDT. Carson's meticulously researched work revealed how chemical pollutants disrupted ecosystems, harmed wildlife, and posed serious risks to human health. Her writing challenged powerful chemical industries and called for stronger government oversight, sparking widespread public awareness and outrage. The book is credited with launching the modern environmental movement, leading to significant policy changes such as establishing the Environmental Protection Agency (EPA) in 1970 and banning DDT in the United States. Silent Spring also influenced urban and regional planning, highlighting the need for sustainable practices that protect ecological systems and public health. Carson's work inspires efforts to balance development with environmental stewardship, making it a cornerstone of environmental advocacy and planning.

How can urban planning integrate the principles of environmental health and sustainability championed in Silent Spring?

THE FOUNDING OF THE FIRST INTERNATIONAL WORKINGMEN'S ASSOCIATION

"The emancipation of the working class must be conquered by the working class themselves." – Karl Marx, speech at the IWMA's inaugural meeting.

Procession of Match Workers to Westminster, July 1888. By W.D.Almoyd. Source: The Union Makes Us Strong – TUC History Online (TUC Library Collections, London Metropolitan University). Via Wikimedia Commons. Public Domain.

On this day in 1864, the First International Workingmen's Association (IWMA) was founded at St. Martin's Hall in London. Also known as the International, this groundbreaking coalition brought together labor groups, socialists, and trade unionists from across Europe and North America in response to the mounting social inequalities of the Industrial Revolution. One of the IWMA's most enduring legacies was its role in linking labor rights to urban reform. Recognizing the appalling conditions faced by the working class in rapidly growing industrial cities—marked by overcrowded slums, unsanitary housing, and exploitative workplaces—the IWMA advocated for improved housing, sanitation, and public health infrastructure. These early calls for systemic change laid the foundation for the development of social housing policies and equitable urban planning. The IWMA was instrumental in shifting the political conversation toward the right to the city, positioning urban space as a key battleground in the fight for social justice. Its legacy continues in movements for inclusive, worker-centered urban development.

How did the IWMA's advocacy for urban reforms shape the early labor movement, and what lessons can today's urban planners take from their efforts?

SEPTEMBER 29
2008

DOW JONES PLUMMETS:
FINANCIAL CRISIS HITS URBAN ECONOMIES

"This crisis has reminded us of the interconnectedness of the global economy and the responsibility we have to protect our most vulnerable." – Barack Obama. 44th US President.

Aerial View of a stalled subdivision. By Andy Dean. Licensed

On this day in 2008, the Dow Jones Industrial Average plunged 777.68 points, marking the largest single-day point drop in its history after the U.S. House of Representatives rejected a $700 billion bailout plan to stabilize the financial system. This event intensified the 2008 global economic crisis, sending shockwaves through urban economies worldwide. Financial centers like New York, London, and Tokyo faced significant unemployment, halted construction projects, and widespread foreclosures, while smaller cities struggled to maintain services amid dwindling budgets. Vulnerable urban populations were hit hardest as the crisis deepened housing insecurity and strained social safety nets. The economic downturn highlighted weaknesses in urban resilience, prompting reforms in housing policies, urban planning, and financial oversight to mitigate future risks. The crisis remains pivotal in modern urban history, shaping how cities prepare for and adapt to economic and systemic challenges.

How can cities better prepare for economic shocks while ensuring equitable housing, sustainable development, and protections for vulnerable populations?

BERLIN
AIRLIFT ENDS

"Only unity and cooperation can secure freedom and justice."
– Harry S. Truman. 33rd President of the United States. (Adapted).

Berlin - Airport Tempelhof, a key site during the Berlin Airlift of 1948–1949. The airlift supplied West Berlin with food and fuel during the Soviet blockade, marking a pivotal moment in Cold War history and urban resilience. By daskleineatelier. Licensed

On this day in 1949, the Berlin Airlift officially ended, concluding a historic effort to sustain West Berlin during the Soviet blockade. For 15 months, over 277,000 flights transported essential goods such as food, fuel, and medical supplies to the isolated city, preventing a humanitarian disaster. This unprecedented operation showcased the critical role of transportation infrastructure and logistics in maintaining urban resilience under extreme conditions. The airlift's success relied on international cooperation and innovative use of aerial mobility, setting a standard for modern humanitarian relief efforts. Beyond addressing immediate needs, it symbolized a broader commitment to freedom and unity in the face of geopolitical challenges. The Berlin Airlift remains a powerful example of how well-coordinated logistics and transportation systems can support urban populations in times of crisis, inspiring advancements in disaster preparedness and global urban planning.

How can modern urban logistics systems be adapted to ensure resilience in times of crisis or disruption?

OCTOBER 1
1978

FORMATION OF
THE AMERICAN PLANNING ASSOCIATION

"Good planning builds communities of lasting value."
— American Planning Association Motto.

Scale model for a district. By Bizoo_n. Licensed

On this day in 1978, the American Planning Association (APA) was officially established through the merger of the American Institute of Planners (AIP) and the American Society of Planning Officials (ASPO). The APA brought together professional planners, policymakers, and community leaders to promote the principles of urban and regional planning. Its mission emphasized advancing ethical conduct, public engagement, and sustainable, equitable community development. The organization supports the profession through training programs, certification for planners, and advocacy efforts that address pressing urban challenges. With its flagship publication, Planning Magazine, and its annual national conferences, the APA is a hub for innovation, collaboration, and dissemination of best practices in the field. Over the decades, the APA has played a vital role in shaping planning standards and fostering a shared vision for building sustainable, inclusive, resilient cities and regions.

How has the APA shaped the evolution of urban and regional planning practices since its founding in 1978?

PATRICK GEDDES: CITIES IN EVOLUTION

"Think globally, act locally." – Often attributed to Patrick Geddes, Scottish biologist and urban planner, reflecting his regionalist philosophy.

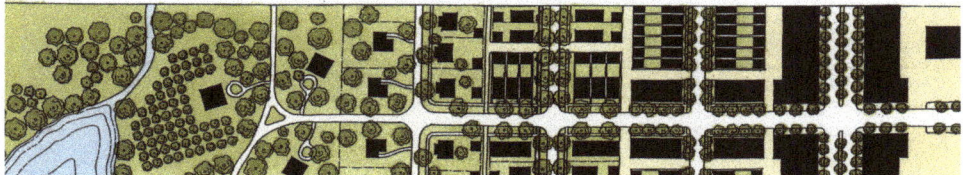

Inspired by Geddes' transect, a Duany Plater Zyberk concept illustration of the Rural-Urban Transect depicting the transition from natural landscapes through rural areas to urban environments, highlighting the continuum of land use and the integration of natural and built environments. Courtesy of DPZ CoDESIGN. With Permission.

On this day in 1854, Patrick Geddes, the pioneering Scottish biologist, sociologist, and urban planner, was born in Ballater, Aberdeenshire, Scotland. Widely regarded as the father of modern urban planning, Geddes championed an interdisciplinary approach that combined ecology, sociology, and civic engagement. He introduced the idea of viewing the "region as a planning unit" and stressed the interconnectedness of people, place, and work in urban design. In 1915, Geddes published Cities in Evolution, a landmark work that laid the foundation for regional planning and the modern town planning movement. The book emphasized his "survey before plan" methodology, urging planners to study a city's history, culture, and environment before proposing changes. Geddes' ideas continue to shape contemporary planning frameworks, including the rural-to-urban transect concept, which organizes land use along a continuum from natural to urban. His legacy endures in sustainable planning practices that treat cities as evolving systems, grounded in both local context and ecological wisdom.

How can Patrick Geddes' holistic and interdisciplinary approach to planning inspire solutions for today's urban challenges, such as rapid urbanization and climate change?

OCTOBER 3
1989

THE RELEASE OF SIMCITY

"SimCity is a game about creating and understanding. It's about the delicate balance that makes cities thrive—or fail." – Will Wright, creator of SimCity.

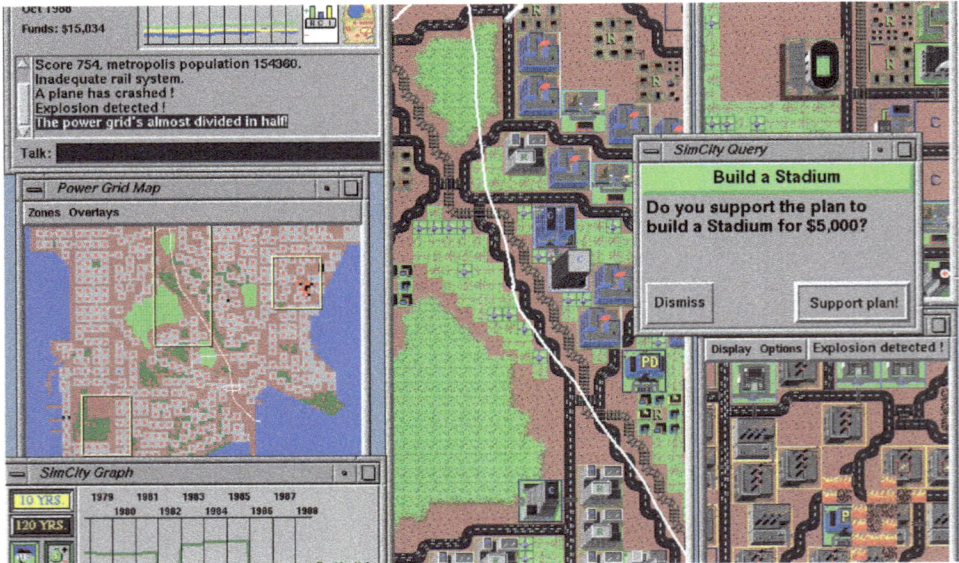

Multi Player SimCity for X11 TCL/Tk running on SGI Indigo workstation. By Don Hopkins. Via Wikimedia Commons. Public Domain.

In October 1989, the first version of SimCity was released by Maxis, co-founded by game designer Will Wright. While not all sources cite October 3 as the release date for the IBM PC version, most agree that the game debuted sometime during that month. This groundbreaking city-building simulation allowed players to design and manage urban environments, engaging with zoning, transportation, taxation, public services, and disasters. By immersing millions in the complexities of city systems, SimCity ignited widespread interest in urban planning, sustainability, and infrastructure. The game invited players to creatively experiment with city growth while responding to real-world challenges, providing a compelling platform for learning through play. Its legacy extends beyond entertainment—SimCity has inspired generations of urban planners, architects, and policymakers to explore the interconnected nature of city life. Decades later, it remains a cultural milestone, shaping public understanding of cities and the importance of thoughtful, adaptive planning.

How has SimCity and similar games impacted the way people understand urban planning, and what lessons can professional planners learn from these simulations?

OCTOBER 4
1720

BIRTH OF
GIOVANNI BATTISTA PIRANESI

"Let us consider the grandeur of the ruins; it is not by war or by fire that they are reduced to this condition; it is by the hand of time." – Giovanni Battista Piranesi. Italian architect.

Giardino Colonna nel clivo del Quirinale. By Giovanni Battista Piranesi (1720–1778). Source: Yale Center for British Art. Via Wikimedia Commons. CC0 1.0 Universal

On this day in 1720, Giovanni Battista Piranesi, the renowned Italian architect, engraver, and visionary artist, was born in Venice. Piranesi is best known for his Vedute di Roma (Views of Rome), a series of intricate etchings capturing the grandeur of ancient Roman ruins, and his Carceri d'Invenzione (Imaginary Prisons), which depicted vast, surreal architectural spaces. These works blended meticulous detail with boundless imagination, redefining the relationship between architecture and artistic expression. Piranesi's fascination with ruins and monumental forms preserved the legacy of ancient Rome and influenced Romanticism, modern architecture, and urban planning.

His visionary interpretations of space and structure encouraged architects and planners to explore innovative ideas while respecting historical context. Piranesi's legacy endures, celebrating cities as living, layered entities where the past and future coexist in dynamic interplay, inspiring creativity in design and urbanism.

How can Piranesi's blend of history and imagination encourage architects and urban planners to embrace both preservation and creativity?

OCTOBER 5
1970

ADOPTION OF THE FIRST
REGIONAL FAIR-SHARE HOUSING PLAN IN DAYTON

*"Fair housing is not just a policy—it's a planning responsibility shared across the region." –
Inspired by the principles of the Dayton plan.*

Housing is a human right sign being painted on fence. By Dennis M. Swanson. Licensed

On this day in 1970, the Miami Valley Regional Planning Commission in Dayton, Ohio, adopted the United States' first fair-share regional housing allocation plan aimed at low- and moderate-income households. At a time when exclusionary zoning and suburban resistance to affordable housing were widespread, the plan represented a bold and collaborative step toward regional equity. It required each municipality in the Dayton metropolitan area to accommodate its fair share of affordable housing, thereby addressing entrenched patterns of racial and economic segregation. The initiative established common housing targets, a detailed policy toolkit, and mechanisms for implementation—spanning zoning reform, infrastructure alignment, and interjurisdictional coordination. Its success in expanding affordable housing access to Dayton's surrounding counties and townships made it a national model for regional housing justice. The plan prefigured later debates around suburban exclusion, housing affordability, and the role of metropolitan governance in ensuring inclusive, balanced growth across city and suburb alike.

What are the challenges and opportunities of implementing equitable housing goals across fragmented suburban jurisdictions?

BIRTH OF
LE CORBUSIER

"The city is a tool for human activity, not a constraint upon it."
– Le Corbusier. Swiss-French architect and urban planner.

Detail of the facade of the Unité d'Habitation in Berlin by Le Corbusier, showcasing its systematic, cell-like modules. This impersonal grid of stacked living units embodies the architect's vision of a "machine for living," emphasizing efficiency and uniformity over individual expression. By: photoopus - stock.adobe.com. Licensed.

On this day in 1887, Le Corbusier (born Charles-Édouard Jeanneret), a revolutionary architect, urban planner, and theorist, was born. A key figure in modernist urban design, he introduced the Radiant City (Ville Radieuse) concept in the 1920s, proposing high-density housing within a structured grid system emphasizing functionality, zoning efficiency, and expansive green spaces. Le Corbusier advocated for towering skyscrapers surrounded by parks, aiming to maximize urban density while improving urban residents' air, light, and living conditions. His ideas, though controversial, shaped many urban renewal projects and influenced zoning and planning debates throughout the 20th century. His principles are exemplified in iconic projects like Chandigarh, India's planned capital city. Le Corbusier's work continues to inspire and provoke discussion about modernism's impact, highlighting the tension between large-scale urban visions and the need for human-centered, community-driven, and sustainable design approaches.

How can cities balance the efficiency of modernist design with the need for human-scale, livable communities

OCTOBER 7
1593

FOUNDING OF PALMANOVA

"A city's design should reflect the harmony of the cosmos and the security of its people."
– Vincenzo Scamozzi. Italian architect and city planner. (Paraphrased).

Palmanova Friuli. By Pierluigi. Licensed

On this day in 1593, Palmanova, a visionary utopian city in present-day Italy, was founded by the Republic of Venice. Designed by Vincenzo Scamozzi, the city epitomized Renaissance ideals of harmony, order, and geometric precision. Its distinctive nine-pointed star-shaped layout, with radial streets converging on a central plaza, symbolized unity and balance. Conceived as a military fortress and a self-contained urban utopia, Palmanova blended advanced fortifications with civic amenities, including public spaces and efficient infrastructure. This dual-purpose design reflected Renaissance humanism, where geometry and function served societal needs. Built to defend against Ottoman expansion, Palmanova also represented an idealistic vision of urban living, inspiring future city designs rooted in symmetry and integration. Today, Palmanova is a UNESCO World Heritage Site, celebrated as a masterpiece of early modern urban planning and a lasting symbol of utopian aspirations in city design.

How do utopian ideals shape the planning and legacy of cities in history and modern times?

THE GREAT CHICAGO FIRE BEGINS

"What we need is an architecture that will stand the test of time and fire—one that serves both beauty and safety." – Louis Sullivan. American architect. (Adapted).

The Great Chicago Fire, an artists rendering, Chicago in Flames -- The Rush for Lives Over Randolph Street Bridge, 1871. Source: Originally from Harper's Weekly. Via Wikimedia Commons. Public Domain.

On this day in 1871, the Great Chicago Fire broke out, devastating much of Chicago, Illinois, and burning for two days. The fire destroyed over 17,000 structures, killed approximately 300 people, and left more than 100,000 residents homeless. The fire spread rapidly in a barn due to high winds and the city's wooden construction. Despite its destruction, the fire became a turning point in urban development, leading to stricter building codes, fireproof materials like steel and brick, and innovations in urban planning. Chicago's rebuilding efforts attracted renowned architects, resulting in groundbreaking designs and the rise of modern skyscrapers, including the 1885 Home Insurance Building, considered the first skyscraper. The disaster also prompted improved fire safety regulations and expanded public services. Today, the Great Chicago Fire is remembered for its tragic impact and its transformative role in shaping Chicago as a resilient, forward-thinking city.

How can cities today learn from historical urban disasters to build more resilient and adaptive infrastructure in the face of climate change and urban risks?

OCTOBER 9
1888

THE OPENING OF
THE WASHINGTON MONUMENT

"The preservation of the sacred fire of liberty… is the fundamental objective of the people."
– George Washington. First President of the United States.

A view of The Boulevard in Potomac Park, Washington, D.C., showing a wide road with trees lining both sides and cars driving along it (1905 - 1924). Source: The New York Public Library. Postcard series number: 70064. Public Domain.

On this day in 1888, the Washington Monument was officially opened to the public in Washington, D.C., after decades of planning and construction. Standing at 555 feet, the marble obelisk honors George Washington, the first President of the United States, and symbolizes the nation's ideals of unity and democracy. Designed by Robert Mills and completed in 1884, the monument's construction faced significant delays due to funding shortages, the Civil War, and engineering challenges. Located on the National Mall, it became the world's tallest structure at the time and remains one of the most iconic landmarks in the U.S. The monument's opening marked a milestone in American civic architecture, reinforcing Washington, D.C.'s identity as a capital city rooted in history and symbolism. Today, the Washington Monument inspires millions of visitors annually and is a focal point of the city's urban landscape.

How do monumental structures like the Washington Monument shape the identity of a city and foster civic pride?

DEATH OF
ANTONIO SANT'ELIA

"The decorative value of Futurist architecture depends solely on the use and original arrangement of raw or bare or violently colored materials." – Antonio Sant'Elia. Italian architect and Futurist.

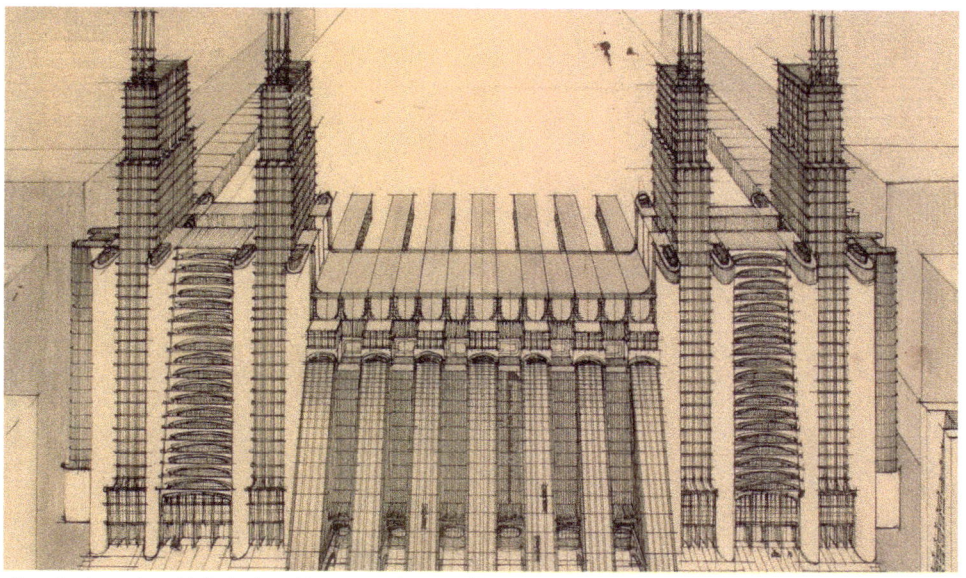

Air and train station with funicular cableways on three road levels. Part of the series La Città Nuova, 1914. By Antonio Sant'Elia. Source: Utopie metropolitane, la mostra (in Italian). Style & Design. l'Espresso (2013-03-28). Via Wikimedia Commons. CC BY-SA 4.0

On this day in 1916, Antonio Sant'Elia, a visionary Italian architect and key figure in the Futurist movement, died in combat during World War I. Though his career was tragically brief, Sant'Elia left an enduring legacy through his radical ideas and designs that reimagined modern cities. His 1914 Manifesto of Futurist Architecture envisioned dynamic, functional urban environments defined by bold geometric forms, towering structures, and seamless integration with modern technologies like elevators, power plants, and advanced transportation systems. His unbuilt designs, captured in striking sketches, portrayed cities of movement, speed, and innovation, emphasizing architecture as a reflection of a rapidly evolving industrial society. While Sant'Elia's concepts were never realized, they inspired generations of architects and urban planners to think beyond traditional forms and embrace the transformative potential of modern technology in shaping cities of the future.

How can Sant'Elia's visionary concepts of futurism and functionality inspire contemporary urban planning in the face of rapid technological change?

OCTOBER 11
1884

BIRTH OF
ELEANOR ROOSEVELT

"The future belongs to those who believe in the beauty of their dreams."
— Eleanor Roosevelt. Former First Lady of the United States.

U.S. First Lady Eleanor Roosevelt addressing the Cumberland Homesteaders near Crossville, Tennessee, an early New Deal project, 1935. Author unknown; either Ben Shahn, Carl Mydans, or Arthur Rothstein. Source: Wikimedia Commons. Public Domain.

On this day in 1884, Anna Eleanor Roosevelt, a champion of social justice and housing reform, was born in New York City. As First Lady during the Great Depression, Roosevelt became a staunch advocate for New Deal public housing programs, addressing urban poverty and deteriorating slum conditions. She supported groundbreaking initiatives such as the Arthurdale project in West Virginia, which aimed to provide struggling families with dignified housing and a sense of community. Roosevelt believed housing was a fundamental human right to personal dignity and societal progress. She also brought national attention to racial and economic inequalities in urban areas, influencing federal housing reforms to reduce homelessness and improve urban living standards. Her tireless advocacy helped shape housing policy in the United States, and her legacy continues to inspire movements for equitable, inclusive urban development that prioritizes human dignity and opportunity.

How did Eleanor Roosevelt's advocacy for housing and social justice influence urban policies in the United States, and what lessons can be drawn for housing reforms today?

PASSAGE OF
THE COMMUNITY REINVESTMENT ACT

"Access to credit is the cornerstone of economic opportunity."
— Jimmy Carter. 39th President of the United States.

Downtown Provo, Utah. The image shows the area managed by the Provo City Redevelopment Agency (RDA), which oversees development projects using Tax Increment Financing (TIF) to stimulate economic growth and improve urban infrastructure.. By SeanPavonePhoto. Licensed

On this day in 1977, President Jimmy Carter signed the Community Reinvestment Act (CRA) into law, a landmark effort to combat discriminatory lending practices like redlining and promote equitable access to financial services. The CRA required federally regulated banks to meet the credit needs of low- and moderate-income communities, ensuring fair access to loans, investments, and banking services across all neighborhoods, regardless of race or income. This legislation marked a critical step in addressing systemic disparities, helping to increase homeownership, support small businesses, and spur economic development in underserved areas. While the CRA has faced criticism over enforcement gaps and its evolving relevance in a changing financial landscape, it remains a foundational policy for promoting economic equity. By encouraging community reinvestment, the CRA continues to play a vital role in fostering inclusive growth and empowering historically marginalized communities across the United States.

How can policies like the CRA be strengthened to address persistent inequities in access to credit and financial services in underserved communities?

OCTOBER 13
1931

ENACTMENT OF
THE FIRST HISTORIC DISTRICT ORDINANCE

"Preserving the past is a way of building for the future."
— Charleston Historic Preservation Principle.

St. Michael's Church and Broad Street, Charleston, South Carolina. The area is part of the first historic district established by ordinance in the United States (Charleston Historic District, 1931), reflecting early efforts to preserve architectural heritage and urban character. By Susanne2688. Licensed

On this day in 1931, Charleston, South Carolina, became the first U.S. city to enact a Historic District Ordinance, establishing a legal framework to protect its architectural and cultural heritage. The ordinance created the Charleston Old and Historic District, preserving iconic colonial and antebellum-era homes, churches, and public buildings. To oversee preservation efforts, the city formed the Board of Architectural Review (BAR), responsible for regulating changes and ensuring that new construction complemented the district's historic character. This groundbreaking legislation set a national standard, showcasing how cities could balance development pressures while safeguarding their historical identity. Charleston's ordinance not only preserved its unique character but also inspired the modern historic preservation movement in the United States. By highlighting the cultural, aesthetic, and economic value of historic sites, Charleston demonstrated the enduring importance of preservation in fostering civic pride and maintaining the integrity of urban landscapes.

How has the concept of historic preservation evolved since Charleston's ordinance, and how can it address modern challenges like climate change and urban growth?

BIRTH OF
DWIGHT D. EISENHOWER

"The Interstate System is essential to the defense, economy, and cultural growth of the United States." – Dwight D. Eisenhower. 34th President of the United States.

Aerial view of a large highway intersection in Los Angeles, California, USA. The image illustrates the impact of mid-20th-century freeway construction on urban form and mobility patterns in American cities. By Tierney. Licensed

On this day in 1890, Dwight D. Eisenhower, the 34th President of the United States and a visionary in infrastructure development, was born in Denison, Texas. His 1919 experience in a cross-country military convoy exposed the inadequacy of America's road network, shaping his commitment to modernizing transportation. Eisenhower signed the Federal-Aid Highway Act of 1956 during his presidency, creating the Interstate Highway System, a transformative network connecting cities and suburbs. This ambitious infrastructure project revolutionized urban development, fostering economic growth, enhancing mobility, and reshaping the American landscape. However, it also accelerated urban sprawl, environmental degradation, and the decline of many city centers, prompting debates about equity and sustainability in transportation planning. Eisenhower's vision remains a cornerstone of urban and regional planning, influencing modern mobility systems and infrastructure development globally while highlighting the need to balance growth with environmental and social considerations.

How can modern cities address the challenges created by highway systems while transitioning to more sustainable and equitable transportation networks?

OCTOBER 15
1966

PASSAGE OF THE NATIONAL HISTORIC PRESERVATION ACT

"The spirit and direction of the Nation are founded upon and reflected in its historic heritage." – Lyndon B. Johnson. 36th President of the United States.

Historically designated Victorian Townhouses in Cincinnati Ohio. By Nicholas J. Klein. Licensed

On this day in 1966, President Lyndon B. Johnson signed the National Historic Preservation Act (NHPA) into law, a landmark in the effort to protect America's cultural and architectural heritage. The NHPA created the National Register of Historic Places and the Advisory Council on Historic Preservation and provided a framework for state and local preservation programs. It introduced Section 106, requiring federal agencies to assess and mitigate the impacts of their projects on historic properties, ensuring collaboration with stakeholders to minimize harm. This act empowered communities to preserve their heritage while accommodating urban growth and modern development. By integrating preservation into urban planning, the NHPA set a new standard for sustainable development that respects cultural history. It remains a cornerstone of preservation policy, safeguarding historic buildings, neighborhoods, and landscapes across the United States and inspiring global approaches to heritage conservation.

How can the principles of the NHPA be adapted to protect cultural heritage in rapidly growing urban areas?

PIONEERING DECISION FOR BARCELONA'S SUPERILLAS

"Reducing the dominance of cars is not just an environmental necessity; it is about reclaiming public space for people." – Salvador Rueda. Spanish urban ecologist and planner.

Superilla del barri de Sant Antoni, Barcelona – Completed in 2019, this superblock reclaimed over 26,000 m² of street space around the market, transforming the area into a pedestrian-friendly zone, reflecting Barcelona's push for more livable, community-centered urban spaces. By Cataleirxs. Via Wikimedia Commons. CC BY-SA 4.0

On this day in 1997, Barcelona's City Council announced its first major initiative to limit car access on select streets, aiming to improve pedestrian safety and public transportation. Publicly introduced on October 16, this decision marked a turning point in the city's approach to mobility and public space. Though modest in scope, it echoed the original 19th-century vision of Ildefons Cerdà, whose Eixample plan emphasized a balance between transportation, building density, and green space. The 1997 policy represented a renewed commitment to that balance, acknowledging the growing challenges of air pollution, traffic congestion, and diminished public life in the modern city. This early effort laid the conceptual groundwork for what would become the "superblocks" (superilles) model decades later. Developed by urban ecologist Salvador Rueda, superilles restructured traffic flow and reclaimed interior streets for pedestrians, cyclists, and community use. Today, the superblock approach has become a global example of how incremental, visionary urban policy can evolve into transformative change for livability and sustainability.

How can cities globally adapt the superblock model to address challenges of congestion, air pollution, and urban livability?

OCTOBER 17
1814

THE LONDON BEER FLOOD

"The safety of the people shall be the highest law."
– Cicero. Roman statesman and philosopher.

Horseshoe Brewery, London, c. 1800. Author unknown. Source: Brewers' Journal, 15 February 1906, p 55. Via Wikimedia Commons. Public Domain.

On this day in 1814, the London Beer Flood devastated the St. Giles district when a giant vat at the Meux and Company Brewery burst, releasing over 320,000 gallons of beer into the streets. The torrent destroyed multiple buildings, flooded basements, and tragically killed eight people, many of whom lived in working-class homes ill-equipped to withstand such a disaster. The incident highlighted the dangers of inadequate safety measures in industrial operations, particularly in densely populated urban areas where infrastructure was often poorly maintained. It also drew attention to the vulnerability of working-class neighborhoods, which bore the brunt of industrial accidents. While the

flood did not immediately lead to stricter regulations, it raised public awareness of the need for improved oversight and governance in urban-industrial settings. The London Beer Flood remains a somber reminder of the intersection of industrial growth and urban safety, emphasizing the importance of proactive planning and regulation.

How can modern urban planning ensure that industrial safety and infrastructure protect communities, especially in high-density areas?

THE TRANSFER OF ALASKA FROM RUSSIA TO THE UNITED STATES

"The acquisition of Alaska is a grand step in the onward march of our Republic."
– William H. Seward, U.S. Secretary of State.

Main St., Ft. Wrangell, Alaska. Nowell Photo, 475, 1850 - 1950. Source: Frank H. Nowell Photographs of Alaska. Via Wikimedia Commons. Public Domain.

On this day in 1867, Alaska was formally transferred from Russia to the United States in a ceremony held in Sitka, an event now celebrated annually as Alaska Day. This territorial acquisition, often called "Seward's Folly" after then-Secretary of State William H. Seward, expanded U.S. sovereignty into a vast, resource-rich, and strategically significant region. At the time, Alaska was sparsely populated, but it would later see the development of cities such as Juneau, Anchorage, and Fairbanks, which became centers of governance, commerce, and culture. Urbanization in Alaska posed unique challenges, requiring innovative approaches to infrastructure and settlement in a remote and often harsh environment. The acquisition highlighted the importance of integrating new territories into national planning frameworks and managing natural resources responsibly. Today, Alaska's cities embody a delicate balance between urban development and preserving its stunning natural landscapes, reflecting its frontier legacy.

How can modern urban planning address the challenges of developing remote regions like Alaska while preserving their cultural and environmental heritage?

OCTOBER 19
1895

BIRTH OF
LEWIS MUMFORD

"A city is not only a place of trade but a theater of social action."
– Lewis Mumford. American historian, sociologist, and philosopher of technology.

An aerial view of Esch-sur-Sûre, a medieval town in Luxembourg, where human settlement remains closely integrated with the natural landscape – a living example of the 'organic city' championed by Lewis Mumford. By Radu79. Licensed.

On this day in 1895, Lewis Mumford, a visionary urban historian, sociologist, and critic, was born. Mumford profoundly reshaped how we understand cities and their impact on human life. His landmark work, The City in History (1961), traces the rise and fall of urban civilizations, arguing that cities are not just physical structures, but reflections of their cultures, values, and relationships with nature. Mumford sharply criticized modern urban sprawl, automobile dependency, and unchecked industrialization, seeing them as forces that isolate people and erode the social fabric. He admired the medieval city as a model for urban design, with its tight-knit communities, walkable streets, and deep connection to the surrounding landscape – qualities he believed fostered a richer civic life. In contrast, he warned that cities disconnected from their natural surroundings and spiritual roots risk the same fate as ancient Rome – collapse. Today, his ideas continue to guide architects, planners, and policymakers working to create more sustainable, humane, and connected cities.

How can cities balance economic growth with cultural and social vitality in the 21st century

U.S. SENATE RATIFIES
THE LOUISIANA PURCHASE

"The acquisition of New Orleans would be of great importance to the United States."
– Thomas Jefferson. 3rd President of the United States.

Map of the Louisiana Purchase, 1803. By I.P. Berthrong and C. J. Helm. Source: Records of the Bureau of Land Management, Record Group 49; National Archives at College Park. Via Wikimedia Commons. Public Domain.

On this day in 1803, the United States Senate ratified the Louisiana Purchase, a landmark agreement that doubled the nation's size and paved the way for westward expansion. Acquired from France for $15 million, the vast territory encompassed land that would later host major urban centers such as New Orleans, St. Louis, and Kansas City. These cities became vital hubs for trade, transportation, and culture, shaping the nation's economic and social landscape. The Louisiana Purchase also raised critical issues, including the governance of newly acquired lands, the displacement of Indigenous peoples, and the expansion of slavery into western territories. This transformative acquisition highlighted the interplay between territorial growth and urban development, illustrating how land policies and expansionism can influence the trajectory of cities and national identity. It remains a defining moment in the history of American urbanization and governance.

How can historical territorial expansions inform modern strategies for sustainable urban growth and equitable land use?

OCTOBER 21
1987

PUBLICATION OF
THE SEASIDE CODE

"The heart of a community is its public realm; it is where we come together to share our lives." – Andrés Duany. American architect and urban planner.

Early Seaside FL. Form-Based Code 1987. By Duany Plater-Zyberk. Courtesy of DPZ-CO With permission.

On this day in 1987, the zoning code for Seaside, Florida, was published—a groundbreaking document that helped redefine the future of urban planning. Created by Duany Plater-Zyberk & Company (DPZ), the Seaside Code became one of the first modern form-based codes and a foundational text of the New Urbanism movement. Unlike traditional zoning, which emphasized the separation of land uses, this code focused on the physical form and design of the built environment. It introduced principles such as the transect and required design elements like front porches, narrow streets, mixed-use neighborhoods, and walkable public spaces. Central parks and civic squares were deliberately integrated to foster social interaction and a sense of place. The Seaside Code represented a bold shift away from suburban sprawl and automobile dependency, promoting instead compact, human-scaled, and visually coherent urbanism. Its influence continues to shape zoning reforms and inspire planners around the world.

How can modern cities balance flexibility with design codes to create livable and sustainable urban spaces?

ADOPTION OF
THE MIAMI 21 ZONING CODE

"Miami21 is a blueprint for a sustainable, connected, and people-focused future."
– Elizabeth Plater-Zyberk. American architect and urban planner.

Downtown Miami. By Fotoluminate LLC. Licensed

On this day in 2009, the City of Miami adopted the Miami 21 Zoning Code, the first large-scale form-based code implemented in a major U.S. city. Replacing traditional zoning laws, Miami 21 introduced a forward-thinking framework focused on urban form, emphasizing pedestrian-friendly, mixed-use, and sustainable development. Spearheaded by urban planner Elizabeth Plater-Zyberk, the code redefined the relationship between buildings, streets, and public spaces, fostering vibrant and livable communities. Grounded in New Urbanism principles, Miami 21 promotes transit-oriented development, walkability, and the preservation of neighborhood character, aiming to create a more human-scale urban environment. Its adoption marked a transformative shift in urban planning by prioritizing the quality and functionality of urban spaces over rigid land-use categories. Miami 21 has since served as a model for cities worldwide, demonstrating how form-based codes can guide equitable, sustainable, and community-focused urban development.

How can cities apply the principles of form-based codes like Miami21 to balance urban growth with livability and sustainability?

OCTOBER 23
1915

WOMEN'S SUFFRAGE PARADE ON FIFTH AVENUE

"Whatever women do, they must do twice as well as men to be thought half as good."
— Charlotte Whitton. Canadian feminist and mayor of Ottawa. (Commonly attributed).

Suffragists "march in October 1917, displaying placards containing the signatures of over one million New York women demanding to vote." Author unknown. Source: The New York Times photo archive. Via Wikimedia Commons. Public Domain.

On this day in 1915, more than 25,000 women marched up Fifth Avenue in New York City, demanding the right to vote. The decision to hold the parade on Fifth Avenue was deeply symbolic—this grand, prestigious thoroughfare represented power, influence, and wealth. By occupying this space, suffragists sent a clear message that their fight for equality could not be ignored. Marching past some of the city's most prominent landmarks, dressed in white and carrying banners, the women strategically used public space to amplify their cause. Occurring just weeks before a state referendum on women's voting rights, the parade brought visibility to the movement, uniting participants from all walks of life. Although the referendum failed in 1915, this act of public solidarity helped pave the way for the 19th Amendment's ratification in 1920.

How does the use of prominent urban spaces, like Fifth Avenue, shape the visibility and impact of social movements?

RELEASE OF GATTACA, A FUTURISTIC URBAN DYSTOPIA

"There is no gene for the human spirit."
– Gattaca. Film (1997) tagline.

Image inspired by the Movie Gattaca. By Plusurbia Design. Created using MidJourney.

On this day in 1997, Gattaca, directed by Andrew Niccol, premiered, offering a striking vision of a genetically engineered society. The film's urban landscapes are sleek, minimalist, and meticulously ordered, embodying a utopian aesthetic that belies a dystopian reality marked by genetic discrimination. Filmed in locations like the Marin County Civic Center, designed by Frank Lloyd Wright, the architecture emphasizes precision and control but feels sterile and devoid of humanity. Gattaca critiques the pursuit of perfection in futuristic urban planning, highlighting inequality, exclusion, and the human cost of progress. The cityscapes become a character in themselves, reflecting societal rigidity while serving as the stage for the protagonist's defiance of genetic determinism. The film questions whether highly controlled urban environments can accommodate creativity and individuality, challenging audiences to consider the balance between order and the human spirit in the cities of the future.

How can cities ensure that technological and scientific advancements in urban environments are balanced with inclusivity, equity, and opportunities for all residents?

OCTOBER 25
1701

FOUNDING OF
PHILADELPHIA BY WILLIAM PENN

"Let every house be placed... with a free and open prospect."
— William Penn. Founder of the Province of Pennsylvania.

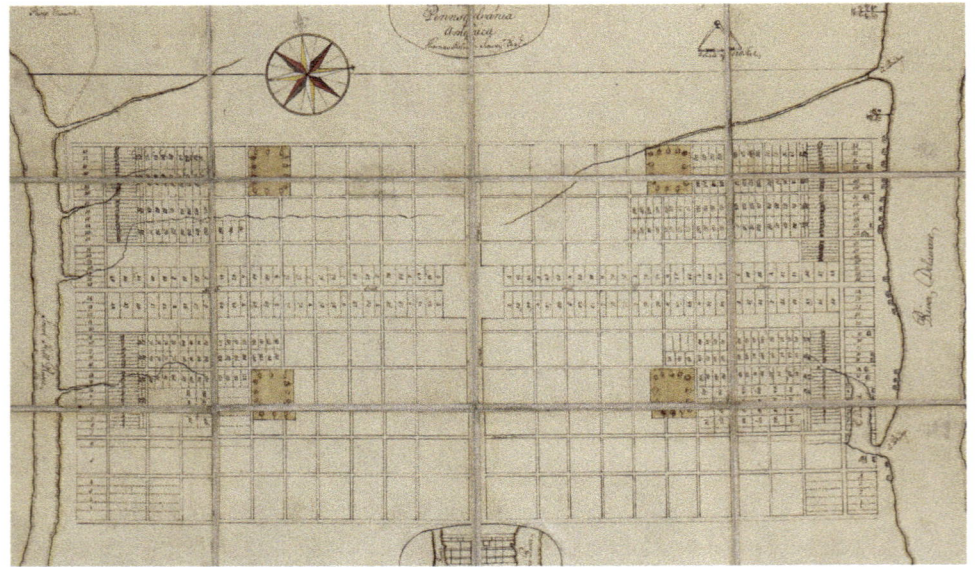

Map of the Original City of Philadelphia in 1682. By Thomas Holme. Source: Historic Society of Pennsylvania. Via Wikimedia Commons. Public Domain.

On this day in 1701, William Penn, an English Quaker and founder of the Province of Pennsylvania, formally established the city of Philadelphia. Penn envisioned the city as a "greene country towne," offering religious freedom and refuge from the congestion and disorder of European cities. Drawing on Enlightenment ideals and influenced by classical planning principles, he designed Philadelphia with a rectilinear grid of wide streets and generous open spaces. Central to the plan were five public squares, including Rittenhouse and Logan Squares, intended to promote health, safety, and civic engagement. This layout prioritized equity and public access, reflecting Penn's commitment to egalitarianism and long-term urban order. Philadelphia's design became a lasting model for urban planning in America, influencing cities across the colonies and beyond. As the "City of Brotherly Love," it soon flourished into a thriving commercial and intellectual center and played a defining role in the birth of American democracy, hosting the Continental Congress and the signing of the Declaration of Independence.

How can Penn's vision of combining open spaces with urban growth guide the design of more livable and sustainable cities today?

OCTOBER 26
1825

OPENING OF
THE ERIE CANAL

"Let us now begin this work, which will unite us in bonds of social and commercial interest."
— Governor DeWitt Clinton. 6th Governor of New York.

Erie Canal, Syracuse, New York, postcard, 1906. The image shows the canal's integration into the urban landscape, reflecting the role of the Erie Canal in shaping trade, transportation, and city development in 19th-century America. 1906. By Archivist. Licensed

On this day in 1825, the Erie Canal was officially opened, connecting the Hudson River in Albany to Lake Erie in Buffalo. Spanning 363 miles, the canal was a monumental engineering achievement and a transformative infrastructure project for the United States. By dramatically reducing transportation costs and travel time, the canal facilitated the efficient movement of goods and people across New York State, establishing New York City as the nation's premier port and commercial hub. Its construction spurred economic growth along its route, leading to the rise of cities such as Syracuse, Rochester, and Buffalo. As the first major infrastructure project of its kind in the U.S., the Erie Canal underscored the critical role of transportation networks in urban development and regional economies. Its success inspired similar projects nationwide, setting a precedent for modern infrastructure planning and integration.

How can the Erie Canal's success inform modern infrastructure planning and regional economic integration efforts?

OCTOBER 27
1275

FOUNDING OF AMSTERDAM

"Amsterdam does not build for the present alone; it builds for eternity."
– Inspired by Pieter Oosterhuis documentation. Dutch photographer and documentarian.

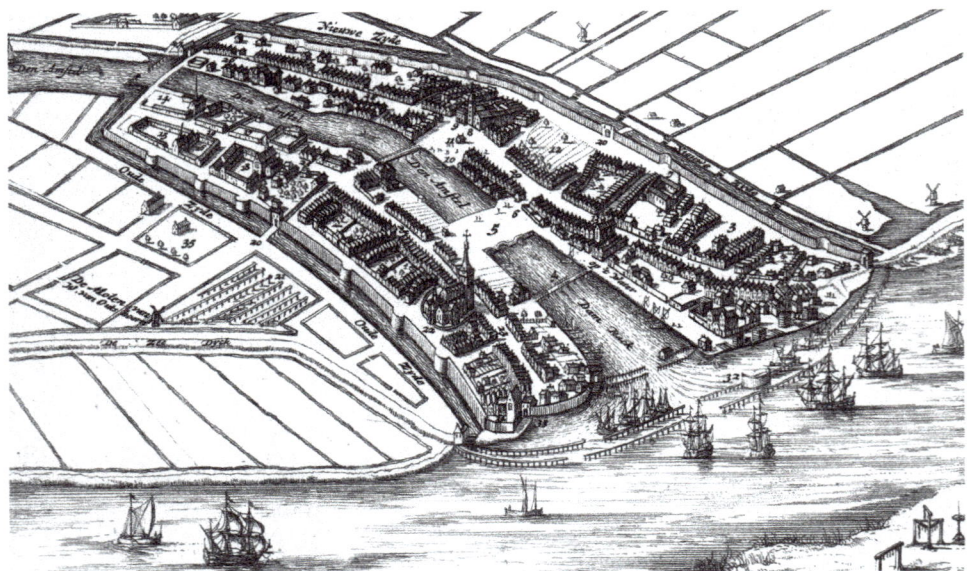

Map of Amsterdam with cityscape in 1300. Attributed to Jan Luyken. Source: Rijksmuseum. Via Wikimedia Commons. Public Domain.

On this day in 1275, the traditional founding of Amsterdam is commemorated, tied to a toll exemption granted to residents by Count Floris V of Holland. At the Amstel River's mouth, Amsterdam began as a small fishing village but evolved into a major trade hub and global city. Its innovative urban planning, particularly the creation of its iconic canal network during the 17th-century Dutch Golden Age, facilitated commerce and defined its unique urban character. The canals, now a UNESCO World Heritage Site, reflect Amsterdam's blend of functionality and beauty. Over centuries, the city has maintained its historical charm while embracing modern sustainability practices, progressive transportation systems, and vibrant street life. Amsterdam continues to be a model for balancing historical preservation with forward-thinking urban innovation, showcasing the enduring importance of thoughtful city planning in fostering livability, economic resilience, and a rich cultural identity.

How can modern cities balance historical preservation with the need for innovation and sustainable urban growth?

COURT FINDS
ZONING ORDINANCE EXCLUSIONARY

"A municipality may not exclude low- and moderate-income families through its land use regulations." — New Jersey Supreme Court, Mount Laurel Decision

Zoning (land use) map displaying typical color-coded classifications used in urban planning. The image illustrates the composition of a variety of landuses within a city's urban fabric. Image by Olivier-Tuffé. Licensed

On this day in 1971, the New Jersey Supreme Court issued a landmark decision in Southern Burlington County NAACP v. Mount Laurel Township, ruling that the township's zoning ordinance was exclusionary and violated its constitutional obligation to provide affordable housing. The ordinance restricted development to large single-family lots, barring low- and moderate-income families from living in the community. This decision, known as Mount Laurel I, established that municipalities must meet their "fair share" of regional housing needs, setting a precedent for challenging exclusionary zoning practices. However, widespread resistance and implementation difficulties led to a follow-up ruling in 1983, Mount Laurel II, strengthening enforcement and introducing mechanisms to promote affordable housing development. Together, these decisions became pivotal in the fight for housing equity, influencing planning and zoning policies nationwide by highlighting the role of municipalities in addressing regional housing disparities.

What role should zoning policies play in addressing systemic housing inequities and promoting inclusive communities?

OCTOBER 29
1929

BLACK TUESDAY:
THE URBAN IMPACT OF THE GREAT DEPRESSION

"The autumn of 1929 was, perhaps, the first occasion when men succeeded on a large scale in swindling themselves." — John Kenneth Galbraith. Canadian-American economist and diplomat.

CCC workers constructing a road in what is now Cuyahoga Valley National Park, 1933. Source: U.S. National Archives and Records Administration Author unknown. Source: National Archives and Records Administration. Franklin D. Roosevelt Library (NLFDR). Via Wikimedia Commons. Public Domain.

On this day in 1929, known as Black Tuesday, the U.S. stock market crashed, triggering the Great Depression—the most severe economic downturn in modern history. The crash devastated financial markets, but its ripple effects profoundly shaped urban environments. Cities faced widespread unemployment, housing foreclosures, and a sharp decline in public services. Urban centers like New York, Chicago, and Detroit experienced massive population shifts as people sought work, while shantytowns known as "Hoovervilles" sprang up on city fringes. The crisis eventually spurred transformative urban policies under the New Deal, including public housing programs, large-scale infrastructure projects, and the Federal Housing Administration (FHA) creation. Black Tuesday highlighted the vulnerability of urban economies to financial instability, shaping how governments approached urban planning, social safety nets, and housing policy in the following decades.

How did the urban challenges of the Great Depression influence the development of modern housing and social welfare policies in cities?

PASSAGE OF THE DISASTER MITIGATION ACT OF 2000

"Mitigation is the foundation of resilience, ensuring communities are prepared to weather the storms of tomorrow." – Federal Emergency Management Agency (FEMA) statement.

Environmental researchers investigate the condition of canal water for toxic spills and river wastewater sampling. By VStudio. Licensed

On this day in 2000, President Bill Clinton signed the Disaster Mitigation Act (DMA 2000) into law, amending the Stafford Act and transforming the nation's approach to disaster preparedness. The act prioritized pre-disaster planning and mitigation to reduce future loss of life and property, shifting from reactive to proactive disaster management. It required state and local governments to develop Hazard Mitigation Plans as a prerequisite for receiving federal disaster assistance, fostering a culture of risk assessment and resilience planning. Communities were encouraged to identify vulnerabilities and implement measures to address hazards such as flooding, hurricanes, and earthquakes. DMA 2000 established a new framework for integrating disaster resilience into urban and regional planning by tying mitigation planning to federal funding eligibility. Its legacy shapes how cities prepare for and adapt to natural hazards, promoting safer and more sustainable communities.

How can communities enhance disaster mitigation planning to address the increasing frequency and severity of climate-related events?

OCTOBER 31
1913

DEDICATION OF THE LINCOLN HIGHWAY, THE FIRST TRANSCONTINENTAL ROAD IN THE U.S.

"The Lincoln Highway is an object lesson in road building that all can understand."
– Carl G. Fisher, principal promoter of the Lincoln Highway

"Across the continent by the Lincoln Highway", 1915. A motorist's journey on the newly established Lincoln Highway, circa 1915, capturing the spirit of early automobile travel across America's first transcontinental road. By Effie Price Gladding (Brentano's, 1915); original held by the New York Public Library. Source: Wikimedia Commons.

On this day in 1913, the Lincoln Highway was officially dedicated as the first transcontinental automobile road in the United States, stretching from Times Square in New York City to Lincoln Park in San Francisco. Conceived by entrepreneur Carl G. Fisher, the highway was envisioned as a "Coast-to-Coast Rock Highway" that would unify the nation and promote automobile travel. At a time when most roads were unpaved and poorly maintained, the Lincoln Highway became a symbol of progress and connectivity, inspiring future road-building efforts across the country. Its route influenced the location of towns, the growth of roadside commerce, and ultimately helped establish the U.S.

Highway System. The dedication marked a turning point in American urban development, as cities began to adapt to the needs of the automobile. The Lincoln Highway's legacy lives on in the urban sprawl, zoning laws, and planning priorities that emerged in the 20th century, highlighting the profound impact of transportation infrastructure on urban form.

How did early national roadways like the Lincoln Highway shape the growth patterns of American towns and influence the development of car-centric urban planning?

JOHN ADAMS
MOVES INTO THE WHITE HOUSE

"I pray Heaven to bestow the best of blessings on this house and all that shall hereafter inhabit it." – John Adams. 2nd President of the United States.

NORTH FRONT OF THE PRESIDENTS HOUSE

Exterior view of the north front of the White House. Engraved for the National Calendar 1822. Source: Library of Congress Prints and Photographs Division. Public Domain.

On this day in 1800, President John Adams became the first U.S. president to reside in the White House, marking a pivotal moment in establishing Washington, D.C., as the nation's capital. Designed by architect James Hoban, the White House was a key element in Pierre Charles L'Enfant's urban plan, which envisioned the capital as a city embodying democratic ideals and national unity. Adams' move into the White House symbolized the transition of Washington, D.C., from a fledgling town to the center of American governance and identity. Over time, the White House became a powerful symbol of leadership, resilience, and the aspirations of a growing republic. Its location and design highlighted the role of thoughtful urban planning in creating a capital that functions as a political, cultural, and symbolic hub, setting a precedent for how cities can reflect and support the values of a nation.

How does the design and placement of government buildings shape a city's identity and civic purpose?

NOVEMBER 2
1863

BIRTH OF
SIR RAYMOND UNWIN

"The great object of the planner should be to create a place to live in, not merely a place to live." – Raymond Unwin. British urban planner and architect.

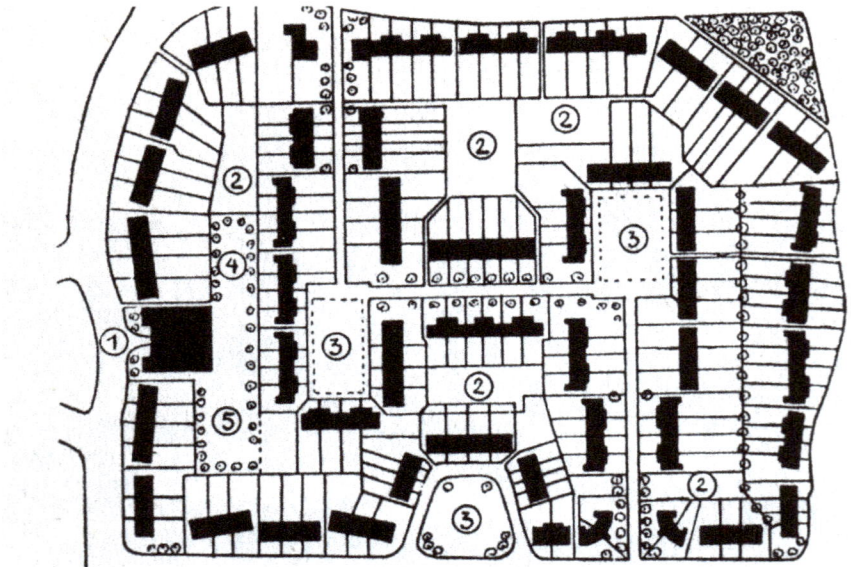

Part of the urban plan for the garden city of Letchworth, 1903. By Raymond Unwin. Source: Ebenezer Howard Gartenstädte von morgen. Via Wikimedia Commons. Public Domain.

On this day in 1863, Sir Raymond Unwin was born—a pioneering urban planner whose work profoundly shaped the Garden City Movement and modern planning practice. Committed to creating healthier, more equitable communities, Unwin championed urban designs that prioritized green space, walkability, and social cohesion. In collaboration with Barry Parker, he co-designed Letchworth Garden City (1903) and Hampstead Garden Suburb (1907), influential models that blended beauty, functionality, and social purpose. His seminal book, Town Planning in Practice (1909), bridged theory and implementation, offering a comprehensive vision for humane and well-ordered cities. Unwin advocated for design that supported both individual dignity and community life—ideas that helped establish planning as a professional discipline. His emphasis on integrating housing, landscape, and public space continues to inspire planners today, reinforcing his enduring legacy as a visionary who reimagined urban environments to serve both people and place.

How can Raymond Unwin's principles of equitable and community-focused urban design inspire solutions to modern challenges like housing inequality and sprawl?

ESTABLISHMENT OF
THE MODEL CITIES PROGRAM

"Model Cities was an effort to ensure that every citizen shared in the promise of American prosperity." — Lyndon B. Johnson. 36th President of the United States.

Community members actively engage in a planning charrette for the 'Little Havana Me Importa' Revitalization Master Plan, embodying the Model Cities Program's legacy of inclusive urban development. Image by Plusurbia Design. Own Work.

On this day in 1966, the Model Cities Program was officially launched as part of President Lyndon B. Johnson's Great Society initiative to combat urban poverty and revitalize struggling neighborhoods. Established under the Demonstration Cities and Metropolitan Development Act, the program aimed to integrate housing, education, healthcare, and job creation into a cohesive urban renewal strategy. Unlike earlier urban renewal efforts, Model Cities prioritized community participation, giving residents a voice in shaping redevelopment plans. Despite its innovative approach, the program faced significant challenges, including limited funding, bureaucratic hurdles, and resistance from local governments. While discontinued in the 1970s, the Model Cities Program influenced later urban policies by emphasizing holistic planning and collaboration between federal and local entities. Its legacy endures in the principles of community engagement and integrated urban development, which continue to shape efforts to create equitable and sustainable cities.

What lessons from the Model Cities Program can be applied to address contemporary challenges in urban revitalization?

CAIRO HOSTS
THE 12TH WORLD URBAN FORUM

"The city is not a problem; it is the solution."
— Jaime Lerner. Brazilian architect and urban planner.

Collage. Image by Andrey Popov. Licensed

On this day in 2024, Cairo, Egypt, hosted the opening of the 12th World Urban Forum under the patronage of President Abdel Fattah El-Sisi. Organized by UN-Habitat, the forum brought together over 20,000 participants from 179 countries, including urban planners, policymakers, and scholars, to discuss sustainable and inclusive urban development. Since its inception in 2002 in Nairobi, Kenya, the World Urban Forum has become a crucial platform for addressing global urban challenges such as climate change, housing inequality, and urban resilience. Hosting the forum in Cairo highlighted the city's efforts in urban regeneration and its role as a model for innovative solutions in the Global South. These gatherings are vital for shaping the future of urban living, fostering international collaboration, and emphasizing the transformative power of thoughtful urban planning in creating livable, resilient, and equitable cities.

How can local actions and community-led initiatives drive sustainable urban development in today's rapidly urbanizing world?

LAUNCH OF
THE BOARD GAME "MONOPOLY"

"Monopoly is the great American game because it deals with the great American concept of property ownership." – Charles Darrow. American board game designer.

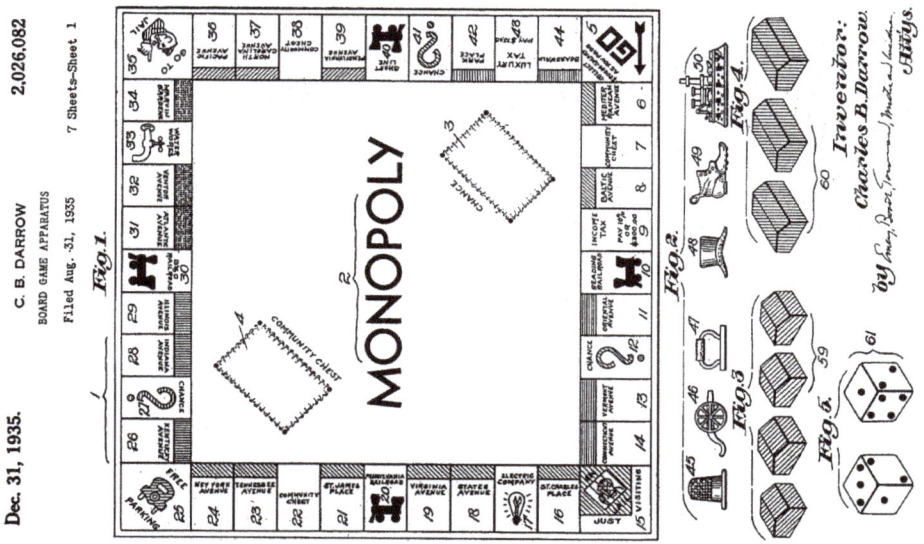

First page of U.S. Patent No. 2,026,082, granted to Charles Darrow for the board game Monopoly on February 6, 1935. Source: Image from the U.S. Patent and Trademark Office, converted to PNG by John D. Buell. Via Wikimedia Commons. Public Domain.

On this day in 1935, Parker Brothers officially launched Monopoly, a board game that became a cultural phenomenon. Monopoly, simulating urban real estate development, financial strategy, and competition, reflects themes of capitalism, property ownership, and economic ambition. Elizabeth Magie's earlier creation inspired The Landlord's Game, initially intended to critique wealth concentration and economic inequality. However, Monopoly evolved into a celebration of real estate acquisition and financial success, popularizing urban growth, infrastructure management, and economic risk-taking concepts. By incorporating railroads, utilities, and housing, the game provides a simplified yet engaging representation of the complexities of city-building and economic systems. Monopoly continues to influence how people understand urban development and financial strategy, serving as both a playful exploration and a reflection of the forces that shape cities and economies. Its enduring legacy underscores the interplay of competition and opportunity in urban life.

How has the cultural impact of games like Monopoly shaped public perceptions of urban real estate and city planning?

NOVEMBER 6
1920

DEATH OF
ARTURO SORIA Y MATA

"The Linear City will bring about the harmonious coexistence of civilization and nature."
– Arturo Soria y Mata. Spanish urban planner and engineer.

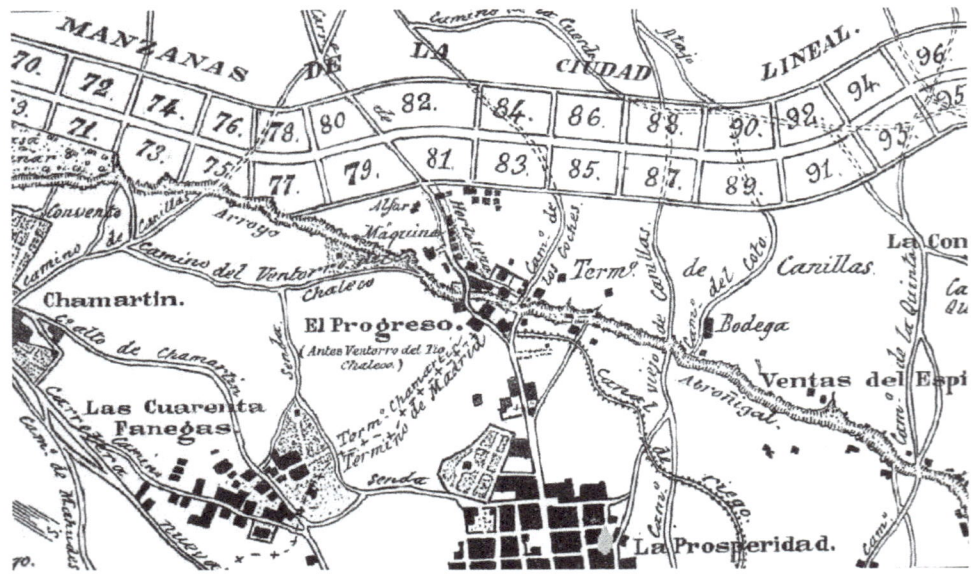

Urban development project for the "Ciudad Lineal" between 1895 and 1910; planning and drawings published in the "La Dictadura" newspaper of the Madrid Urban Development Company. By Arturo Soria (1844-1920). Source: Wikimedia Commons. Public Domain.

On this day in 1920, Arturo Soria y Mata, a pioneering urban planner, passed away in Madrid, Spain. Soria is renowned for his visionary Linear City (Ciudad Lineal) concept, which proposed organizing urban development along transportation corridors. His plan integrated residential, commercial, and green spaces in a continuous linear structure to address the overcrowding and disorganization of traditional city designs. Soria's model sought to create more balanced and efficient urban environments by emphasizing equitable access to resources and mobility. Although his ambitious vision was only partially realized in Madrid through the Ciudad Lineal project, his ideas had a lasting influence on urban planning. Soria's concepts inspired movements such as transit-oriented development and sustainable urbanism, highlighting the importance of integrating transportation and land use. His legacy is a testament to innovative thinking in designing cities that prioritize mobility, equity, and livability.

How can the principles of the Linear City be adapted to address modern urban challenges such as climate change, population growth, and housing affordability?

OCTOBER REVOLUTION:
THE TRANSFORMATION OF SOVIET CITIES

"We must create a new social order, a new everyday life, and new forms of settlement that embody the ideals of socialism." – Nikolai Milyutin, Soviet architect and urban planner.

Aerial view over Soviet-era apartment block houses in Jelgava, Latvia. The image highlights the uniform, prefabricated residential architecture typical of Soviet urban planning, characterized by functional design, centralized layouts, and mass housing. By Darius SUL. Licensed

On this day in 1917, the October Revolution began in Russia (dated October 25 by the Julian calendar then in use, which corresponds to November 7 on today's Gregorian calendar), setting the stage for a radical transformation of urban planning under the Soviet regime. The Bolsheviks saw cities as instruments of socialist change, designed to promote equality and collective life. They prioritized public housing, industrial zones, and shared open spaces, rejecting private ownership as a foundation for urban development. Cities like Moscow, Leningrad (now St. Petersburg), and Magnitogorsk were reimagined as models of socialist urbanism. Innovations such as communal apartments (kommunalkas), large-

scale housing blocks, and monumental public buildings embodied these ideals, though often at the cost of overcrowding and uniformity. Centralized planning became a defining feature, influencing not only the Soviet Union but also city-building across socialist states globally. The October Revolution's legacy in urban design illustrates how ideology can shape the built environment, offering both cautionary lessons and bold examples in the pursuit of equity, cohesion, and collective identity in city-making.

How can cities today reconcile the legacy of centralized urban planning with the modern push for equity, sustainability, and community-driven development?

NOVEMBER 8
1949

CELEBRATION OF 'WORLD TOWN PLANNING DAY'

"Cities are more than places in space, they are dramas in time."
– Patrick Geddes. Scottish biologist and urban planner.

Planners and stakeholders collaborating around a model of a city. Created by Plusurbia Design using MidJourney.

On this day in 1949, World Town Planning Day was established by Professor Carlos María della Paolera of the University of Buenos Aires. Recognized in over 30 countries, this annual observance highlights the vital role of urban planning in creating sustainable, equitable, and livable communities. Lectures, workshops, and community discussions focus on pressing issues like climate resilience, affordable housing, and inclusive development. World Town Planning Day emphasizes the transformative potential of thoughtful planning to address urban challenges and enhance quality of life. It also fosters global collaboration by encouraging the exchange of innovative ideas and best practices among planners and communities. Celebrated each year, the day serves as a tribute to the essential contributions of urban planners in shaping healthy, inclusive, and thriving cities, reflecting the ongoing evolution of the profession in meeting contemporary urban needs.

How can World Town Planning Day inspire greater public participation in the planning process?

FALL OF
THE BERLIN WALL

"The fall of the Berlin Wall shows us that dreams can come true, that nothing is impossible."
– Richard von Weizsäcker, President of West Germany.

Berlin wall memorial, Berlin, Germany. Segments of the reinforced concrete wall have been left as a reminder of events leading up to the fall of the wall. By AlexGo. Licensed

On this day in 1989, the Berlin Wall, a stark symbol of Cold War division, was opened, and crowds from East and West Berlin dismantled it by hand, ending nearly three decades of separation. Built in 1961, the wall had not only split a city but deepened the divide between two different social, political, and economic systems. Its fall marked the start of German reunification and set Berlin on a challenging path of reconstruction—reconnecting fractured infrastructure, harmonizing laws and services, and addressing stark economic disparities. Culturally and socially, the city faced the task of merging identities shaped by vastly different experiences under democracy and authoritarianism. Planners worked to revive neglected neighborhoods and integrate transport networks, while citizens navigated the complexities of building trust and shared purpose. Over time, Berlin emerged as a vibrant global capital of creativity and renewal. Today, remnants of the wall stand as powerful reminders of division overcome and the enduring effort required to rebuild unity.

How can cities with divided histories overcome physical and ideological barriers to create inclusive and unified urban environments?

KRISTALLNACHT: THE URBAN DESTRUCTION OF JEWISH COMMUNITIES

"Wherever they burn books, they will also, in the end, burn people."
– Heinrich Heine. German poet and essayist. Paraphrased from Almansor (1821).

Jews rounded up in Stadthagen after Kristallnacht Author unknown. Via Wikimedia Commons. CC0

On this day in 1938, Kristallnacht—known as the "Night of Broken Glass"—began in the evening hours of November 9 and continued into the early morning of November 10. This coordinated, state-sanctioned attack targeted Jewish synagogues, homes, schools, and businesses across Nazi Germany and Austria. Thousands of buildings were vandalized, looted, and set ablaze, with shards of broken glass strewn across urban streets, giving the event its name. Kristallnacht marked a devastating escalation in the Nazi regime's persecution of Jewish communities, transforming cityscapes through destruction and terror. It left once-thriving neighborhoods in ruins, forced countless families from their homes, and erased cultural and religious landmarks from the urban fabric. The event stands as a grim reminder of how cities can become instruments of political violence and ideological enforcement. Its memory today underscores the importance of protecting vulnerable communities and preserving historical sites tied to justice, diversity, and remembrance.

How can cities preserve the memory of marginalized and persecuted communities while fostering inclusive urban environments today?

ARMISTICE DAY AND
THE URBAN REBUILDING OF EUROPE

"The Great War through has swept away all illusions, and now we are ready to rebuild our cities in the spirit of peace." – Georges Clemenceau, Prime Minister of France. (Paraphrased).

Berlin's Breitscheidplatz in 1954 illustrates the city's postwar reconstruction, with the shattered spire of the Kaiser Wilhelm Memorial Church standing as a symbol of memory amidst renewal. The image reflects the resilience of Berlin's urban landscape after World War II. By Wschmock. Source: Wikimedia Commons. CC0 1.0.

On this day in 1918, the Armistice of Compiègne was signed, ending fighting on the Western Front of World War I and signaling a profound moment of change for cities across Europe. The war left cities like Ypres, Reims, and Verdun devastated, requiring extensive reconstruction in the postwar years. Beyond rebuilding, many cities incorporated new urban forms and public spaces dedicated to commemorating the war, including memorials, monuments, and military cemeteries. The devastation also inspired movements to improve living conditions, focusing on housing, hygiene, and urban planning to create healthier environments. Armistice Day continues to be marked by ceremonies at war memorials in cities worldwide, highlighting the enduring connection between urban spaces and collective memory. This historical moment underscores how cities evolve in response to conflict, using reconstruction as an opportunity for reflection, renewal, and the integration of shared history into urban landscapes.

How can cities balance honoring their history with creating inclusive and resilient urban environments in the face of past conflicts?

NOVEMBER 12
2003

SHANGHAI MAGLEV
SETS WORLD SPEED RECORD

"The train of the future moves not just through space, but through ambition."
– Inspired by the Shanghai maglev vision

Shanghai Maglev high speed train station, China. By Francis Longhurst/Wirestock. Licensed

On this day in 2003, the Shanghai Transrapid maglev train set a world speed record for commercial rail systems, reaching 501 kilometers per hour (311 mph). Developed through a partnership between China and German engineering firms, it became the first high-speed magnetic levitation line to enter commercial operation. The train connects Shanghai Pudong International Airport to the city center in just under eight minutes, spanning a distance of 30 kilometers. This milestone symbolized more than technological prowess—it marked a new era of urban mobility, where ultra-fast transit redefined proximity, regional integration, and metropolitan reach. The Shanghai maglev was an ambitious demonstration of China's infrastructural and urban planning ambitions at the turn of the 21st century. Though the system serves a single corridor, its performance continues to influence high-speed rail discourse worldwide, pushing planners to consider how speed, connectivity, and innovation might shape the next generation of sustainable and dynamic urban regions.

How does ultra-high-speed transport reshape regional equity, land value, and the meaning of proximity in today's cities?

BIRTH OF AUGUSTINE OF HIPPO

"Peace is the tranquility of order."
– Augustine of Hippo. Roman African theologian and philosopher.

Augustine: De civitate dei, woodcut. Petri for A. Koberger (Nuremberg), 1515 (Isny Preachers' Library) – the open city of God, Zion, hostile to the closed city of Babylon. Source: Helmut Schmid: "Ain Liebrey zu den büchern." The medieval Preachers' Library of the St. Nicholas Church in Isny (Kleinode; Vol. 7). Ravensburg 2000 (DNB). Originally published in 426 AD. Via Wikimedia Commons. Public Domain.

On this day in 354 CE, Augustine of Hippo was born in Thagaste, a Roman city in present-day Algeria. As a bishop, theologian, and philosopher, Augustine became one of the most influential thinkers in Western history. His seminal work, The City of God, offered a profound framework by contrasting the "City of Man," focused on material concerns, with the "City of God," centered on spiritual and eternal values. Augustine's ideas deeply influenced medieval urban development, highlighting the role of religious institutions in governance, education, and community life. His reflections on justice, civic duty, and the moral dimensions of city life laid a foundation for understanding urban centers' ethical and spiritual responsibilities. Notably, The City of God includes what may be one of the earliest allusions to NIMBYism—an implicit critique of those who exclude undesirable elements from their cities in favor of self-interest or moral superiority. Augustine's writings continue to shape debates on the interplay between faith, morality, and governance, offering timeless insights into cities' spiritual and ethical foundations.

How can Augustine's vision of the "City of God" inspire contemporary urban planners to create cities that balance material needs with moral and spiritual aspirations?

NOVEMBER 14
1994

CHANNEL TUNNEL OPENS FOR FULL PASSENGER SERVICE

"The Channel Tunnel has made the impossible possible, uniting two nations through innovation and determination." – Jacques Delors. French economist and politician.

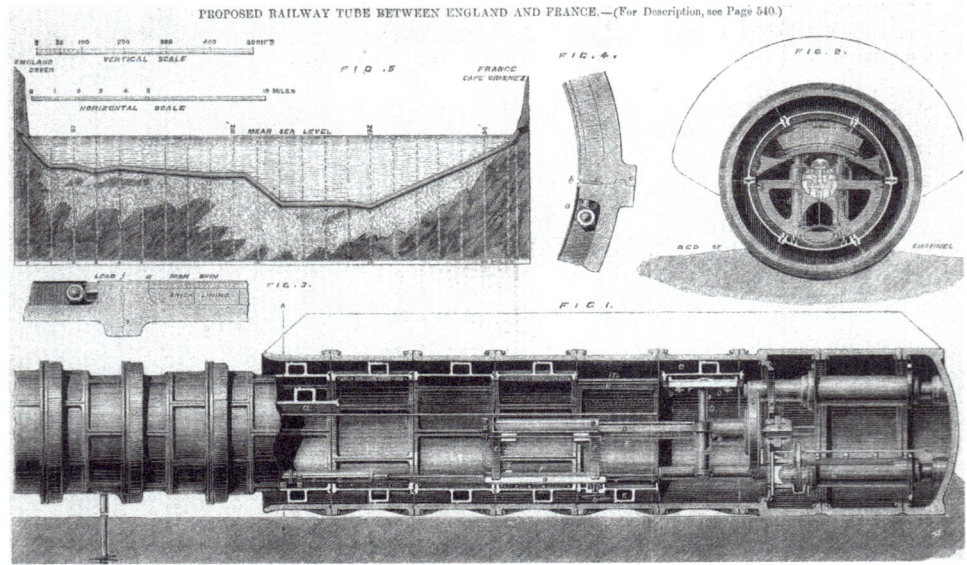

1869 proposal by John F. La Trobe Bateman and Julian Revy for a submerged cast-iron railway tube beneath the English Channel—a visionary precursor to the modern Channel Tunnel. Drawings by La Trobe Bateman and Julian J. Rèvy, 1869. Illustration from The Engineer, August 27, 1869. Source: Adobe Stock, by Archivist.

On this day in 1994, the Channel Tunnel (Chunnel) began full passenger service, fulfilling a long-standing dream of linking the United Kingdom and mainland Europe. Stretching 31.4 miles beneath the English Channel, the tunnel connects Folkestone, England, with Coquelles, France, significantly reducing travel time and enhancing regional integration. A feat of engineering and diplomacy, the Chunnel overcame enormous technical and financial challenges, symbolizing the potential of international collaboration. The idea dates back to 1869, when engineers John F. La Trobe Bateman and Julian Revy proposed a cast-iron railway tube powered by pneumatic pressure—an unbuilt but visionary concept that laid the groundwork for today's tunnel. The Chunnel now stands as both an infrastructure triumph and a model of cross-border cooperation, advancing mobility, sustainability, and cultural exchange in an increasingly interconnected world.

How can large-scale infrastructure projects like the Channel Tunnel inspire future advancements in sustainable regional connectivity?

CELEBRATION OF NATIONAL RECYCLING DAY

"The Earth is what we all have in common."
– Wendell Berry. American novelist, poet, and environmental activist.

Modern city trash cans Ljubljana. By YuryGulakov. Licensed

On this day in 1997, National Recycling Day—also known as America Recycles Day— was established, highlighting the critical role of recycling in fostering urban sustainability. Established in 1997 by the National Recycling Coalition and now spearheaded by Keep America Beautiful, the initiative encourages individuals and communities to reduce waste, conserve resources, and adopt sustainable practices. Recycling mitigates landfill overuse, lowers greenhouse gas emissions, and protects ecosystems while creating economic opportunities in resource recovery industries. In urban areas, effective recycling programs enhance public spaces, promote environmental stewardship, and strengthen community engagement, improving overall quality of life. The day underscores the importance of integrating waste management into urban planning as cities strive to build resilient and sustainable environments. It serves as a call to action, reminding everyone of their role in shaping a cleaner, greener future through mindful consumption and waste reduction.

How can urban communities enhance recycling initiatives to create more sustainable and livable cities for future generations?

NOVEMBER 16
1945

FOUNDING OF U.N.E.S.C.O.

"Since wars begin in the minds of men, it is in the minds of men that the defenses of peace must be constructed." – UNESCO Constitution.

Aerial view of Vilnius Old Town – a UNESCO World Heritage Site, celebrated for its rich architectural history and centuries-old cultural layers. By Top Lithuania. Licensed.

On this day in 1945, the United Nations Educational, Scientific, and Cultural Organization (UNESCO) was founded in London to promote peace, cultural understanding, and sustainable development through education, science, and culture. One of its most impactful initiatives, the World Heritage Program, launched in 1972, identifies and protects culturally significant sites like Venice, the Historic Center of Kyoto, the Medina of Fez, and the medieval Old Town of Vilnius, Lithuania. With its winding cobblestone streets, Gothic spires, Baroque facades, and diverse cultural influences, Vilnius exemplifies the rich urban heritage that UNESCO seeks to preserve. These historic urban landscapes reflect centuries of human creativity and resilience and serve as living reminders of the importance of safeguarding cultural identity in the face of modern challenges like globalization, climate change, and rapid urbanization. Today, UNESCO's work underscores the critical role of cities as hubs of history, culture, and human progress, inspiring future generations to value and protect their shared heritage.

How can cities balance preserving their cultural heritage while adapting to modern urbanization and the challenges of climate change?

STRØGET:
PIONEERING URBAN PEDESTRIANIZATION

"The car is an intrusive guest in our cities, and we must find ways to limit its dominance."
– Jan Gehl, Danish urbanist.

Strøget, Copenhagen, Denmark. The image shows one of the world's longest pedestrian streets, a central example of urban design prioritizing walkability and public space in city centers.. By Hernán Piñera. Via Flickr. CC BY-SA 2.0

On this day in 1962, Copenhagen's Strøget was transformed into one of the world's longest pedestrian streets, stretching approximately 1.1 kilometers through the heart of the city. Initially introduced as a temporary experiment to alleviate growing vehicular congestion and improve urban livability, the plan faced resistance from local merchants who feared losing business. However, the pedestrianization of Strøget proved transformative, significantly increasing foot traffic, boosting retail activity, and revitalizing the area. The initiative became a milestone in urban planning, demonstrating the economic and social benefits of prioritizing people over cars in city design. Strøget's success has since inspired cities worldwide to create pedestrian-friendly zones, showcasing how car-free spaces can enhance public life, promote sustainability, and redefine urban experiences. Today, it stands as a model for innovative urban design, highlighting the power of human-centric planning in fostering vibrant, accessible, and thriving city centers.

How can modern cities balance the needs of pedestrians and vehicles to create more livable urban environments?

NOVEMBER 18
1626

DEDICATION OF
ST. PETER'S BASILICA

"Upon this rock I will build my church."
– Jesus Christ (Gospel of Matthew 16:18).

Saint Peter in Vatican City, 1710 - 1783. By Francesco Polanzani. Source: Rijksmuseum. CC0 1.0 Universal

On this day in 1626, St. Peter's Basilica, one of the most iconic architectural achievements in history, was consecrated by Pope Urban VIII in Vatican City. The basilica represents centuries of innovation in religious and urban architecture, designed by celebrated architects such as Michelangelo, Gian Lorenzo Bernini, and Donato Bramante. Its monumental dome and the grandeur of St. Peter's Square exemplify the integration of sacred spaces into the urban fabric, influencing city planning and church design worldwide. The basilica serves as the spiritual and administrative center of the Catholic Church and symbolizes the enduring connection between faith and urban form. As a cultural and architectural landmark, it attracts millions of pilgrims and visitors annually, embodying the historical and artistic legacy of the Renaissance and Baroque periods while remaining a focal point of Vatican City's urban identity.

How can cities today balance the preservation of iconic historical landmarks with the need to modernize urban infrastructure and meet contemporary demands?

BIRTH OF
HANS MONDERMAN

"If you treat people like idiots, they will behave like idiots."
— Hans Monderman. Dutch traffic engineer and innovator.

Exhibition Road, London – Retrofitted between 2010 and 2012, this iconic street near the city's major museums exemplifies shared space design, where pedestrians, cyclists, and vehicles coexist in a single-level, decluttered public realm inspired by Hans Monderman's principles. By Romazur. CC BY-SA 3.0

On this day in 1945, Hans Monderman was born in Leeuwarden, Netherlands. A pioneering traffic engineer, Monderman is best known for developing the "shared space" concept in urban design—a radical departure from conventional traffic planning. Rather than relying on traffic lights, signs, curbs, and road markings, Monderman's approach integrates all modes of transport within a unified public realm. By blurring the boundaries between pedestrian and vehicular zones, he believed that users would be more attentive and negotiate movement through social cues rather than strict controls. His designs, implemented in towns like Drachten and Haren, demonstrated that reducing formal regulation could paradoxically improve both safety and quality of life. The results often showed fewer accidents, lower speeds, and enhanced civic interaction. Monderman's philosophy emphasized trust in human behavior and called for streets to be designed not just for movement, but as social and democratic spaces. His influence continues to shape contemporary debates about livable streets, traffic calming, and urban equity worldwide.

How can cities adapt shared space design to suit different cultural, climatic, and density contexts while preserving safety and equity?

NOVEMBER 20
1920

BIRTH OF
LANDSCAPE ARCHITECT IAN MCHARG

"Design with nature, not against it."
— Ian McHarg. Scottish landscape architect and regional planner.

Manila city skyline in Philippines. Ermita and Paco districts seen from Intramuros. By Yooranpark. Licensed

On this day in 1920, Ian McHarg, a visionary landscape architect and urban planner, was born. Widely regarded as the father of ecological urbanism, McHarg revolutionized urban planning with his seminal book Design with Nature (1969), which advocated for integrating ecological principles into development. He emphasized that cities should harmonize with the natural environment, proposing a scientific analysis of landscapes to inform planning decisions. By combining geography, ecology, and design, McHarg pioneered sustainable approaches that preserved natural resources and minimized environmental damage. His work laid the foundation for modern concepts like green infrastructure, ecological zoning, and climate-conscious urbanism. McHarg's legacy continues to shape planning practices prioritizing resilience, habitat preservation, and sustainable growth, offering critical solutions for challenges like climate change and urban expansion. His enduring influence demonstrates that development and conservation can coexist, creating sustainable and livable cities.

How can McHarg's ecological principles help cities adapt to climate change and build resilience?

FIRST MANNED
HOT AIR BALLOON FLIGHT OVER PARIS

"The moment mankind first left the earth was the moment cities began to dream of a future without limits." – Paraphrased from the spirit of the Montgolfier brothers.

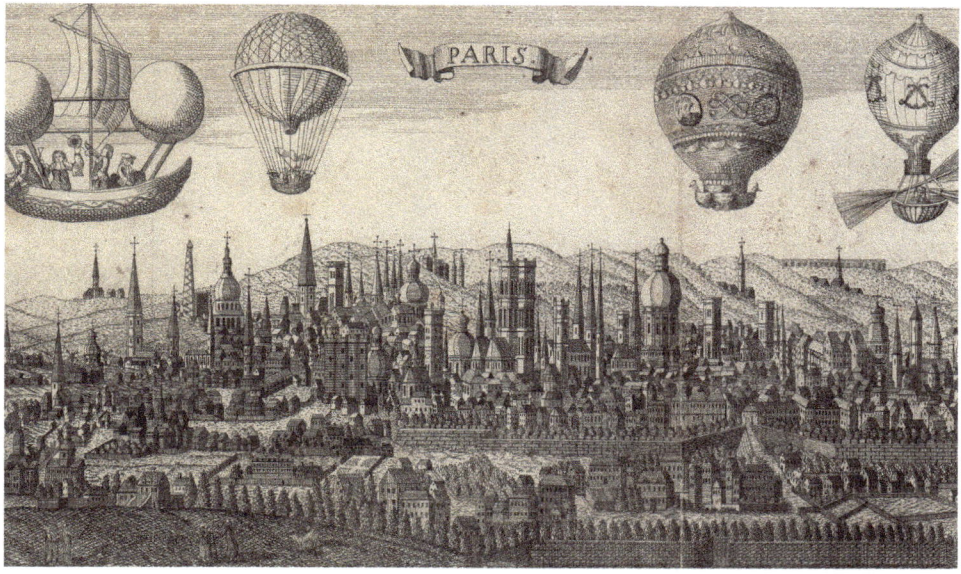

A late 18th-century view of Paris with hot air balloons drifting above the city, likely inspired by the Montgolfier brothers' pioneering 1783 flights. The scene reflects the Enlightenment era's embrace of science, innovation, and the expanding possibilities of urban life. Author unknown. Source: Wikimedia Commons. Public Domain.

On this day in 1783, the Montgolfier brothers achieved a historic milestone in human flight by launching the first manned hot air balloon over Paris, piloted by Jean-François Pilâtre de Rozier and François Laurent d'Arlandes. The flight began in the gardens of the Château de la Muette and covered approximately 9 kilometers before landing outside the city. This groundbreaking event showcased the potential of flight and sparked new ideas about urban mobility and exploration. Paris, already a center of scientific innovation and public spectacle, provided the perfect stage for this transformative achievement. The flight not only captivated the imagination of citizens but also inspired visions of how air transport could one day influence urban connectivity, accessibility, and expansion. The Montgolfier brothers' success heralded a new era of technological ambition, setting the stage for future advancements that would reshape cities and redefine human movement.

How can innovations in mobility, from the hot air balloon to modern-day drones, influence the way cities are designed and connected in the future?

NOVEMBER 22
1954

SUPREME COURT EXPANDS EMINENT DOMAIN IN BERMAN V. PARKER

"The concept of public welfare is broad and inclusive."
— Justice William O. Douglas, Majority Opinion.

Aerial views of Boston's West End, between 1959-1964. Source: West End Urban Renewal project, Boston Redevelopment Authority photographs, Collection # 4010.001. Via Wikimedia Commons. CC BY 2.0

On this day in 1954, the U.S. Supreme Court issued its landmark decision in Berman v. Parker, significantly expanding the scope of eminent domain. The case arose when the District of Columbia used eminent domain to seize private property for a redevelopment plan targeting urban blight. Property owners contested the taking, arguing it was unconstitutional since their land was not blighted. In a unanimous ruling, the Court upheld the seizure, affirming that eliminating blight and promoting urban renewal served a legitimate public purpose under the Fifth Amendment. This decision set a precedent for using eminent domain to reshape cities, facilitating widespread urban redevelopment projects to modernize infrastructure and improve housing conditions. However, the ruling also drew criticism for disproportionately displacing low-income and minority communities, raising enduring questions about equity and fairness in urban planning. Berman v. Parker remains a pivotal moment in the history of urban renewal policy.

How can urban planners balance the use of eminent domain with the need to protect vulnerable communities from displacement?

NATIONAL ESPRESSO DAY

"The city is not a concrete jungle, it is a human zoo."
– Desmond Morris. English zoologist, ethologist, and author.

Café in Paris, France. The image captures the quintessential Parisian café culture, highlighting the integration of small-scale public spaces into the urban fabric, fostering social interaction and community life. By Ekaterina Belova. Licensed

On this day in 2010, National Espresso Day was first celebrated, highlighting coffee's cultural and social significance in urban life. Cafés and terraces have long been vibrant centers of connection, creativity, and engagement within cities. These spaces have profoundly influenced city culture, from the intellectual coffeehouses of Vienna and Paris to modern urban cafés that double as coworking and social hubs. Sidewalk cafés and outdoor terraces enliven streetscapes, encouraging walkability, fostering interaction, and cultivating a sense of community. With its quick preparation and bold flavor, Espresso reflects the fast-paced rhythm of urban living while offering moments of pause and reflection amid the city's energy. Beyond their cultural role, cafés contribute to local economies and urban vibrancy, showcasing the importance of shared public spaces in shaping dynamic, inclusive, and socially connected cities. National Espresso Day reminds us of coffee's enduring role in enriching urban life and fostering human connection.

How can cities design more inviting and accessible public spaces to foster the vibrant street life associated with café culture?

NOVEMBER 24
1859

PUBLICATION OF
DARWIN'S ON THE ORIGIN OF SPECIES

"In the long history of humankind... those who learned to collaborate and improvise most effectively have prevailed." – Charles Darwin. English naturalist, geologist, and biologist.

Modern adaptation of Darwin's evolution of man. By Olena. Licensed

On this day in 1859, Charles Darwin published On the Origin of Species, introducing the theory of natural selection and transforming our understanding of adaptation and interconnected systems. While primarily a scientific breakthrough, Darwin's ideas profoundly influenced fields beyond biology, including urban planning and design. His emphasis on interconnectedness and resilience inspired planners like Frederick Law Olmsted, whose projects, such as New York's Central Park, sought harmony between urban development and natural landscapes. These green spaces prioritized ecological balance and human well-being, embodying principles aligned with Darwin's vision of adaptation and coexistence. Darwin's theories also laid the conceptual groundwork for sustainable urbanism, where cities integrate natural systems to address climate change, resource conservation, and resilience. His legacy continues to inform how we approach urban challenges, emphasizing the need for adaptive, balanced designs that support human life and the environment.

How can cities adapt to modern environmental challenges by embracing principles of resilience and sustainability inspired by natural systems?

BIRTH OF
ANDREW CARNEGIE

"The man who dies rich dies disgraced."
– Andrew Carnegie. Scottish-American industrialist and philanthropist.

Carnegie Hall at Night, New York City, USA. The image captures the historic concert venue's iconic façade, illuminated against the urban skyline. Carnegie Hall has been a key cultural landmark in the city's development since its opening in 1891. By Victor Prataviera. Licensed

On this day in 1835, Andrew Carnegie was born in Dunfermline, Scotland. After emigrating to the United States as a child, Carnegie became one of the most influential figures of the 19th century, reshaping urban infrastructure through his dominance in the steel industry. Carnegie's steel empire fueled the construction of bridges, railroads, and skyscrapers, accelerating the rapid urbanization of American cities and enabling their vertical and horizontal expansion. Later in life, he turned to philanthropy, donating much of his fortune to create public libraries, universities, and cultural institutions in urban centers. His libraries provided free access to knowledge, empowering working-class communities and promoting education as a pathway to self-improvement. Carnegie's investments in physical infrastructure and intellectual resources left an indelible mark on cities, reflecting his belief in using wealth to benefit society and shape thriving, equitable urban environments.

How can modern philanthropists and businesses contribute to the cultural and educational enrichment of urban communities?

NOVEMBER 26
1876

BIRTH OF
WILLIS CARRIER

"Air conditioning changed cities, making hot climates livable and fueling urban growth."
– Gail Cooper. American historian and author.

Air conditioner units filling the side of buildings. The image illustrates the integration of mechanical systems into the urban fabric, reflecting the impact of climate control technologies on building design, energy use, and city life. By Mediaimag. Licensed

On this day in 1876, Willis Carrier, the inventor of modern air conditioning, was born in Angola, New York. Carrier's 1902 invention transformed urban life by making it possible to control indoor climates, revolutionizing architecture and city planning. Air conditioning enabled the rise of skyscrapers and sprawling indoor complexes, allowing cities to expand vertically and host large populations in dense urban centers. It played a pivotal role in the rapid growth of cities in hot climates, such as Houston, Phoenix, and Dubai, which became viable urban hubs due to climate control. Carrier's innovation also shaped industries critical to urban economies, including healthcare, manufacturing, and entertainment, by creating environments conducive to productivity and comfort. Beyond practical applications, air conditioning reshaped urban lifestyles, enabling year-round use of public and cultural spaces in all climates. Carrier's work continues to influence how cities adapt to environmental challenges and ensure livable spaces for growing populations.

How can modern cities leverage innovations in climate control to promote energy efficiency and sustainability in urban design?

THE BERNERS STREET HOAX

"The great secret of success in life is for a man to be ready for his opportunity when it comes." – Benjamin Disraeli, British Prime Minister.

Illustration of the Berners Street Hoax of 1810. By Alfred Concanen, 1883.. Source: The choice humorous works, ludicrous adventures, bons mots, puns and hoaxes of Theodore Hook, published by Chatto and Windus, 1883. Via Wikimedia Commons. Public Domain.

On this day in 1810, London witnessed the Berners Street Hoax, a notorious prank orchestrated by Theodore Hook. Hook arranged for tradespeople, dignitaries, and workers to converge on a single address in Berners Street under false pretenses, overwhelming the area and creating chaos. The prank exposed the fragility of urban order and how misinformation could disrupt city systems. Streets became congested, services were paralyzed, and the commotion revealed communication and coordination challenges in densely populated areas. Though intended as a joke, the incident highlighted the importance of efficient urban management, emphasizing the need for robust systems to maintain public order and service delivery. The Berners Street Hoax remains a fascinating episode in London's history, an early example of how cities must adapt to vulnerabilities. Its lessons about resilience and misinformation resonate in today's complex urban environments.

How can modern cities improve communication systems to prevent disruptions caused by misinformation or hoaxes?

NOVEMBER 28
1911

PUBLICATION OF
THE MANUAL OF THE PLAN OF CHICAGO

"The plan is not merely a plan for a big city. It is a plan for a great city."
— Walter D. Moody. American civic leader and author.

Proposed Twelfth Street Improvement at its Intersections with Michigan Avenue and Ashland Avenue, 1912. Source: Wacker's Manual by Walter Moody, p. 104. Via Via Archive.org. Public Domain.

On this day in 1911, Walter D. Moody completed his introduction to the Manual of the Plan of Chicago, an educational text designed to teach Chicago's schoolchildren about urban planning and the transformative vision of the 1909 Plan of Chicago by Daniel Burnham and Edward Bennett. The manual was distributed to schools citywide, detailing Chicago's history, its urban challenges, and the 1909 plan's proposed solutions, such as improved transportation systems, expanded public spaces, and city beautification. This initiative marked the first formal effort to integrate urban planning into civic education. It aimed to instill pride in Chicago's progress and inspire young citizens to participate in its future development. Between 1912 and 1924, six editions of the manual were published, reflecting the growing importance of civic education in fostering collective responsibility for urban growth. The Manual of the Plan of Chicago remains a milestone in connecting education with city planning.

How can urban planning education in schools today encourage students to participate in shaping the future of their communities?

FIRST US PATENT
FOR TRAFFIC LIGHTS SYSTEM

"The automobile has not merely taken over the street, it has transformed our way of life."
– Marshall McLuhan. Canadian philosopher and media theorist.

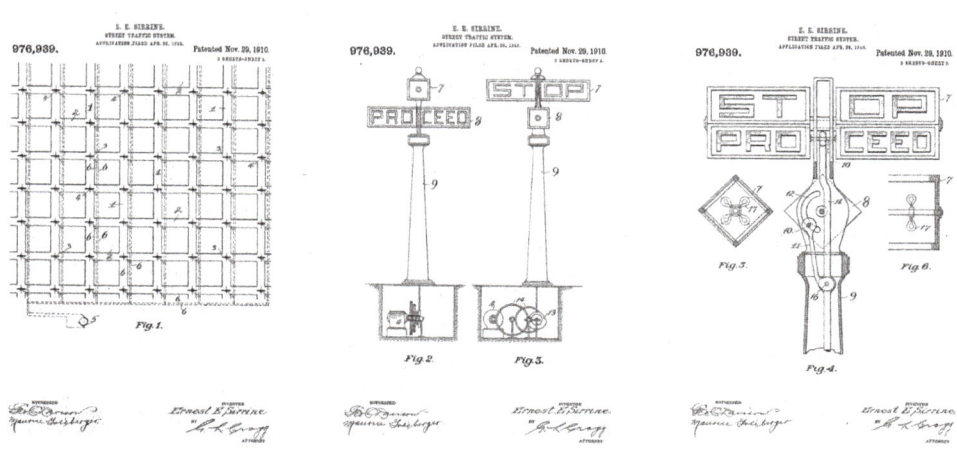

Street-traffic system patent #US976939A By Ernest E Sirrine. Source: U.S. Patent and Trademark Office. Public Domain.

On this day in 1910, the first U.S. patent for a traffic light system was issued to Ernest Sirrine. His invention featured non-electric, mechanically rotating signs displaying "Stop" and "Proceed" to manage the increasing congestion in early 20th-century urban centers. Though basic compared to today's technology, Sirrine's traffic system addressed the challenges posed by the rapid rise of automobiles, providing a framework for safer and more organized streets. As cities grew and car ownership expanded, efficient traffic control became vital to urban mobility. Sirrine's innovation laid the groundwork for developing electric traffic lights, later revolutionizing transportation infrastructure worldwide. By improving the flow of vehicles and protecting pedestrians, traffic signals have become indispensable to modern cities, enhancing the safety, efficiency, and functionality of urban environments. Sirrine's contribution marks an early step in the evolution of transportation management.

How can innovations in traffic management today address the challenges of congestion and prioritize pedestrian-friendly urban design?

NOVEMBER 30
1965

RALPH NADER'S
UNSAFE AT ANY SPEED PUBLISHED

"The automobile has brought death, injury, and the most pervasive kind of pollution to the United States." – Ralph Nader, American political activist and consumer advocate.

Diagram of the effects of vehicular traffic, illustrating the relationship between vehicle speed, accident likelihood, and pedestrian fatalities. The graphic underscores the critical role of speed management in urban planning for improving traffic safety.. By Plusurbia Design.

On this day in 1965, Ralph Nader's groundbreaking book Unsafe at Any Speed was published, exposing the auto industry's prioritization of profits over safety. Nader criticized car design flaws, particularly the Chevrolet Corvair, and highlighted the lack of accountability in automotive manufacturing. The book sparked a national outcry, leading to the passage of the National Traffic and Motor Vehicle Safety Act in 1966 and the establishment of the National Highway Traffic Safety Administration. These developments introduced new safety standards for vehicles and roadways, significantly reducing traffic-related fatalities over time. Beyond its impact on automobile design, Unsafe at Any Speed underscored the importance of integrating safety considerations into urban planning, advocating for infrastructure that protects public welfare. Nader's work reshaped consumer advocacy and transportation planning, leaving a lasting legacy in cities and industries prioritizing safety in designing mobility systems.

How can modern transportation systems balance innovation with safety and sustainability in urban environments?

BUENOS AIRES
METRO BEGINS OPERATION

"A modern city moves with the rhythm of its people, powered by innovation beneath its streets." – Carlos Pellegrini. Argentine statesman and former president. (Paraphrased).

Despedir al Subte "A", 2013. By Camila Molinari. Via Wikimedia Commons. CC BY-SA 4.0

On this day in 1913, the Buenos Aires Metro (Subte) inaugurated its first line, becoming the first underground railway system in the Southern Hemisphere and Latin America. Modeled after European systems such as those in London and Paris, the Subte reflected Buenos Aires' ambition to modernize and address the challenges of rapid urban growth. Incorporating advanced technologies for its time, including electric traction and innovative subterranean construction, the metro connected key urban areas, reducing congestion and facilitating efficient transportation for a growing population. The stations were designed with ornate tilework, marble finishes, and artistic details, showcasing the city's cultural aspirations and its identity as a global city. The success of the Subte set a benchmark for urban transit in Latin America, inspiring similar systems across the region. Today, the Subte remains integral to Buenos Aires' infrastructure, symbolizing the city's historical commitment to innovation and public transit excellence.

How does public transit transform urban development and accessibility in growing cities?

DECEMBER 2
1851

LOUIS-NAPOLÉON BONAPARTE'S COUP AND PARIS' TRANSFORMATION

"Paris is the city of light because we dared to destroy the old to create the new."
– Attributed to Baron Haussmann. French civic planner and urbanist.

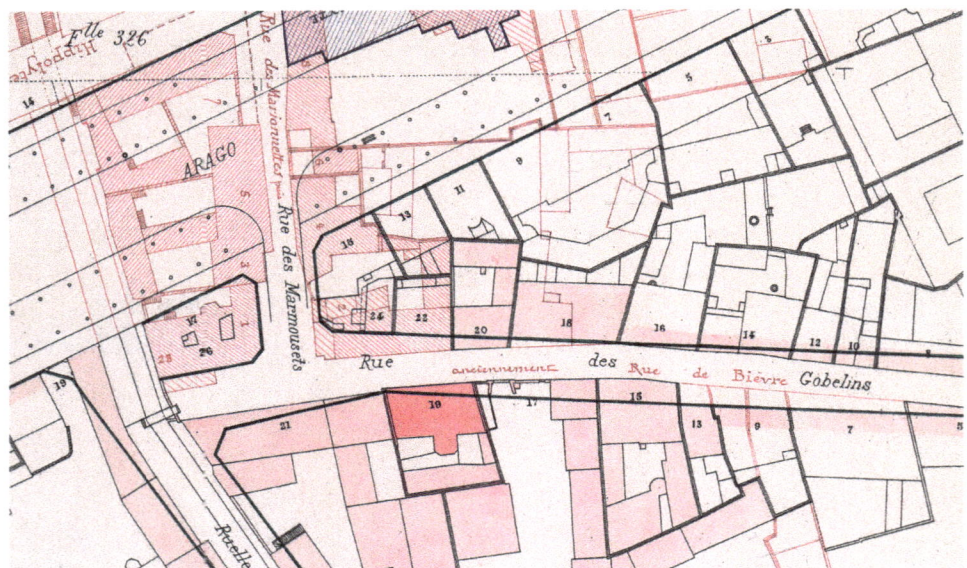

Reconfiguration of Boulevard Arago, c. 1860. The image shows an overlay of Haussmann's Plan over the existing streets of Paris, illustrating the transformation of the city's medieval street network into a modern, gridded system of boulevards and avenues. Unkown Author. Image courtesy of Paris Musées. CC0.

On this day in 1851, Louis-Napoléon Bonaparte staged a coup d'état, dissolving France's National Assembly and consolidating power as Emperor Napoleon III, setting the stage for the transformative Haussmannian renovation of Paris. Beginning in 1853 under Baron Georges-Eugène Haussmann, the city underwent radical redesigns, including wide boulevards, uniform building facades, expansive parks, and advanced water and sewer systems. These changes addressed public health issues, improved urban mobility, and strengthened military control by preventing barricades in narrow streets. The project modernized Paris, inspiring urban planning worldwide, but it also displaced thousands of working-class residents, sparking debates about equity and gentrification. Haussmann's vision profoundly shaped Paris, creating its iconic boulevards and public spaces that define the city today. These achievements serve as enduring symbols of innovation in urban design while reminding us of the social complexities inherent in large-scale urban renewal projects.

How can modern cities balance the need for infrastructure modernization with protecting vulnerable communities and preserving historical fabric?

ILLINOIS
ENTERS THE UNION

"Chicago is an idea, an ambition, a world within itself."
– Carl Sandburg. American poet, writer, and editor.

Kaskaskia, Illinois, in 1857 – a historic river town and the state's first capital, capturing the spirit of the American frontier before the rise of modern urban centers. Source: Meyer's Universe, or Illustration and Description of the Most Interesting and Remarkable Things in Nature and Art on the Entire Earth, Volume 18 (1857), Bibliographical Institute, Hildburghausen. Via Wikimedia Commons. Public Domain.

On this day in 1818, Illinois became the 21st state to join the United States, marking a pivotal moment in the nation's westward expansion. In the early 19th century, Kaskaskia, the first capital of Illinois, played a crucial role in the state's political and economic development. Located on the Mississippi River, Kaskaskia was a key trading hub and a symbol of frontier life before the rise of Chicago transformed the state's urban landscape. This early settlement reflects a time when the Midwest served as the gateway to the American frontier, connecting eastern markets to the untamed West. Though much of Kaskaskia was lost to the river's shifting course, its legacy endures as a reminder of the early struggles and aspirations that shaped Illinois. Today, Illinois remains a leader in urban innovation, blending its deep historical roots with a forward-looking approach to economic growth and sustainable development.

How can Illinois' history of urban innovation inspire solutions for modern challenges like sustainability and equitable growth?

DECEMBER 4
1924

BIRTH OF
JOHN C. PORTMAN JR.

"Buildings should serve people, not the other way around."
– John C. Portman Jr. American architect and real estate developer.

The atrium in the Bank of Canada building, ca. 2017. By Bank of Canada - Banque du Canada Via Wikimedia Commons. CC BY 2.0

On this day in 1924, John C. Portman Jr., a trailblazing American architect, was born. Known for his innovative atrium-centered designs, Portman redefined the relationship between architecture and urban life. His landmark projects, such as the Hyatt Regency Atlanta and the Renaissance Center in Detroit, integrated commercial, hospitality, and social spaces, breathing new life into urban cores and revitalizing city centers. Portman's designs emphasized human-centric environments within towering structures, transforming skyscrapers into vibrant hubs of connectivity and interaction. By merging functionality with aesthetic ingenuity, he set a new standard for urban architecture, fostering dynamic public spaces in vertical environments. His work addressed the evolving needs of modern cities, blending bold design with practicality to enhance livability. Portman's visionary approach inspires architects and urban planners, demonstrating how thoughtful design can transform cities and create spaces that connect people and communities.

How can modern architects continue to design urban spaces that foster community, connectivity, and inclusivity?

START OF
THE MONTGOMERY BUS BOYCOTT

"You must never be fearful about what you are doing when it is right."
– Rosa Parks. American civil rights activist.

Rosa Parks at her Congressional Gold Medal ceremony seated with assistant Elaine Steele (left); President Bill Clinton, Representatives Dennis Hastert, Dick Gephardt and others stand behind them. By Rebecca Roth. Source: Roll Call portion of CQ Roll Call Photograph Collection. Library of Congress Prints and Photographs Division. CC0.

On this day in 1955, the Montgomery Bus Boycott began in Montgomery, Alabama, marking a watershed moment in the American Civil Rights Movement. Sparked by Rosa Parks' arrest on December 1 for refusing to surrender her bus seat to a white passenger, the boycott lasted 381 days, drawing national attention to the injustices of segregation in urban public transportation. The boycott demonstrated the power of grassroots organization, with the African American community uniting to challenge systemic racism through sustained resistance. It underscored the role of urban transit systems as battlegrounds for civil rights and the deep ties between transportation planning and social equity. The eventual desegregation of Montgomery's buses in December 1956 was a historic victory, highlighting how cities can serve as arenas for transformative social change. This moment reshaped urban policy discussions, emphasizing the need for equitable and inclusive public services.

How can cities today ensure that their public transportation systems are equitable, inclusive, and accessible to all, regardless of social or economic background?

DECEMBER 6
1897

LONDON LICENSES
TAXICABS FOR THE FIRST TIME

"The organization of transport is the organization of the city itself."
– Herbert Morrison. British Labour politician.

London Taxi, hand drawn sketch. By Oleksandr Pokusai. Licensed

On this day in 1897, London became the first city in the world to introduce a licensing system for taxicabs, revolutionizing urban transportation. Early motorized "hansom cabs" provided a faster and more reliable alternative to horse-drawn carriages, and the new licensing system ensured safety, standardized fares, and professionalized drivers. This innovation brought order and accountability to London's bustling streets and set a global precedent for public transportation regulation. Over the years, licensed taxis have played a vital role in urban mobility, with their legacy influencing modern ride-sharing platforms like Uber and Lyft. While these services have improved convenience, they have also increased congestion and highlighted the need for better curbside management and fair regulation. London's 1897 decision underscores how transportation systems continuously evolve and the importance of balancing innovation with thoughtful urban planning to ensure safety, efficiency, and equitable access in ever-changing cities.

How can cities better manage modern mobility innovations, such as ride-sharing and micro-mobility, to ensure they contribute to sustainable and equitable urban transportation?

DECEMBER 7
1987

INSCRIPTION OF BRASÍLIA
AS A UNESCO WORLD HERITAGE SITE

"Architecture is the art of organizing space."
– Oscar Niemeyer. Brazilian architect.

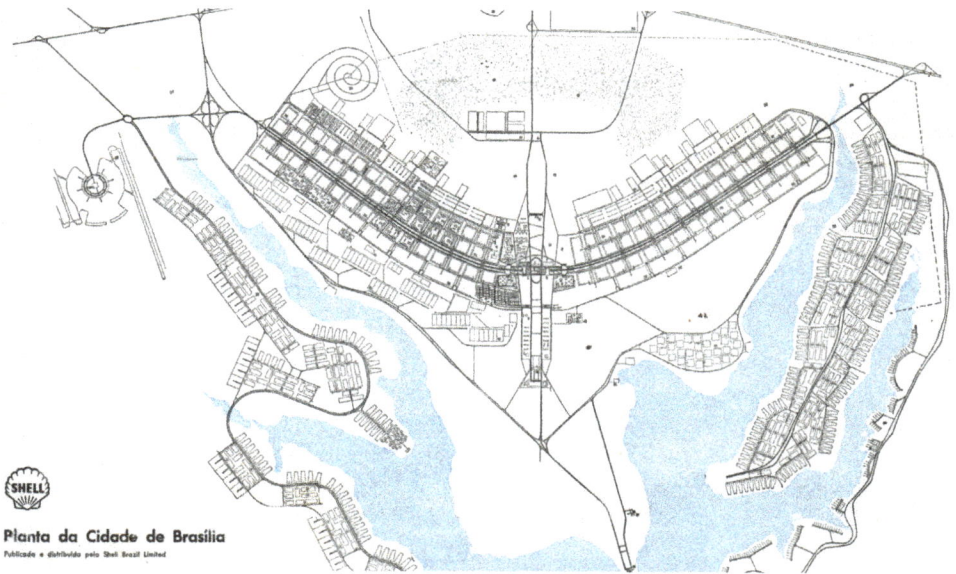

Planta da Cidade de Brasília
Publicado e distribuído pelo Shell Brazil Limited

Map of Brasília by Lúcio Costa in Brasília (edited image). Source: Unknown Author. Via Wikimedia Commons. Public Domain.

On this day in 1987, Brasília, the capital of Brazil, was inscribed as a UNESCO World Heritage Site for its groundbreaking and visionary urban design. Planned by urbanist Lúcio Costa and architect Oscar Niemeyer, Brasília was inaugurated in 1960 to symbolize Brazil's modernization and ambition. Its layout, resembling an airplane or bird, embodies modernist zoning principles, with distinct sectors for government, residential, and commercial functions. The city features monumental architecture, expansive green spaces, and a strong emphasis on symmetry and functionality, reflecting modernist ideals. However, Brasília has faced criticism for its car-centric design and the socioeconomic disparities between its meticulously planned areas and surrounding informal settlements. Despite these challenges, Brasília is an enduring example of innovative urban planning, inspiring planned cities worldwide and showcasing the potential of architecture and design to shape national identity and future aspirations.

How can the lessons of Brasília's design—both its successes and limitations—inform the development of planned cities in emerging economies today?

DECEMBER 8
1794

FIRE DEVASTATES
NEW ORLEANS' FRENCH QUARTER

"New Orleans makes it possible to go to Europe without leaving the United States."
– Franklin D. Roosevelt. 32nd President of the United States.

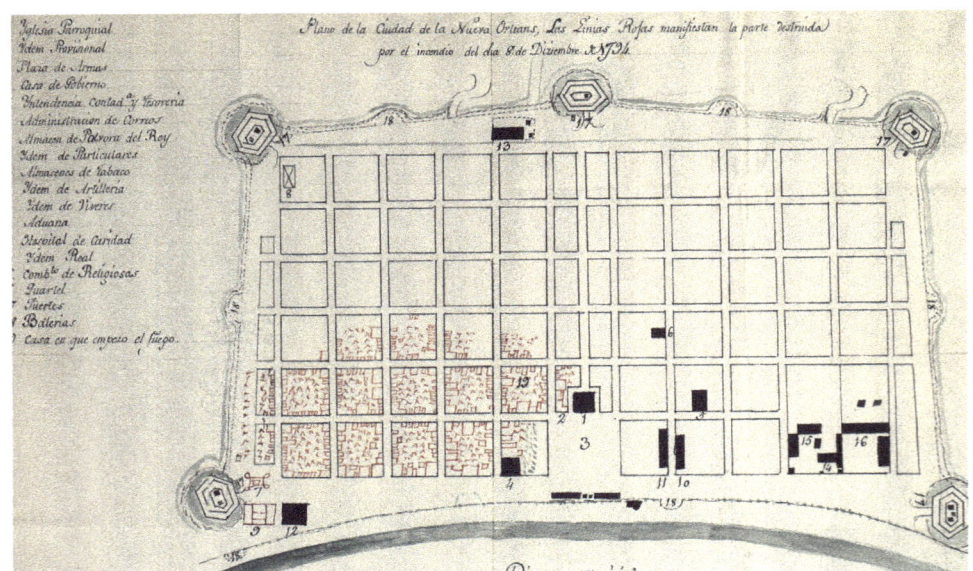

Plan of the City of New Orleans, the red lines indicate the part destroyed by the fire of 8 December 1794. Source: Preserved at the Archivo General de Indias (Seville, Spain), MP-FLORIDA_LUISIANA,150BIS. Via Wikimedia Commons. Public Domain.

On this day in 1794, a catastrophic fire swept through New Orleans' French Quarter, destroying much of the historic district and marking a transformative moment in its urban history. Established in 1718 by French colonists and laid out in a European-style grid, the French Quarter (Vieux Carré) underwent a major rebuilding under Spanish rule after the fire. This reconstruction introduced the architectural features that define the Quarter today, including stuccoed facades, wrought-iron balconies, and enclosed courtyards, blending French and Spanish influences into a distinctive urban fabric. Over time, the French Quarter evolved into a cultural and historical hub, maintaining its 18th-century layout while adapting to modern urban demands. Today, the district stands as a testament to New Orleans' resilience and rich heritage, embodying the city's ability to preserve its unique identity while navigating change and renewal.

How can cities balance preserving historical neighborhoods with meeting the needs of modern urban growth and resilience?

ENACTMENT OF THE HIGHWAYS ACT 1555

"A well-maintained road is the thread that weaves communities and commerce together."
– Queen Elizabeth I. English monarch. (Paraphrased).

The picturesque village of Castle Combe, Wiltshire, with its historic bridge over the River Bybrook – a reminder of England's early transportation infrastructure, shaped by the 1555 Highways Act, which required local parishes to maintain public roads. By John Corry. Licensed.

On this day in 1555, the Highways Act was enacted in England, marking a significant milestone in the development of transportation infrastructure. The legislation required local parishes to take responsibility for road maintenance, mandating that residents provide labor for repairs. Though rudimentary by today's standards, this community-based approach to infrastructure management underscored the growing importance of road networks in connecting towns, facilitating trade, and driving economic growth. The act laid the foundation for a more organized approach to transportation, paving the way for professionalized road-building practices and early urban planning strategies. Over time, the system evolved to accommodate the increasing demands of commerce and mobility, influencing the development of more comprehensive legislation. The Highways Act of 1555 was a pivotal step in recognizing transportation as a critical component of urban and regional development, shaping the future of infrastructure and its role in economic and social progress.

How have historical transportation policies influenced the way modern cities prioritize and maintain their infrastructure?

DECEMBER 10
1870

BIRTH OF
ARCHITECT ADOLF LOOS

"The house has to please everyone. Unlike a work of art, it is not meant to be admired."
– Adolf Loos. Austrian architect and theorist.

Looshaus am Michaelerplatz in Vienna. By Reichhartfoto. Licensed

On this day in 1870, Adolf Loos, a pioneering Austrian architect and theoretician, was born. Loos revolutionized architecture by rejecting excessive ornamentation, advocating for a functional, minimalist design prioritizing practicality over decoration. His groundbreaking 1908 essay Ornament and Crime criticized traditional aesthetics and championed simplicity, marking a pivotal shift toward modernist principles in urban design. Loos's projects, such as the iconic Looshaus in Vienna, emphasized clean lines, unadorned surfaces, and practical forms, reflecting the needs of rapidly modernizing cities. His work challenged established norms, influencing the global modernist movement and inspiring architects to embrace efficiency and purpose in their designs. Loos's ideas remain highly relevant, offering enduring insights into creating urban environments that balance aesthetic integrity with functional demands. His legacy continues to shape contemporary architecture, embodying the spirit of innovation and adaptation in city-building.

How can modern architects balance functional minimalism with the cultural and historical context of urban spaces?

U.S. SUPREME COURT ESTABLISHES CONCEPT OF REGULATORY TAKING

"If regulation goes too far, it will be recognized as a taking."
— Justice Oliver Wendell Holmes Jr.. Associate Justice of the U.S. Supreme Court.

A view of Ewen Breaker of the Pennsylvania Coal Co. in South Pittston, PA, 1927-1930. By Lewis Wickes Hine. Source: National Child Labor Committee collection, Library of Congress. Public Domain.

On this day in 1922, the U.S. Supreme Court issued its landmark ruling in Pennsylvania Coal Company v. Mahon, establishing the concept of regulatory taking. The court ruled that government regulations affecting property value could constitute a "taking" under the Fifth Amendment, requiring compensation to the property owner. The case involved a Pennsylvania law restricting mining activities to prevent subsidence under homes. The Pennsylvania Coal Company argued that the regulation rendered their mining rights useless, depriving them of property without compensation. Justice Oliver Wendell Holmes Jr., writing for the majority, stated, "If regulation goes too far, it will be recognized as a taking." This decision became a cornerstone of property law, balancing the rights of property owners against the need for public regulation, with far-reaching implications for land-use planning and zoning.

How can planners and policymakers balance the need for public regulation with property owners' rights to ensure equitable and sustainable development?

DECEMBER 12
1968

REPORT FROM THE
NATIONAL COMMISSION ON URBAN PROBLEMS

"The crisis of the American city is a crisis of unprecedented proportions."
– National Commission on Urban Problems, 1968.

Derelict street. By Philip J. Openshaw. Licensed

On this day in 1968, the National Commission on Urban Problems—established by President Lyndon B. Johnson the previous year—transmitted its final report, Building the American City, to the president. Commonly known as the Douglas Commission after its chair, Senator Paul Douglas, the body was tasked with investigating the mounting challenges facing American cities, including inadequate housing, failing infrastructure, and deepening racial segregation. The report offered a groundbreaking analysis of urban issues and proposed ambitious reforms to zoning, federal housing policy, and urban governance. It emphasized the urgent need for equitable development and called for expanded federal leadership in shaping the future of American urbanization. Building the American City became a foundational document for late 20th-century urban policy, influencing planners, legislators, and advocates seeking to address inequality through thoughtful, coordinated urban investment. Its recommendations remain relevant today as cities continue to grapple with affordability, segregation, and systemic disinvestment.

How can the findings of the Douglas Commission inform current urban planning practices to address contemporary challenges such as affordable housing and social equity?

DECEMBER 13
1577

FRANCIS DRAKE DEPARTS ON HIS CIRCUMNAVIGATION OF THE GLOBE

"Great things have small beginnings."
– Sir Francis Drake. English explorer and sea captain. (Commonly attributed).

Replica of the Golden Hinde, the UK's famous 16th-century ship, located in London. The vessel commemorates Sir Francis Drake's historic circumnavigation and is a cultural landmark linking maritime exploration to urban history. By Coward_lion. Licensed

On this day in 1577, Francis Drake departed from Plymouth, England, embarking on his historic voyage to circumnavigate the globe. This journey marked a significant milestone in maritime exploration and set the stage for the global networks that later influenced urban development. Drake's expedition expanded trade routes and contributed to the rise of colonial cities, with port cities like Plymouth, Cape Town, and Manila emerging as critical hubs in the interconnected urban systems of the early modern period. These developments fostered economic growth and urban expansion but also facilitated the exploitation of resources and labor in colonized regions, leaving a complex legacy.

Drake's voyage underscores the profound impact of exploration on global urbanism, highlighting the dualities of connectivity and commerce alongside colonialism and inequity—tensions that continue to shape the evolution of cities and global networks today.

How can cities today acknowledge the colonial legacies of exploration and trade while fostering equitable global connections?

DECEMBER 14
1994

CONSTRUCTION BEGINS ON THE THREE GORGES DAM

"The Three Gorges Dam is a dream of generations, a grand project that demonstrates the strength of the Chinese people." – Zhu Rongji, Premier of China.

Three Gorges Dam area at the Yangtze River, China. The image highlights the world's largest hydroelectric dam and its impact on regional landscapes, urban development, and flood control infrastructure. By Cacaroot. Licensed

On this day in 1994, construction began on the Three Gorges Dam on the Yangtze River in China. This project would become one of history's largest and most ambitious infrastructure undertakings. Designed to generate hydroelectric power, improve flood control, and enhance navigation, the dam has profoundly reshaped the region, providing clean energy to millions and supporting China's rapid industrial and urban growth. However, the project came with significant challenges, including the displacement of over a million residents, the submersion of historical and cultural sites, and ecological concerns affecting river ecosystems and biodiversity. The

Three Gorges Dam symbolizes both the transformative potential and the complexities of large-scale infrastructure. Its legacy underscores the importance of pursuing sustainable development strategies that balance economic, environmental, and social considerations, offering critical lessons for worldwide urban and regional planning efforts.

How can modern infrastructure projects balance economic growth with environmental and social responsibility?

DECEMBER 15
1974

LAUNCH OF
BOGOTÁ'S CICLOVÍA INITIATIVE

"Urban streets should serve as spaces of connection, not congestion."
– Enrique Peñalosa. Former Mayor of Bogotá, Colombia.

Sunday Cycling day in downtown Bogota (Colombia). By MacAllenBrothers. Via Wikimedia Commons. CC BY-SA 2.0

On this day in 1974, Bogotá, Colombia, launched its first Ciclovía initiative, reclaiming city streets for people by temporarily closing them to cars and opening them for cyclists, pedestrians, and recreational activities. Initially informal, the program gained government support in the late 1970s, evolving into a global model for sustainable urban mobility. Today, Ciclovía operates every Sunday and public holiday, covering over 120 kilometers of streets and attracting more than 1.5 million participants weekly. This initiative has redefined urban streets as community, health, and recreation spaces, fostering social interaction and promoting active lifestyles. Ciclovía's success has inspired similar programs in cities worldwide, such as Open Streets in New York and CicLAvia in Los Angeles, demonstrating how people-centered urban design can transform public spaces. Bogotá's innovation highlights the potential of reimagined streetscapes to enhance urban living and advance sustainable transportation goals.

How can cities reallocate street space to prioritize community interaction, sustainable transportation, and recreation for all residents?

DECEMBER 16
1773

BOSTON
TEA PARTY

"Boston Harbor, a teapot tonight!"
– Newspaper headline, 1773

A trading brig drifting into a Continental harbour, circa 1900. By C.J. De Lacy. Source: Wikimedia Commons. Public Domain.

On this day in 1773, the Boston Tea Party took place in Boston Harbor, an iconic event in American history and a powerful example of the role of urban public spaces in political protest. Colonial activists, angered by Britain's imposition of taxes without representation, boarded British ships and dumped 342 chests of tea into the harbor. The event was staged near Faneuil Hall, one of Boston's key civic spaces, underscoring the importance of accessible public areas in mobilizing social and political action. As centers of trade, governance, and communication, cities have long served as focal points for protest movements, with their streets, plazas, and marketplaces facilitating the exchange of ideas and organized dissent. The Boston Tea Party exemplifies the profound connection between urban form, accessibility, and the collective power of people to assemble, challenge authority, and shape their society. This principle remains essential for contemporary urban planning and the preservation of democratic engagement in public spaces.

How can modern urban spaces support democratic ideals and provide platforms for civic engagement while balancing concerns about safety and order?

DECEMBER 17
1903

FIRST POWERED FLIGHT
BY THE WRIGHT BROTHERS

"The airplane has unveiled for us the true face of the earth."
– Antoine de Saint-Exupéry. French writer and pioneering aviator.

The Wright Brothers; first powered flight, 1903. By John T. Daniels. Source: Wikimedia Commons / Library of Congress. Public Domain.

On this day in 1903, Orville and Wilbur Wright achieved the first powered, heavier-than-air flight at Kitty Hawk, North Carolina. Their aircraft, the Wright Flyer, flew 120 feet in 12 seconds, marking the beginning of modern aviation. This breakthrough revolutionized transportation and profoundly impacted cities, reshaping urban planning and connectivity. Air travel reduced travel times, linked distant cities, and facilitated global economic and cultural exchange. Airports emerged as critical urban infrastructure, transforming surrounding areas into economic hubs and influencing the spatial organization of cities. The aviation industry also played a role in suburbanization, enabling people to live farther from urban centers while remaining connected to workplaces and cultural hubs. The Wright brothers' invention laid the foundation for global networks and continues to inspire innovations in sustainable mobility, underscoring the transformative power of aviation in urban development.

How has the rise of aviation reshaped urban development, and how might future innovations like green aviation impact city planning and connectivity?

DECEMBER 18
1888

BIRTH OF
ROBERT MOSES

"Those who can, build. Those who can't, criticize."
– Robert Moses. American public official and and influential urban developer.

Robert Moses with the Battery Bridge model. (edited for format). By C.M. Stieglitz, World Telegram staff photographer. Source: Library of Congress. New York World-Telegram & Sun Collection. Via Wikimedia Commons. Public Domain.

On this day in 1888, Robert Moses, a transformative yet controversial figure in American urban planning, was born in New Haven, Connecticut. Dubbed the "master builder" of modern New York City, Moses shaped the city's infrastructure through ambitious projects, including highways, bridges, parks, and housing developments. His vision prioritized large-scale urban renewal, emphasizing automobile accessibility and public recreation. Iconic works like the Triborough Bridge and the Robert F. Kennedy Bridge stand as testaments to his influence. However, Moses's projects often came at a cost, displacing marginalized communities and sidelining public input, sparking enduring debates about equity and accountability in planning. His career underscores the tension between visionary ambition and the social impacts of urban development. While his legacy transformed New York's urban landscape, it also serves as a reminder of the importance of balancing infrastructure progress with community needs and participation.

How can modern urban planners balance large-scale infrastructure development with the needs and voices of local communities?

DEPARTURE OF
SHIPS TO FOUND JAMESTOWN

"He that will not work, shall not eat."
– Captain John Smith. English explorer and leader of the Jamestown colony.

Jamestown in 1622, vintage illustration. By Morphart. Licensed

On this day in 1606, the ships Susan Constant, Godspeed, and Discovery departed England (though some sources cite December 20) bound for what would become Jamestown, Virginia, the first permanent English colony in North America. This pivotal journey marked the beginning of sustained European urban settlement in the Americas, introducing fortified layouts, centralized marketplaces, and structured civic governance. Although the Jamestown colonists faced extreme hardships—food shortages, disease, and violent conflict with Indigenous peoples—the settlement laid a foundation for future colonial cities. Its urban planning efforts reflected a pragmatic adaptation of European principles to a new and often hostile environment, prioritizing defense, survival, and communal organization. The influence of Jamestown extended beyond its modest scale, shaping early patterns of governance and infrastructure in colonial America. Its legacy highlights the enduring challenges of creating sustainable communities in unfamiliar settings and continues to inform discussions on resilience and city-building today.

How can the lessons from early colonial settlements inform modern approaches to resilience and sustainability in urban planning?

DECEMBER 20
1999

MACAU RETURNED TO CHINESE SOVEREIGNTY

"Macau is a place where East meets West—a living testament to cultural coexistence."
– UNESCO

The Ruins of St. Paul's, Macau, China. The image depicts the remains of the 17th-century Portuguese church, symbolizing Macau's colonial history and its role as a cultural crossroads between East and West. By Javarman. Licensed

On this day in 1999, Macau, a former Portuguese colony and one of Asia's oldest European settlements, was officially returned to China under the "one country, two systems" framework. For over 400 years, Macau's urban landscape evolved as a fusion of Portuguese and Chinese cultures, seen in landmarks like the Historic Centre of Macau, a UNESCO World Heritage Site featuring plazas, churches, temples, and winding streets. Since the handover, Macau has experienced rapid urbanization and economic growth, driven primarily by its booming casino industry, while facing challenges in preserving its colonial-era heritage. The integration of Macau into modern Chinese governance has underscored the complexities cities with colonial legacies face in balancing cultural preservation with development. Today, Macau remains a unique urban entity, blending its historical identity with contemporary growth, exemplifying the dynamic interplay between heritage and modernization in urban planning.

How can cities with complex colonial legacies, like Macau, balance economic growth, modern governance, and the preservation of cultural heritage?

PRESIDENT COOLIDGE SIGNS
THE BOULDER CANYON PROJECT ACT

"A great civilization is not conquered from without until it has destroyed itself from within."
– Will Durant. American historian and philosopher.

Nevada - Boulder Dam through Boulder City, 1917 – 1964. Source: National Archives and Records Administration. National Archives at College Park. Via Wikimedia Commons. Public Domain.

On this day in 1928, President Calvin Coolidge signed the Boulder Canyon Project Act, authorizing the construction of the Hoover Dam on the Colorado River. This monumental infrastructure project was designed to provide flood control, hydroelectric power, and a stable water supply to rapidly growing urban centers in the southwestern United States, including Los Angeles, Las Vegas, and Phoenix. The act transformed the arid region, enabling urban expansion, agricultural development, and economic growth. The Hoover Dam became a symbol of American engineering and a catalyst for regional development, supporting millions of residents and industries. However, it also raised questions about environmental impacts and equitable water distribution, challenges that continue today. The Boulder Canyon Project Act remains a landmark in urban infrastructure history, highlighting the transformative potential of large-scale public works in shaping cities and addressing the complexities of modern urbanization.

How can modern infrastructure projects balance environmental sustainability with the needs of urban growth and resilience?

DECEMBER 22
1882

FIRST CHRISTMAS TREE WITH ELECTRIC LIGHTS

"Electricity is the genie of the modern world, transforming night into day, and changing the character of cities." – Thomas Edison. American inventor and businessman. (Paraphrased).

Christmas tree in Midtown Manhattan in Madison Square Park, New York. By Lazyllama. Licensed

On this day in 1882, Edward H. Johnson, a colleague of Thomas Edison, lit the first electric Christmas tree lights in his New York City home, marking a milestone in urban electrification. The event replaced traditional candles with electric lights, reducing fire hazards and symbolizing a shift toward modern city electric infrastructure. At a time when urban areas were rapidly adopting electricity, this innovation revolutionized lighting in homes, streets, and public spaces. By the early 20th century, electric holiday displays became a beloved tradition, with cities like New York and Paris creating dazzling public spectacles. These displays celebrated the festive season and showcased advancements in technology and their integration into urban life. Today, holiday lights remain a vibrant expression of urban culture, blending technological innovation with community celebration and illuminating the evolving relationship between cities and their cultural traditions.

How have innovations in urban lighting systems, from electric lights to modern LEDs, shaped the identity and experience of public spaces in cities?

BIRTH OF ILDEFONS CERDÀ

"Urban planning must balance the needs of the individual with those of the collective."
— Ildefons Cerdà. Spanish engineer and urban planner.

Blocks of the Eixample of Barcelona, Spain. The image shows the iconic urban grid layout designed by Ildefons Cerdà, with chamfered corners for better visibility, light, and ventilation in the city's streetscape. By Ildefons Cerda. Image by ikuday. Licensed.

On this day in 1815, Ildefons Cerdà, a visionary Spanish urban planner and engineer, was born. Renowned for his design of Barcelona's Eixample district, Cerdà revolutionized modern city planning. His groundbreaking grid layout featured chamfered corners, wide streets, and integrated green spaces, addressing overcrowding, sanitation, and mobility challenges in the rapidly industrializing 19th-century city. The chamfered intersections improved air circulation, visibility, and traffic flow, concepts that remain influential in urban design today. Cerdà envisioned the Eixample as a socially equitable space, incorporating mixed-income housing and public areas to foster community. His ideas, elaborated in his 1867 text The General Theory of Urbanization, established him as one of the pioneers of modern urban planning. Cerdà's legacy continues to shape urban design worldwide, inspiring cities to prioritize livability, accessibility, and sustainability while addressing the evolving needs of their populations.

How can Cerdà's integration of infrastructure and livability guide urban development in rapidly growing cities

DECEMBER 24
1889

PATENT FOR
BACK-PEDAL BRAKE BICYCLE

"The bicycle is a simple tool of freedom, transforming how we move through our cities."
– H.G. Wells. English writer and social commentator.

Patent drawing for the Stover Bicycle, 1889 – illustrating an early rear-wheel braking mechanism developed by Daniel C. Stover and William A. Hance, a significant innovation in late 19th-century bicycle engineering. U.S. Patent No. 418,142, issued December 24, 1889. Public domain. Image courtesy of the United States Patent and Trademark Office via Google Patents. Public Domain.

On this day in 1889, Daniel Stover and William Hance patented a bicycle with a back-pedal brake, a key innovation that improved cycling safety and usability. This brake allowed riders to stop by pedaling backward, eliminating the need for more complex hand-operated systems. The design simplified cycling, making it more accessible for beginners and safer for navigating busy urban streets. This advancement paved the way for bicycles to become a practical mode of transportation, particularly as other innovations—such as lighter frames, pneumatic tires, and multi-speed gearing—further enhanced usability. Today, bicycles remain essential to urban mobility, valued for their sustainability and efficiency in reducing congestion and emissions. However, modern cities must carefully plan for safe and accessible cycling infrastructure, balancing the rise of e-bikes, scooters, and shared micro-mobility systems with pedestrian and motor vehicle needs. Stover and Hance's innovation set the stage for cycling's enduring role in shaping urban transportation.

How can cities create flexible infrastructure that can adapt to new mobility technologies like e-bikes and scooters?

FIRST RECORDED
CELEBRATION OF CHRISTMAS IN ROME

"Cities are the stage where the stories of our faith, our culture, and our communities unfold."
– Paraphrased from the spirit of St. Augustine's City of God.

Christmas in Vatican City, Rome. By Vadim. Licensed

On this day in 336 CE, the first recorded celebration of Christmas took place in Rome, marking a significant shift in the city's cultural and religious landscape as it transitioned from pagan traditions to Christian observances. This event laid the foundation for Christmas to become a central feature of urban cultural life, influencing how cities adapted their spaces for communal and religious gatherings. In medieval and Renaissance Europe, cities designed public squares and cathedrals to host Christmas festivities, blending spiritual rituals with social interaction. These celebrations integrated religious traditions into the urban fabric, reinforcing cities as cultural and communal expression hubs. Rome's early observance of Christmas mirrored the broader Christianization of urban centers, transforming them into stages for shared identity and faith. Today, cities worldwide continue to adapt their public spaces for Christmas and other festivities, reflecting how urban environments evolve to meet cultural and communal needs.

How can cities balance preserving traditional celebrations, like Christmas markets, while adapting to the diverse cultural needs of modern urban populations?

DECEMBER 26
2004

INDIAN OCEAN
TSUNAMI AND ITS IMPACT ON CITIES

"The Indian Ocean Tsunami taught us that preparedness and resilience must be at the heart of every city's planning process." – Ban Ki-moon. Former Secretary-General of the United Nations.

A photograph of the 2004 sunami in Ao Nang, Krabi Province, Thailand. By David Rydevik. Via Wikimedia Commons. Public Domain.

On this day in 2004, a powerful undersea earthquake off the coast of Sumatra triggered the Indian Ocean Tsunami, one of the deadliest natural disasters in history. The tsunami impacted 14 countries, including Indonesia, Sri Lanka, India, and Thailand, devastating coastal cities and towns, causing over 230,000 deaths, and displacing millions. Urban areas suffered catastrophic damage to infrastructure, housing, and livelihoods, highlighting the vulnerability of coastal cities to seismic and climate-related events. The disaster prompted affected countries to adopt critical measures, including early-warning systems, stricter building codes, and enhanced urban disaster preparedness plans to mitigate future risks. Globally, the tragedy spurred conversations about resilience, equitable urban reconstruction, and prioritizing vulnerable populations in recovery efforts. The tsunami remains a sobering reminder of the importance of integrating disaster risk management into urban planning to protect communities from similar events in the future.

How can urban planners incorporate lessons from disasters like the Indian Ocean Tsunami to build safer, more climate-resilient cities for the future?

DECEMBER 27
1512

LAWS OF BURGOS
ISSUED BY THE SPANISH CROWN

"Laws are made to guide humanity, but their strength lies in their enforcement."
– King Ferdinand II of Aragon. (Paraphrased)

Detail from Diego Rivera's Epic of the Mexican People depicting the Spanish conquest and the exploitation of Indigenous peoples. Diego Rivera (1929–1935), National Palace, Mexico City. Public domain (CC0 1.0 Universal).

On this day in 1512, the Laws of Burgos were enacted by the Spanish Crown, becoming the first legal code to govern the treatment of Indigenous peoples in the Americas. These laws sought to regulate the conduct of Spanish settlers under the encomienda system, addressing labor practices and the rights of Native Americans. While provisions included limiting forced labor, mandating fair treatment, and requiring religious instruction, the laws were poorly enforced and failed to prevent widespread exploitation and abuse. Nevertheless, the Laws of Burgos represented an early attempt at social and urban governance in colonial settlements, influencing labor organization and resource management in towns and cities across the New World. As the first legal framework for Spain's colonial administration, these laws laid the groundwork for subsequent policies, shaping urban planning and governance while highlighting the challenges of balancing economic interests with ethical considerations in colonial rule.

How can modern urban policies address historical legacies of exploitation and inequality in post-colonial contexts?

DECEMBER 28
1908

MESSINA EARTHQUAKE
DEVASTATES SOUTHERN ITALY

"In the ruins of Messina, we are reminded that cities are fragile, but human resilience is unbreakable." – Paraphrased from contemporary reports.

A view of the widespread destruction caused by the Messina earthquake and tsunami. Charles Farrugia & Ian Ellis,Images, Context and Structure: The Richard Ellis archive (Malta) revisited, Revista Photo & Documento No. 1, 2016; section "Visual essay". Via Wikimedia Commons. Public domain.

On this day in 1908, the Messina Earthquake devastated southern Italy, registering a magnitude of 7.1 and nearly leveling the cities of Messina and Reggio Calabria. Over 80,000 lives were lost as the quake and subsequent tsunamis caused catastrophic destruction. The disaster highlighted the vulnerabilities of urban centers to natural disasters and spurred debates about reconstruction and resilience. In response, Italy introduced stricter building codes and implemented earthquake-resistant design principles, marking a significant shift in urban planning and safety regulations. Messina was rebuilt with modernized infrastructure and a redesigned city layout to improve functionality and reduce future risks.

This tragedy underscored the importance of urban resilience and proactive disaster planning, serving as a critical example for cities worldwide. The Messina Earthquake remains pivotal in understanding how urban centers can recover and adapt to catastrophic events while enhancing safety and sustainability.

How can modern cities learn from historical reconstruction efforts like Messina's to create more resilient and disaster-prepared urban environments?

BIRTH OF
GARCÍA DE SILVA FIGUEROA

"I saw nothing in the world that compares to the beauty and order of these Persian cities."
– García de Silva Figueroa. Spanish diplomat and traveler.

Naranjestan Garden, Shiraz, Iran. The image captures the traditional Persian garden's symmetrical layout and water features, reflecting the type of urban beauty and architectural order described by García de Silva Figueroa in his 17th-century accounts of Persian cities. By Matyas Rehak. Licensed

On this day in 1550, García de Silva Figueroa was born, a Spanish diplomat and traveler whose observations of cities during his diplomatic mission to Persia from 1614 to 1624 significantly enriched European understanding of urban planning and architecture. As the Spanish ambassador to the Safavid court of Shah Abbas I, Figueroa meticulously documented the sophisticated designs of Persian cities, particularly Isfahan. He praised their advanced water management systems, expansive gardens, and vibrant public squares, demonstrating a harmonious blend of aesthetics and functionality. His accounts introduced Renaissance Europe to Persia's intricate urban design principles, emphasizing the importance of integrating natural elements with civic spaces. Figueroa's writings highlight how cultural exchange through diplomacy shaped the evolution of urban planning, influencing approaches to city building in different regions and fostering a greater appreciation of global urban traditions.

How did travel and diplomacy contribute to the exchange of urban planning ideas across cultures?

DECEMBER 30
1924

OPENING OF
BARCELONA'S FIRST METRO LINE

"The Barcelona metro is the city's pulse, linking neighborhoods, people, and opportunities."
– Ada Colau. Former Mayor of Barcelona.

Construction work on Via Laietana, Barcelona, January 7, 1912. This photograph captures the early stages of developing one of Barcelona's major thoroughfares. Author unknown. Source: Revista Semanal Ilustrada, issue number 448, January 7, 1912. Via Wikimedia Commons. CC0.

On this day in 1924, Barcelona inaugurated its first metro line, connecting the city center at Catalunya station to Lesseps. Now part of the L3 (green line), this milestone began a transportation network essential to Barcelona's growth and modernization. The upcoming 1929 Barcelona International Exposition spurred the project, which underscored the need for efficient urban mobility in a rapidly expanding city. Over the decades, the metro system expanded significantly, enhancing connectivity and accessibility while reducing congestion and encouraging more sustainable urban development. By reshaping Barcelona's urban form, the metro supported the city's transformation into a modern metropolis, integrating neighborhoods and improving the quality of life for residents. Today, Barcelona's metro stands as a model of effective public transit, demonstrating the enduring role of mass transit systems in fostering equitable, sustainable, and dynamic urban environments worldwide.

How has the development of metro systems influenced the growth and sustainability of cities around the world?

FIRST NEW YEAR'S EVE CELEBRATION IN TIMES SQUARE

"It was the greatest crowd of New Yorkers ever assembled to celebrate the dawn of a new year." — The New York Times, January 1, 1905

"Happy New Year" glitter bunting hangs festively above the vibrant neon glow of Times Square, capturing the energy and spectacle of New York City's iconic year-end celebration. By lazyllama. Licensed.

On this day in 1904, New York City held its first-ever New Year's Eve celebration in what would become Times Square. Organized by Adolph Ochs, publisher of The New York Times, the event commemorated the newspaper's move to its new headquarters in the newly constructed Times Tower at the intersection of Broadway and 42nd Street. Ochs had successfully advocated for the area's renaming from Longacre Square to Times Square earlier that year. To mark the occasion, he sponsored a grand fireworks display that drew over 200,000 spectators, transforming the space into a major civic gathering point. Although the famous ball drop would not debut until 1907, the 1904 celebration laid the foundation for what would become one of the world's most iconic annual traditions. Today, Times Square's New Year's Eve festivities attract millions of global viewers, symbolizing unity, renewal, and the cultural power of public space in the heart of the city. It remains a vivid reflection of urban celebration and identity.

How can cities design and manage public spaces that foster shared cultural rituals and civic identity on both everyday and extraordinary occasions?

www.ingramcontent.com/pod-product-compliance
Lightning Source LLC
Chambersburg PA
CBHW050440150626
46551CB00028B/786